Domestic and Family V

Domestic and family violence (DFV) is an enduring social and public health issue of endemic proportions and global scale, with multiple and lasting consequences for those directly affected. This book tackles current debates in the field and addresses the social norms and settings that perpetuate this type of violence, along with implications for service delivery.

The book offers a thorough introduction into the nature and extent of DFV in contemporary social contexts and serves as a foundation for informed practice. It provides a firm theoretical and empirical overview of core issues, covering the challenges and support needs experienced by those affected, along with the implications this raises for the range of relevant response services. The authors also offer insight into the predominantly gendered nature of DFV and its influence beyond the traditional couple context, across age, gender, sexual orientation, cultural background, and family relationships. Drawing on theoretical explanations, international research, and practice experience, they highlight examples of good practice and holistic responses, including primary, secondary, and tertiary prevention.

Written in a clear and direct style, this book will appeal to students and scholars of criminology, sociology, and social work engaged in studies of domestic and family violence, violence against women, and intimate partner violence. It will be an invaluable resource for those designing, coordinating, and conducting service responses.

Silke Meyer is Associate Professor at Monash University and Adjunct Associate Professor at CQUniversity, Australia. Silke is a criminologist and social worker by training, bringing practical and theoretical expertise to her research, teaching, and writing. Her research centres on different aspects of domestic and family violence, including women and children's safety and wellbeing, men's accountability in their role as perpetrators and fathers, experiences specific to Aboriginal and Torres Strait Islander communities and the role of domestic and family violence-informed practice in child protection, policing, and court proceedings. Silke's research has been published and cited widely and continues to inform policy and practice in areas of victim- and perpetrator-related service delivery.

Andrew Frost leads a team of educators in the Domestic and Family Violence Practice program at CQUniversity, Australia. Andrew has been working, teaching, and researching in offender rehabilitation since 1993. His practice and award-winning research into group work with violent offenders, along with the establishment of a forensic therapeutic community, has spawned a range of publications across books and academic journals. Theoretical models and other outcomes from this work have been used by state, NGO, and independent service providers to inform practice.

"This book, intended for students and practitioners, will be extremely valuable to each of these audiences. However, it also has the potential to reach other audiences both policy makers and academic. It is clear, accessible and incisive in its coverage of the complex issues surrounding domestic violence. The authors do not shy away from the hotly contested debates within this field but work through them for and with the reader. As a result, it offers the reader a refreshingly honest critical appreciation of what is known, what is yet to be known, and what might be doable as a consequence. Anyone interested in domestic family violence will learn much from it."

Professor Sandra Walklate, Eleanor Rathbone
Chair of Sociology, University of Liverpool, UK

"Meyer and Frost have created a book that provides a refreshing look at domestic and family violence. The authors address head on the tensions and challenges that exist in current theorising and practice approaches, and provide effective strategies for addressing domestic and family violence. The result is a book that is comprehensive and holistic. It is a must read for domestic and family violence professionals, educators, researchers and students."

Dr Yvonne Crichton-Hill, Senior Lecturer, Department of Human
Services and Social Work, University of Canterbury, New Zealand

"This book is as scholarly as it is practical. Administration and practitioners alike will find this book accessible, informative, and thought provoking. It will undoubtedly be an important resource that will serve as a guide to our efforts to reduce domestic and family violence."

Dr Jayson Ware, Group Director, Offender Services & Program
Corrective Services New South Wales, Department of Justice, Australia

"Given the expansive, complex, and multi-faceted literature of this field, this book contributes a much-needed summary and reformulation of our current knowledge and best understanding of domestic and family violence. It is brilliantly organized to enable readers to find given subjects of interest, while conveying a sensitive 'inside' portrayal of victimhood and perpetratorhood alike."

Jerry L. Jennings, Ph.D., Vice President of Clinical Services,
Liberty Healthcare Corporation, Pennsylvania, USA

"This book is very timely for practitioners, educators and students who need a critical yet reflective approach to responding to domestic and family violence. Importantly the book shows constructive ways to respond to perpetrators and victims. It highlights the need for a gendered approach as well as extending to other occurrences of violence such as in same sex relationships and those living with a disability. I fully recommend this book as a practical and thoughtful guide to this complex field of practice."

Patrick O'Leary, Professor of Social Work, Griffith Criminology
Institute, School of Human Services and Social Work,
Griffith University, Australia

Domestic and Family Violence

A Critical Introduction to Knowledge and Practice

Silke Meyer and Andrew Frost

Routledge
Taylor & Francis Group

LONDON AND NEW YORK

First published 2019
by Routledge
2 Park Square, Milton Park, Abingdon, Oxon OX14 4RN

and by Routledge
52 Vanderbilt Avenue, New York, NY 10017

Routledge is an imprint of the Taylor & Francis Group, an informa business

British Library Cataloguing-in-Publication Data
A catalogue record for this book is available from the British Library

Library of Congress Cataloging-in-Publication Data
A catalog record has been requested for this book

ISBN: 978-1-138-55272-2 (hbk)
ISBN: 978-1-138-55273-9 (pbk)
ISBN: 978-1-315-14828-1 (ebk)

Typeset in Goudy
by Apex CoVantage, LLC

To our colleagues in research and practice and students, with appreciation of their enthusiasm and dedication to this field of work and study

Contents

Acknowledgements

This book would not have been possible without the input and support of a number of people. We would therefore like to acknowledge the voices of our many research participants. Without their input and willingness to share their personal and professional experiences, research and knowledge building would not be possible in this field. Thank you.

We would also like to acknowledge the contribution of one of our amazing research assistants, Ms Lorelei Hine. Lorelei's editing support for this book has been invaluable. We cannot thank her enough for her attention to detail and for saving our sanity.

Chapter 1

Introduction

Conduct amounting to what we collectively refer to as domestic and family violence (DFV) has historically been regarded as a private and individual matter, occurring within the context of a traditional husband and wife relationship. From this long perspective, cultural attitudes towards DFV could be described as largely semi-tolerant; eyes averted, voices unheard, acts excused. Contemporary understandings, however, portray the phenomenon as a complex and diverse social issue involving persons who are bound together across a range of intimate and kin relationships. While much of the focus of expanding research and intervention efforts still concern adult partners in an intimate relationship – regardless of the identities of those partners and the social status of their relationship – there is increasing recognition of the direct involvement of, and impact upon, children, siblings, seniors, and extended family members. Cultural attitudes have also hardened, and DFV is now recognised as pernicious and widely condemned. Nevertheless, its prevalence endures.

DFV has been identified as an issue of endemic proportions. The consequences for those directly affected is both pervasive and enduring. Lives of individuals can be devastated and the social fabric of families and communities damaged, often for generations. There are significant global implications for public health, criminal justice, and economic systems. Responding to this problem has become a social policy priority, and prevention efforts are organised at the primary, secondary, and tertiary levels.

It is clear that DFV is associated with the entangled and often protracted nature of domestic and kinship arrangements. Grandparents, parents, children, partners, siblings, and cousins – including non-related "family" – are commonly enmeshed in the variable arrangements of their family constellations, as well as their cultural histories and community relationships. However, it also clear that, despite the ubiquity and institutional status of the family, the explanation as to why DFV arises in some family systems and not others remains highly contestable. For, despite advances in our appreciation of the scale and diversity of the DFV problem, progress in understanding – and therefore in advancing policy and practice – has been hindered by slow progress in making conceptual sense of it. In other words, in the study of DFV, theory lags behind research. Progress continues to be confounded by fierce theoretical and ideological debate, the dynamics of which have been characterised less by dialectical development and more by conflict and polarisation. As a result, for the most part, groups of theorists remain locked in mutual opposition. While there have been attempts to reconcile the extremes, researchers have tended to favour one end or the other of a continuum of views. At one pole of this continuum is the belief that DFV arises out of inequality and oppression, with deep roots in social structure across time and place. This perspective, sometimes referred to as structural feminist, focuses its analysis on patriarchal social systems that, by definition, support narrow, rigid, and hierarchical gender roles. Such restrictive roles serve to privilege and legitimise the power of men over women and children. Under these conditions, the sanctity accorded the institution of the family by society serves to provide "privacy", and therefore the captive context, whereby abusive conditions might thrive. This conditional case ("might thrive"), however, provides the chink in the armour of the structural feminist position, in that such an argument cannot account for why DFV arises in some families and not others. At the opposing end of the spectrum of DFV theory and ideology, then, is what has been referred to as the family systems position. Proponents of this position take the view that DFV arises out of poorly managed or uncontrolled conflict. Conflict, according to this view, is an inevitable product of the dynamics inherent in family systems. This view, while acknowledging the disproportionate impact of DFV on women by men, maintains that unequal or oppressive gender power relations is neither an essential cause nor an inevitable outcome of DFV. A chief weakness of this position, therefore, is that it cannot successfully account for the fact that the preponderance of harm from DFV is perpetrated by men towards women.

This division in theoretical perspectives has profound consequences for how DFV is studied and portrayed. While approaches based on the family systems perspective are intent on the microanalysis of discrete episodes and incidents within a circumscribed family context, a structural feminist analysis tends to favour attention to the patterning of violence and the perpetrator's intentional abusive tactics over time. While the former analysis emphasises the sequence of events contained within a bounded system, the latter is more concerned with the agency of an abusive actor conducting a more or less deliberate regime of subjugation. Intimate partner sexual assault, for example, might be defined from a family systems perspective as behaviour that involves the commission of a specific act or the omission of consent surrounding such an act. From a structural feminist perspective, however – where such behaviour is likely to be viewed within the context of an orchestrated and protracted pattern of domination, isolation, coercion, and surveillance – *any and all* sexual activity occurring within that context might be considered abusive.

Neither the structural feminist perspective nor the family systems perspective, however, directly confront the issue raised in the opening of this introductory chapter: the increasing recognition of the complexity and diversity surrounding DFV. How can these mean of conceptualising DFV account for people with diverging sexualities and genders, such as homosexual, bisexual, queer, intersex, or transgender people? How can notions of gender and the nuclear family system accommodate the extended family household or active and committed tribal affiliation where such violence and abuse occur? One principle of service in this sector that appears to have gained widespread acceptance is that, regardless of the nuances of ideology, effective intervention is best supported by an integrated response. In other words, victim advocacy, criminal justice, perpetrator programs, child protection, local community, and other relevant agencies and services across the DFV sector should form an information sharing, collaborative, and coordinated system in order to address the problem.

Primary-level (or preventative) prevention refers to community-wide educational and consciousness-raising strategies to tackle the problem at a foundational level. In this way, it seeks to align behaviour with beliefs and commitments by providing resources to promote information and public debate. Secondary-level responses take the form of early intervention in situations where a high risk of DFV is identified, such as in vulnerable communities, in families, or among their members. Tertiary responses attempt to address DFV harm that has already occurred and to avert its worsening or repetition. The proliferation of shelters for women who have been victimised and behaviour change programs for men are testimony to the growth in services at this level. Each of these prevention levels requires its own set of knowledge, techniques, and skills. While, for instance, human rights education might be an appropriate approach in primary prevention contexts, such as schools, that same approach might be less effective, as an initial gambit at least, in working with a man who is apparently astonished at an order that he attend a program to address his regime of coercive control over his partner and children.

In the end, however, good theory is a necessity. It is needed to offer the overarching conceptual means to explore and to account for the gaps and debates in our understanding and service strategies. Good theory should offer means of resolving apparent contradictions across diverse cases and multiple sectors. It informs strong policy, and strong policy shapes concerted action and effective practice. In this book, we aim, ultimately, to equip students with the conceptual clarity that provides a pathway to make sense of DFV, and to equip practitioners with the means to both analyse policy and inform inclusive and collaborative service intervention involving those affected by DFV, either as victims or as perpetrators, across age, gender, and status. We acknowledge that victim and perpetrator identities may at times overlap; violators may at some time have been violated. However, we utilise these terms throughout the book, referring to those exercising the role of primary aggressors as perpetrators and those disproportionately affected by DFV as victims.

The book is divided into sections that address the four aspects critical to its intentions: the context of DFV, the protagonists, the diversity among them, and our responses to this "wicked" problem. We begin by traversing the evolution of thinking in relation to DFV, discussing diverse examples, including DFV experienced by young people and the elderly, heterosexual and LGBTIQ couples, and people from different cultural backgrounds. We provide a theoretical understanding of the concepts underpinning different views of DFV, including the family system and structural feminist perspectives. We explore gender and power in private spaces as factors in shaping the problem, as well as the controversy over matters concerning causality, volition, and victimhood. We examine children's exposure to parental DFV, including how children can become enmeshed in parental violence, the impact it has on their short- and long-term safety, development, and wellbeing, and the role of child-centred responses. This book concludes with an illustration of strategies used to tackle the problem, including the role of prevention and examples of national and international good practice in working with those affected.

Chapter 2

The nature and prevalence of domestic and family violence

Estimating prevalence rates: data challenges and other considerations

The way in which we define a social phenomenon has implications for how we define and measure its existence. If limiting the definition of DFV to physical and sexual abuse within intimate relationships, prevalence rates would be substantially lower than when expanding the definition to include non-physical behaviours, such as emotional, psychological, social, and economic abuse. When identifying prevalence rates, it is therefore important to closely examine the definitions applied to describe the phenomenon being measured as well as the nature and diversity of target populations asked to self-report their experiences.

In addition to definition-related variations for prevalence rates of DFV, variations are also likely to be observed across different data sources. While administrative data (e.g. police, courts, or hospital data) provide us with "official statistics" around a certain social phenomenon (e.g. DFV) where it presents itself, this can be strongly impacted by the issue of underreporting. As a result, most global estimates of phenomena that are highly sensitive and often private in nature (such as DFV, sexual abuse, or child abuse) rely on self-report data to provide a more accurate estimate of prevalence.

Examples of self-report data used to estimate the extent of DFV across international jurisdictions include components of the International Violence Against Women Survey (IVAWS), conducted in Australia, the US, Hong Kong, the Philippines, Mozambique, and a number of European countries (see, for example, Mouzos & Makkai, 2004; Tjaden & Thoennes, 2002). In addition, many countries conduct their own national population-based surveys. Examples include:

- The Australian Personal Safety Survey, which captures a diverse range of violent victimisation experiences, including DFV
- The British Crime Survey, which incorporates a component on DFV
- The German Prevalence Study on Violence against Women, which captures similar information to what has been gathered via the IVAWS instrument

Some of these surveys are administered repeatedly (e.g. the Australian Personal Safety Survey, which was conducted in 1996 as the Women's Safety Survey and in 2005, 2012, and 2016 as the amended Personal Safety Survey, further including men's experiences of violence and abuse). The purpose of such repeated waves of survey administration is to identify trends in social issues (e.g. DFV) and how these affect different populations over time.

Most population-based prevalence studies reveal similar prevalence rates of DFV across comparable populations. As an example, prevalence rates of physical and/or sexual violence perpetrated against women by a current or former partner range between 25% and 30% in each of the Organisation for Economic Co-operation and Development (OECD) countries surveyed as part of the IVAWS (Mouzos & Makkai, 2004), the European Union-wide survey (European Union Agency for Fundamental Rights [FRA], 2014), and the Australian Personal Safety Survey (ABS, 2014). This means that between one in three and one in four women experience intimate partner violence (IPV) in the form of physical and/or sexual abuse at some point from the age of 15 years. These national prevalence rates are in line with global estimations of IPV generated by the World Health Organization (WHO, 2013), which are estimated to be around 30%. This estimate is the average of prevalence rates identified across countries globally. Some countries have prevalence rates above 30% (the highest rates have been identified for some of the Southeast Asian, African, and Eastern Mediterranean regions, with up to 37%), whereas other regions have prevalence rates below 30% (e.g. high-income European and Western Pacific regions with 25%; WHO, 2013).

While rates of DFV may vary slightly depending on the social and cultural settings they are measured in, national and global estimates identify a clearly gendered pattern of victimisation experiences, which disproportionately affect women and children (WHO, 2013). However, researchers and men's rights activists who argue that DFV affects men and women equally (Beel, 2013; Straus, 1980) have frequently questioned the gendered nature of DFV. Given these polarising sides of the debate, it is important to critically examine and understand what the data reveal around gender symmetry versus gender imbalance in relation to experiences of DFV victimisation.

Gender symmetry in DFV?

From a structural feminist perspective, DFV is seen as a gendered issue, informed by male patriarchy and female oppression. Within this framework, DFV is primarily a male-to-female perpetrated phenomenon, usually marked by the abuser's desire to strategically manipulate and control the victim (Dobash & Dobash, 1979; Johnson, 2008; Stark, 2007). From a family conflict perspective, on the other hand, DFV is seen as a form of situational conflict associated with different individual and family factors, including financial and housing stress, parental disagreement around parenting practices, unemployment, poor communication, and conflict resolution skills (Straus, 1973, 1980). Family conflict scholars argue that DFV may be used to establish or maintain status within the family structure or hierarchy but that the underlying objective is not to strategically control the victim (Straus, 1973, 1980). While feminist scholars argue that DFV is part of a pattern of manipulative and controlling behaviours, family conflict scholars argue that DFV is an expression of anger and frustration, which may occur as an isolated incident or as the frequent result of an argument (Johnson, 2008).

These opposing views have created tension between those advocating for either perspective. Family conflict scholars accuse feminist scholars of vilifying men, while feminist scholars criticise them for minimising the nature and impact of DFV on its victims (Keating, 2015). The ongoing debate, however, does not stop at the definition of DFV. Both theoretical perspectives hold very different views on the nature and extent of the phenomenon as well as its perpetrators. Scholars and practitioners aligning with the structural feminist perspective frame DFV as a primarily male-to-female perpetrated phenomenon, with women and children suffering the most detrimental physical, emotional, financial, and social impacts (Devries et al., 2013; Johnson, 2008). Those aligning with the family conflict perspective argue that women are equally as violent as men and that the prevailing gendered framework that informs policy and practice in most countries is misplaced and misleading (Beel, 2013).

Since the 1960s, most advocacy and awareness raising around the issue of DFV has been initiated and driven by second-wave feminism (Dobash & Dobash, 1979; Yllö & Bograd, 1988). As such, DFV has been framed and addressed as a gendered issue in research, policy, and practice. Parallel to that, family conflict scholars have raised the idea of family conflict as a systems approach in which multiple players within the family system may be abusive, regardless of their gender (Straus, 1973).

Originally, the family conflict perspective primarily centred on exploring the contextual factors surrounding DFV. Over subsequent decades, it has moved towards an examination of victim and perpetrator roles and the promotion of gender symmetry in DFV (Keating, 2015). Supported by large-scale household survey data, advocates of the family conflict perspective argue that statistics indicate that women use violent tactics in their intimate relationships as often as – if not more often than – men (Beel, 2013; Straus, 1980, 2008, 2009). The late Murray Straus, one of the most vocal and well-known advocates of the gender symmetry debate, frequently argued that social survey data measuring couples' responses to conflict, anger, and frustration reveal that women use violence against a male intimate partner at the same rate as men do against a female intimate partner (Straus, 2008, 2009). While most scholars like Straus make admissions around the impact of DFV, acknowledging that women are more likely to experience manipulation and injuries, some proponents of the gender symmetry framework further deny this imbalance (Beel, 2013). In his review of the literature and data surrounding DFV from family conflict and structural feminist perspectives, Beel

(2013) argues that there is substantial empirical evidence which demonstrates that male victims of DFV are equally as likely to require medical attention when experiencing DFV (Heady, Scott, & DeVaus, 1999, as cited in Beel, 2013) and that equal numbers of men and women experience control as part of the abuse (Ross & Babcock, 2009, as cited in Beel, 2013). He purports that feminist scholars have been misleading in defining DFV as a gendered issue anchored in male patriarchy and gender inequality and, as a result, have created not only a bias in social science research but also a policy and practice landscape that denies male victims their right to suitable services (Beel, 2013). From a structural feminist perspective, the argument has always been the opposite. Beginning with Dobash and Dobash (1979), well-known work framing "a case against the patriarchy" in the late 1970s and followed by many other (male and female) feminist scholars, DFV has primarily been identified as a male-to-female perpetrated problem. A large number of studies, including population-based surveys as well as those drawing their findings from higher risk, clinical samples have repeatedly confirmed a gendered pattern in the experience of DFV (Australian National Research Organisation for Women's Safety [ANROWS], 2017; Keating, 2015; Mouzos & Makkai, 2004). The WHO has repeatedly labelled male-to-female perpetrated violence a global public health issue of endemic proportions (Garcia-Moreno & Watts, 2011).

National and international homicide statistics show that women are three to five times more likely to be killed by an intimate partner than men (Beel, 2013; Keating, 2015; Bryant & Cussen, 2015). The most recent edition of Australia's national prevalence study of DFV conducted in 2016 revealed that women were more than three times more likely to experience physical or sexual violence by a current or former intimate partner than men (ANROWS, 2017). US findings derived from a recent reanalysis of the 2010 National Intimate Partner and Sexual Violence Survey revealed a smaller gender gap but still supported the gendered nature of the issue, with one in four women reporting severe physical abuse by a partner of the opposite sex, compared to one in seven men (Walters, Chen, & Breiding, 2013). The gender gap in experiences of IPV appears to be smaller in general in US data. While US-based domestic homicide statistics also support the gendered nature of DFV, the overrepresentation of women in domestic homicide statistics is slightly lower in the US than in a number of other Western countries (Beel, 2013).

Findings derived from a number of national and global prevalence studies have repeatedly contradicted the argument of gender symmetry put forward by advocates of the family conflict perspective (see, for example, Straus, 2007, 2009). National and global prevalence studies are not subject to limitations associated with research designs employing high-risk clinical samples (e.g. overrepresentation of a wide range of severe and repeat experiences of DFV in high-risk populations often captured in clinical samples). Indeed, respondents to large-scale prevalence surveys are randomly selected and the experiences and perceptions of men and women equally represent those of the broader population. These studies therefore cover a range of individuals and their experiences in past or current intimate relationships. The clear overrepresentation of women in all areas of violent experiences involving a perpetrator of the opposite sex across national and global prevalence studies lends strong support to the structural feminist argument that DFV is an issue that affects women disproportionately.

Is there a way of reconciling the argument?

The significant discrepancies in evidence that both sides of the debate draw on in support of their argument beg the question as to whether there is any common ground between the two perspectives. It seems the closest these two perspectives come to sharing a common ground in their arguments is that some family conflict scholars acknowledge the greater vulnerability of female victims with regards to injuries (Beel, 2013; Straus, 2008), although some negate this observation (Heady et al., 1999). Both sides argue that the opposing perspective generates its findings through biased or flawed sampling designs, which lead to either an alleged overrepresentation of male-to-female perpetrated violence (family conflict argument) or an alleged misinterpretation of female use of violence that is taken out of context (structural feminist argument). Feminist scholars argue that women's admissions of violent tactics in surveys are meaningless unless examined within the situational context in which they occur (Keating, 2015). That is, is women's violence being used as a form of resistance or self-defence? Does the violence being used generate the same impact as the violence being used by a male against a female? Are patterns of control being accounted for? Without addressing these questions, it is difficult to determine whether the gender symmetry observed in some studies reflects genuinely equal experiences of violence and conflict in intimate relationships (Keating, 2015; Kimmel, 2002).

The body of international research evidence shows that female victims of DFV are significantly overrepresented, especially with regard to severe physical violence, including presentation to emergency room departments for DFV-related injuries and domestic homicide (Bryant & Cussen, 2015; Garcia-Moreno & Watts, 2011; Keating, 2015). These observations support the argument that women are disproportionately affected by the experiences and consequences of DFV over the life course. Rather than arguing for one extreme or the other in this debate, it is important to address the needs arising from the gendered pattern of DFV while also acknowledging that men, too, experience violence at the hands of an intimate partner. While research suggests that violence is more likely to be perpetrated by a male than female partner (Walters et al., 2013; University of New South Wales, 2013), these findings still highlight that men need to be considered in practice responses addressing the needs of those affected by DFV. We further examine the role of gender in victimisation experiences in Chapters 3 and 7.

The shift from "family conflict" and "wife beating" towards more inclusive definitions

As stated early on in this chapter, estimating the nature and extent of a problem, such as DFV, is further informed by how we define the issue at hand along with the relationships in which it occurs. Historically, DFV was seen as a private matter that took place behind closed family doors. Early work in defining and examining DFV included perspectives around family conflict as well as gender. Straus, Gelles, and Steinmetz' (1980) early book, *Behind Closed Doors: Violence in the American Family*, for example, focused on DFV from a family perspective and included parental violence as well as child and sibling abuse in its examination and definition of the issue.

The women's movement, on the other hand, has driven the development of more gender-based approaches to understanding and defining DFV, including Dobash and Dobash's (1979) pioneer work, *Violence Against Wives: A Case Against the Patriarchy*. Under early feminist or gender-based frameworks, DFV was often referred to as "wife abuse" or "spousal abuse", setting clear margins for the phenomenon as something which occurs in opposite sex, marital relationships and is male-to-female perpetrated. Feminists documented the widespread occurrences of what police often referred to as "wife beating" throughout the 1970s (Dobash & Dobash, 1979). It was the feminist – or women's – movement that highlighted DFV as a social issue that occurred across social classes. This movement also highlighted the need for adequate crisis responses, including criminal justice responses and access to crisis accommodation for "battered wives" (Clark, 2011). With the change in nature of intimate relationships over time, definitions have evolved to reflect a more diverse range of relationships and a greater awareness of the pervasiveness of DFV.

Contemporary definitions of DFV

When seeking to define DFV, it is easy to become overwhelmed by the plethora of definitions of this phenomenon. To start with, several labels are used interchangeably to describe DFV, including domestic violence, family violence, and IPV. While these may all capture the same behaviours in one context, they may actually refer to different things. A common example is the term "family violence". While it is often used to refer to violence between couples or parents in some settings, in other settings this term may include a wider variety of behaviours, such as child abuse and violence directed at extended family members. It is therefore important to clarify the types of behaviours and relationships included under a relevant definition of DFV, to gain clarity around the context and extent of the behaviour. Throughout this book, we use an inclusive definition of DFV, informed by the approach taken by the United Nations (UN) and WHO. Both organisations highlight the importance of understanding DFV as a gendered phenomenon that – while not exclusively male-to-female perpetrated – affects women and children disproportionately (UN Department of Economic and Social Affairs, 2015; WHO, 2013). In addition, both highlight the need to understand DFV as behaviours that reach far beyond physical and sexual abuse. Their definitions include physical, sexual, emotional, psychological, and economic forms of abuse (UN Department of Economic and Social Affairs, 2015; WHO, 2013). Aside from specifying certain behaviours as abusive, definitions of DFV may further include the impact of such behaviour. The Australian Bureau of Statistics (ABS), for example, describes DFV as behaviours designed to intimidate, control, or manipulate a family member, partner, or former partner (ABS, 2013). Where definitions of DFV are quite broad, they may include any of the following behaviours:

- Physical assault and abuse
- Sexual assault and abuse
- Psychological abuse
- Emotional abuse
- Verbal abuse
- Economic abuse
- Social abuse and isolation
- Property damage
- Harassment or stalking
- Spiritual abuse
- Cultural abuse
- Threats of any of the above behaviours to coerce victims into submission and compliance

Some of these behaviours may appear to be similar in their definitional approach. Take, for example, psychological abuse and emotional abuse. One may argue that behaviours such as blaming the victim for relationship problems can be classified as emotional as well as psychological abuse. While there is no official distinction between the definition of emotional versus psychological abuse, some argue that psychological abuse involves "manipulative behaviour to coerce, control or harm" someone (ABS, 2013, p. 10). The key difference may therefore lie in the element of manipulation. Emotional abuse encapsulates a number of hurtful behaviours, such as putting the victim down and/or undermining their self-esteem. This in itself may not necessarily require a conscious element of manipulation or coercion, whereas "playing mind games", "gaslighting",[1] questioning the victim's ability to parent, or causing the victim to question his/her ability to move on without the abusive partner are strategies to generate and maintain power and control over the victim.

While detailed definitions as the ones offered above may seem to "double up" on capturing different aspects of DFV, they fulfil a particular purpose. Broad definitions help to ensure that any harmful behaviour, no matter how major or minor it may seem to the victim, perpetrator, or people outside the interpersonal relationship, is captured and understood in a way that facilitates a relevant service response. This applies to responses by victim support services, perpetrator interventions, and primary prevention approaches. For the purpose of providing victim support services, for example, definitions benefit from being broad and in-depth to illustrate to victims that a number of behaviours they may be exposed to are not acceptable, even if the victim has not questioned the wrongness of this behaviour up until the point of service provision.

When responding to perpetrators of DFV, service responses designed to deliver behaviour change and educational programs equally benefit from applying a broad definition to incorporate and address any harmful behaviour, no matter how minor it may seem to the program participants at the time. The same applies to definitions in the context of primary prevention. Educational and awareness-raising campaigns benefit from incorporating a diverse number of harmful behaviours in their definition of DFV to illustrate to the target population that even "minor" forms of these behaviours can have a detrimental impact on the victim's wellbeing and can escalate into more severe forms of abuse over time.

For the purpose of this book, we therefore adopt a broad definition of behaviours designed to coerce, manipulate, or control a victim of DFV. We include current and former intimate partner relationships, extended family relationships, and parent–adult child relationships. Extended family relationships are included due to their cultural relevance in some jurisdictions, e.g. among Australia's Indigenous family networks and communities, and their recognition under relevant protection legislations (Phillips & Vandenbroek, 2014). We do not include parent–child relationships where the abuse is directed at minor children (i.e. children under the age of 18). While this form of abuse is at times classified under family violence in the international (primarily North American) literature, it is more commonly referred to as child maltreatment and treated under a separate legislative framework across a number of jurisdictions. The impact of DFV on children is more commonly discussed in the context of exposure to parental DFV from a research, policy, and practice perspective (Kaukinen, Powers, & Meyer, 2016; Richards, 2011), which we explore in Chapter 6. While the primary focus of this book is on DFV in the form of IPV in line with the prevailing research evidence (Phillips & Vandenbroek, 2014; WHO, 2013), we address cultural diversity in Chapter 8 and gender, age, and relationship diversity among victims and perpetrators in Chapter 7.

Defining DFV as a crime: what are the challenges?

Despite attempts to criminalise DFV and/or some of its inherent behaviours across a number of jurisdictions, challenges remain around the legislative frameworks and service responses required to operationalise DFV as criminal behaviour (Douglas, 2008). Labelling DFV as a crime has increasingly been used in public awareness campaigns to highlight the wrongdoing associated with these behaviours and to discourage public tolerance towards perpetrators. While some jurisdictions have one or more offence categories relating specifically to DFV, others may only criminalise behaviour that in and of itself constitutes a crime under a relevant criminal code. A number of countries have DFV-specific legislation that applies at a federal level, such as the Violence Against Women Reauthorization Act of 2013 (originally the 1994 Violence Against Women Act (VAWA)) in the US, the *Opferschutzgesetz* (Victim Protection Legislation) in Germany (Bundesministerium fuer Familie, Senioren, Frauen und Jugend, 2017), and the Domestic Violence, Crime and Victims Act 2004 in the UK (Graca, 2017). In addition, some jurisdictions have state-level legislation addressing DFV, while others, such as Australia, address DFV from a civil or criminal perspective via individual state and territory legislation (Australian Law Reform Commission, 2010). In addition to challenges arising from state versus federal level legislation addressing the issue of DFV, some legislation further distinguishes between civil and criminal matters associated with DFV. The Violence Against Women Reauthorization Act of 2013, for example, specifies civil law responses to DFV, as does the state and territory legislation informing Australia's response. The UK Domestic Violence, Crime and Victims Act 2004, on the other hand, was designed to address both criminal and civil matters related to DFV. However, its implementation faced challenges, with the Act primarily addressing the civil law needs of victims of DFV in its early stages (Graca, 2017). More recent law reforms in the UK have contributed to a greater utilisation of this legislation in relation to criminal law, in line with its initial intentions.

While it is beyond the scope of this chapter to unpack the nature and associated challenges around different civil and criminal DFV-related legislation, it is important to understand that the definition of a certain behaviour as a crime has implications for possible law enforcement responses. Unless a certain behaviour defined as DFV more broadly has also been defined as a criminal offence under relevant legislation, the only recourse available to victims and those responding to experiences of victimisation (such as law enforcement agencies) are civil remedies, such as the issuing of civil protection orders (also referred to as restraining orders in some jurisdictions) (Douglas, 2008). While civil remedies can be important safety measures for victims of DFV, they do not offer avenues of criminal prosecution of the behaviour. To illustrate this, we use the following example. The behaviours listed below were defined as DFV earlier on in this chapter and have also been defined under a number of policies and legislation:

- Physical or sexual abuse
- Emotional or psychological abuse
- Economic abuse
- Threats or coercion
- Control and domination that creates fear for the victims' safety or wellbeing
- Property damage
- Animal abuse and threats thereof
- Unauthorised surveillance and stalking

However, not all of these behaviours necessarily constitute a criminal offence against property or a person, which therefore restricts the nature of available criminal justice responses. While in some cases, acting on physical abuse, sexual abuse, vandalism, or stalking may be straightforward for police, criminal justice responses to other types of DFV can be much more complicated and, in some instances, impossible. Two examples of recent legislative reforms to criminalise specific DFV behaviours include the criminalisation of non-lethal strangulation in the context of DFV in Australia in 2016 (Criminal Law (Domestic Violence) Amendment Act, 2016) and the criminalisation of coercive control in the context of DFV in the UK in 2016 (Graca, 2017). While it is early days for both legislation changes, researchers have already been alerted to some of the challenges associated with translating these laws into practice (Douglas, 2008; Graca, 2017).

Non-lethal strangulation and DFV in Australia

Non-lethal strangulation is increasingly being identified as a high-risk behaviour in DFV cases (Queensland Health, 2017). This form of abusive behaviour is frequently used by perpetrators as means of maintaining power and control over the victim by demonstrating that the perpetrator has the power to end the victim's life in an instant (Strack, McClane, & Hawley, 2001; Douglas & Fitzgerald, 2014). Taking Australia, for example, Queensland has been the first jurisdiction to acknowledge the severe and pervasive nature of this abusive behaviour by creating a law that allows police to charge perpetrators with the DFV-specific offence of non-lethal strangulation. While previously often dismissed as "choking" or "smothering", the new law encourages police (along with the general public) to think differently about a behaviour that may not necessarily leave immediate physical marks but poses substantial short- and long-term risk to victims' brain and cardiovascular functioning (Douglas & Fitzgerald, 2014). However, researchers have highlighted that it is important that an increase in charges further translates into an increase in prosecutions at the same rate to ensure that legislation changes translate into practice at all tiers of the criminal justice system.

Coercive control and DFV in the UK

Coercive control has been identified as a key feature in DFV behaviour used to manipulate and intimidate victims into submission and compliance (Stark, 2007). While coercive control is frequently observed in abusive relationships marked by a range of DFV behaviours, including more severe forms of physical and sexual violence, many victims experience coercive control without necessarily experiencing physical or sexual abuse. Yet, the manipulative nature of this type of behaviour creates ongoing fear and anxiety in victims, which can have a detrimental impact on short- and long-term psychological wellbeing (Stark, 2007). Acknowledging the severe impact on victims exposed to this form of abuse, and in an attempt to offer victims greater protection from what can be "invisible" forms of abuse, the UK introduced the offence of "coercive and controlling behaviour in intimate and family relationships" under the Serious Crimes Act 2015 (Graca, 2017). While such an introduction of legislation acknowledges the insidious nature of coercive and controlling behaviour in intimate and family relationships and sends a public message of intolerance of DFV, even in the absence of physical abuse, such a law comes with its own implementation challenges. One particular challenge arises from the often invisible nature of coercive control and the power it holds over its victims. While perpetrators may leave no visible marks that can be useful in facilitating the policing and prosecuting of DFV, they tend to strategically manipulate and intimidate their victims into silence when coming in contact with external support sources (Stark, 2007; Johnson, 2008).

Summary

In this chapter, we examined the challenges associated with defining DFV, including its nature and extent across different social settings. We unpacked different factors relating to how DFV is defined from a social and legal (or criminal justice) perspective (including the challenges associated with defining DFV as a crime). The gendered nature of DFV, along with its contested views around the construction of DFV as family conflict versus gendered oppression and abuse, was addressed. Throughout this chapter, we highlighted the extent to which definitions of DFV and their measurement affect how we estimate prevalence rates. We discussed the historical shift in different definitions, including the shift from terms such as "wife beating" towards more contemporary and inclusive definitions of DFV. This chapter provides the foundation for our examinations of the origins and contributing factors of DFV, its impact on victims and children, the accountability of those using violence in intimate and family relationships, and the role of different theoretical, practice, and policy responses examined throughout this book.

Note

1 Gaslighting is commonly understood as practices used by perpetrators of DFV to cause the victim to start questioning their sanity (e.g. by purposely misplacing or hiding items belonging to the victim, such as car keys, or remotely switching electronic devices on or off).

References

Australian Bureau of Statistics (ABS). (2013). *Defining the data challenge for family, domestic and sexual violence* (Cat. No. 4529.0). Canberra: ABS. Retrieved from www.abs.gov. au/AUSSTATS/abs@.nsf/DetailsPage/4529.02013?OpenDocument

Australian Bureau of Statistics (ABS). (2014). *Personal safety survey 2012* (Cat. No. 4906.0). Canberra: ABS.

Australian Law Reform Commission (ALRC). (2010). *Family violence: A national legal response* (ALRC Report 114). Sydney, Australia: ALRC. Retrieved from www.alrc.gov. au/sites/default/files/pdfs/publications/ALRC114_WholeReport.pdf

Australia's National Research Organisation for Women's Safety (ANROWS). (2017). *Personal Safety Survey 2016 fact sheet.* Retrieved from http://anrowsnationalconference. org.au/fact-sheet-personal-safety-survey-2016/

Beel, N. (2013). Domestic violence, gender, and counselling: Toward a more gender-inclusive understanding. *Psychotherapy in Australia, 19*(4), 44–52.

Bryant, W., & Cussen, T. (2015). *Homicide in Australia: 2010–11 to 2011–12: National homicide monitoring program report* (Monitoring Report No. 23). Canberra: Australian Institute of Criminology.

Bundesministerium fuer Familie, Senioren, Frauen und Jugend. (2017). *Mehr Schutz bei haeuslicher Gewalt: Informationen zum Gewaltschutzgesetz.* Berlin: Bundesministerium fuer Justiz and Verbraucherschutz. Retrieved from www.bmjv.de/SharedDocs/ Publikationen/DE/Schutz_haeusliche_Gewalt.pdf?__blob=publicationFile&v=12

Clark, A. (2011). Domestic violence, past and present. *Journal of Women's History, 23*(3), 193–202.

Criminal Law (Domestic Violence) Amendment Act 2016. Retrieved from www.legislation. qld.gov.au/view/pdf/asmade/act-2016-016

Devries, K. M., Mak, J. Y. T., Garcia-Moreno, C., Petzold, M., Child, J. C., Falder, G. F., . . ., Watts, C. H. (2013). The global prevalence of intimate partner violence against women. *Science, 340*(6140), 1527–1528.

Dobash, R. E., & Dobash, R. (1979). *Violence against wives: A case against the patriarchy.* New York: Free Press.

Douglas, H. (2008). The criminal law's response to domestic violence: What's going on? *Sydney Law Review, 30*(3), 439–469.

Douglas, H., & Fitzgerald, R. (2014). Strangulation, domestic violence and the legal response. *Sydney Law Review, 36*, 231–254.

European Union Agency for Fundamental Rights. (2014). *Violence against women: An EU-wide survey.* Retrieved from http://fra.europa.eu/en/publication/2014/violence-against-women-eu-wide-survey-main-results-report

Garcia-Moreno, C., & Watts, C. (2011). Violence against women: An urgent public health priority. *Bulletin of the World Health Organization, 89*, 2.

Graca, S. (2017). Domestic violence policy and legislation in the UK: A discussion of immigrant women's vulnerabilities. *European Journal of Current Legal Issues, 23*(1). Retrieved from http://webjcli.org/article/view/531/715

Heady, B., Scott, D., & DeVaus, D. (1999). Domestic violence in Australia: Are women and men equally violent? *Australian Social Monitor, 2*(3), 57–62.

Johnson, M. P. (2008). *A typology of domestic violence: Intimate terrorism, violence resistance and situational couple violence.* Boston: Northeastern University Press.

Kaukinen, C., Powers, R. A., & Meyer, S. (2016). Estimating Canadian childhood exposure to intimate partner violence and other risky parental behaviors. *Journal of Child Custody, 13*(2–3), 199–218.

Keating, B. (2015). Violence against women: A disciplinary debate and challenge. *The Sociological Quarterly, 56*(1), 108–124.

Kimmel, M. S. (2002). "Gender symmetry" in domestic violence: A substantive and methodological research review. *Violence against Women*, 8(11), 1332–1363.

Mouzos, J., & Makkai, T. (2004). *Women's experiences of male violence: Findings from the Australian component of the International Violence against Women Survey (IVAWS)* (Research and Public Policy Series No. 56). Canberra: Australian Institute of Criminology.

Phillips, J., & Vandenbroek, P. (2014). *Domestic, family and sexual violence in Australia: An overview of the issues* (Parliamentary Library Research Paper Series No. 2014–15). Retrieved from http://parlinfo.aph.gov.au/parlInfo/download/library/prspub/3447585/upload_binary/3447585.pdf;fileType=application/pdf

Queensland Health. (2017). *A health response to non-lethal strangulation in domestic and family violence: Literature review*. Brisbane: State of Queensland. Retrieved from www.health.qld.gov.au/__data/assets/pdf_file/0032/689432/lit-review-non-lethal-strangulation-dva-health-response.pdf

Richards, K. (2011). *Children's exposure to domestic violence in Australia* (Trends & Issues in Crime and Criminal Justice No. 419). Canberra: Australian Institute of Criminology.

Ross, J. M. & Babcock, J. C. (2009). Proactive and reactive violence among intimate partner violent men diagnosed with antisocial and borderline personality disorder. *Journal of Family Violence*, 24(8), 607–617.

Stark, E. (2007). *Coercive control: The entrapment of women in personal life*. New York: Oxford University Press.

Strack, G. B., McClane, G. E., & Hawley, D. (2001). A review of 300 attempted strangulation cases Part I: Criminal legal issues. *Journal of Emergency Medicine*, 21(3), 303–309.

Straus, M. A. (1973). A general systems theory approach to violence between family members. *Social Science Information*, 12(3), 105–125.

Straus, M. A. (1980). Victims and aggressors in marital violence. *American Behavioral Scientist*, 23(5), 681–704.

Straus, M. A. (2007). Processes explaining the concealment and distortion of evidence on gender symmetry in partner violence. *European Journal on Criminal Policy and Research*, 13(3–4), 227–232.

Straus, M. A. (2008). Dominance and symmetry in partner violence by male and female university students in 32 nations. *Children and Youth Services Review*, 30, 252–275.

Straus, M. A. (2009). Gender symmetry in partner violence: Evidence and implications for prevention and treatment. In D. J. Whitaker & J. R. Lutzker (Eds.), *Preventing partner violence: Research and evidence-based intervention strategies* (pp. 245–271). Washington, DC: American Psychological Association.

Straus, M. A., Gelles, R. J., & Steinmetz, S. K. (1980). *Behind closed doors: Violence in the American family*. Garden City, NY: Anchor/Doubleday Press.

Tjaden, P., & Thoennes, N. (2000). *Findings from the National Violence against Women Survey: Full report of the prevalence, incidence, and consequences of violence against women*. National Institute of Justice, Center for Disease Control. Retrieved from www.ncjrs.gov/pdffiles1/nij/183781.pdf

United Nations (UN) Department of Economic and Social Affairs. (2015). *The world's women 2015*. Violence against Women, United Nations. Retrieved from https://unstats.un.org/unsd/gender/chapter6/chapter6.html

University of New South Wales (UNSW). (2013). *Calling it what it really is: A report into lesbian, gay, bisexual, transgender, gender diverse, intersex and queer experiences of domestic and family violence*. NSW, Australia: UNSW.

Violence against Women Reauthorization Act of 2013. Retrieved from www.gpo.gov/fdsys/pkg/BILLS-113s47enr/pdf/BILLS-113s47enr.pdf

Walters, M. L., Chen, J., & Breiding, M. J. (2013). *The National Intimate Partner and Sexual Violence Survey (NISVS): 2010 findings on victimization by sexual orientation*. Atlanta, GA: National Center for Injury Prevention and Control, Center for Disease Control and Prevention.

World Health Organization (WHO). (2013). *Global and regional estimates of violence against women: Prevalence and health effects of intimate partner violence and non-partner sexual violence*. Department of Reproductive Health and Research, London School of Hygiene and Tropical Medicine, South African Medical Research Council. Retrieved from www.who.int/reproductivehealth/publications/violence/9789241564625/en/

Yllö, K., & Bograd, M. (1988). *Feminist perspectives on wife abuse*. Thousand Oaks: Sage Publications.

Chapter 3

Theoretical strands

The usefulness of theory and a theory of usefulness

How theory helps

Theory assists any practical endeavour by directing attention to what is important and by suggesting what can be done about it. When investigating concerns about the safety of family members affected by domestic and family violence (DFV), for instance, information needs to be gathered to help understand and determine the type and level of risk involved and how that risk might be minimised. More particularly, theory offers guidance, directing our actions by means of:

- Observation – what to notice and what to look for
- Description – helping to make sense of and arrange observations into an explanatory framework
- Explanation – extending this framework into an account of how events are linked
- Prediction – determining what is likely to happen next
- Intervention – establishing what can be done to effect change

As student, practitioner, or policymaker, you need to be able to engage with theory and fashion it into a set of tools that can be used to conceptualise, assess, and respond to DFV. You have to be able to evaluate the relative usefulness of competing theories for practice based on a critical analysis of their performance in the practice setting. For practitioners, then, and the agencies that employ them, the "proof of the pudding" is in how theories reflect experience in practice. You might decide that some theory fits some aspects of your work better than others. In this chapter, we consider the usefulness to DFV practice of theory in general and of certain theories in particular.

But which theory? Determining utility for the practice field

The DFV field is complex. It combines multiple issues and involves a range of persons and groups, including a wide range of community and government agencies tasked with responding to this immense problem. The kind of responses available are influenced by diverse academic and political interests. This generates competition between attempts to explain DFV and therefore results in competing theories. The nature of this competition, ironically, has become fierce. Such antagonism has fostered increasing divergence among the theoretical perspectives, as each has based its developing theory on the research it sees as appropriate, often generating disparate and contradictory findings. In this way, while research activity has been frantic and outputs voluminous, the state of theorising in the field has become somewhat bogged down (see Groves & Thomas, 2014). This is not a helpful state of affairs for practitioners, and we must strive to disentangle or reconcile the various components of theory.

In this chapter, our goal is to present the current state of play in DFV theory and to provide the means for readers to form an informed perspective. We propose a way of applying theory in an educated but purposeful fashion, such that it can assist students and practitioners in undertaking good practice. We begin by examining a range of different theories with a view to developing both a firm conceptual grasp of DFV and an understanding of its occurrence. We seek to disentangle the knotting that has occurred in DFV theorising and, by referring to what we call strands of theory, re-weave these strands into a practicable approach.

Person-level theory strands

Some theories aim to understand the occurrence of DFV and the response of its victims by way of the background, and certain other features, of the individuals involved. The features of these individuals and their circumstances, which contribute to the likelihood of violence, are often called risk factors. Conversely, those features that support resistance and resilience to the violence are called protective factors. In this book, we refer to this strand of explanation as person-level theory. While the feminist strand of theories in particular (as we describe later in this chapter) has successfully helped to shift the policy conceptualisation of DFV away from its characterisation as a personal problem and establish it as a social issue, there are strong arguments to suggest that, at the level of practice, these individual protective and risk factors are important to understand within the wider social context. Some (such as Lawson, 2012) maintain that, by drawing on both individual level and broader social explanations, practitioners can more easily grasp the bigger picture of DFV.

Social learning theory

Like many person-level theory strands, social learning theory has its origins in psychology. Given that DFV is widely believed to be a heritable risk, social learning theory has primarily been applied to understanding the intergenerational transmission of violence. Both aggression and victimisation might be "learned" through the observation and imitation of the behaviour and responses of members of the original family (Bandura, 1973; Ehrensaft et al., 2003; Griffing, Fish Ragin, Sage, Madry, & Primm, 2005). DFV can, for example, shape the values and behaviours of children who grow up in an environment where they frequently witness violence and abuse, even where they experience no direct physical harm. Such experiences might contribute in the mind of the developing person to the normalisation of such conduct.

Rational choice theory (benefit theory)

Rational choice theory has a longstanding tradition in psychology, economics, political science, and, more recently, criminology. It assumes that people are rational decision-makers and that where a person perceives choice among courses of action, that person will assess the costs and benefits of each (Kohlberg, 1984). The course of action likely to be chosen by the individual actor is that where the benefits of such action are calculated to outweigh the costs. In the context of DFV, rational choice theory can be used to better understand the actions of both perpetrator and victim.

For example, for his sense of social and emotional wellbeing, Zed places a great deal of emphasis on his performance according to a traditional, conservative version of masculinity. His role as what he might call the family "breadwinner" is central to this identity. Recently, Zed lost his job. His partner, Bee, started paid employment for the first time since their children were born to help with the bills. Zed found that he was expected to shift into an unaccustomed role that included childcare and domestic tasks. Faced with the prospect of what he interpreted as declining status, Zed sought to re-establish control. He felt his choices were severely limited. He could initially accept the situation as a way of maintaining the functioning of the household and family – a considerable benefit. But the costs of this adaptation were also high to him, given his feelings of anxiety and depression related to his sense of failing to "measure up as a man". He began to try to recompense by engaging in compensatory actions: controlling family finances, telling Bee whether and how she could spend money, repeatedly insisting that she was useless because she earned less than he used to, and refusing to carry out domestic tasks. The costs of this course of action included increased conflict with Bee. The benefits, however, were in the emotional satisfaction of feeling angry and in somewhat restoring his sense of power and his status in what he perceived to be a household hierarchy. Implicitly calculating benefits to outweigh costs, he persisted with this strategy. When his partner continued to object, Zed often contemplated resorting to acts of physical violence. The contemplated costs associated with this included criminal justice responses, relationship disintegration, and the loss of access to their mutual children. Seen in the light of rational choice theory, then, Zed weighs up the potential costs and benefits of his actions. As an active and rational decision-maker, if Zed were to conclude that the achievement of regained status and power outweighed his calculation of risk, we might predict that Zed would indeed add physical violence to the list of his other abuses.

Bee, on considering her situation, felt she was faced ultimately with one choice: leaving the relationship with Zed or remaining in it. The benefit of leaving was the prospect of escaping the daily experience of dread: of being ground down by constant belittling and fear of physical violence backed up by Zed's continual threats. She then calculated the risks attached to disclosing the abuse: the prospects of finding alternative accommodation while maintaining employment and caring for her children, the threat to the children's wellbeing, and being continually stalked as Zed sought to escalate his violence. She concluded these costs were too great.

There is a widespread misconception that walking out of an abusive relationship is a logical step for victims (Gracia, 2014; VicHealth, 2014). Rational choice theory, however, helps to understand the dilemma for Bee. Many like Bee never seek the support they need to terminate the violence, and those who do often endure years of abuse before taking that step (Ellsberg, Heise, Peña, Agurto, & Winkvist, 2001; Sabina & Tindale, 2008). Further, many victims are aware that ending an abusive relationship does not necessarily end experiences of abuse. As we discuss in Chapter 5, leaving an abusive partner can be the most dangerous point in a carefully considered process for many women, and experiences of post-separation abuse and control are common.

Self-control

Also referred to as the general theory of crime, this theory is an extension of Hirschi's (1969) social control theory (discussed under "The family violence strand" section of this chapter). Gottfredson and Hirschi (1990) incorporate the role of self-control into the theoretical understanding of why some individuals engage in antisocial behaviour while others do not. Their theory proposes that socially acceptable (confirming) behaviour is the result of secure emotional attachments formed during childhood (emotional bonds to parent figures). People who experience low self-control, they argue, are exposed to inconsistent parenting, have developed weak attachments, and are thought, as adults, to be driven primarily by desire for instant gratification (Gottfredson & Hirschi, 1990). Thus, they might be willing to engage in antisocial behaviour if they believe this will help achieve immediate goals by satisfying present urges. Returning to the case of Zed, we learn that he suffered emotional neglect in his early life, resulting in adverse attachment outcomes. As an adolescent, he had poor self-control; he was impulsive and considered a thrill-seeker. Later, as a partner and father, he felt emotionally needy and fragile. The loss of his job was a breaking point, and he felt driven to regain the gratifying and immediate rewards of status and power by resorting to abusive controlling strategies over family members.

Strain theory

General strain theory has its origins in criminology and is traditionally used to explain criminal and/or violent behaviour as a response to the experience of frustration (Agnew, 1992). The experience of "strain" in this sense is linked to potentially destructive emotions, such as anger and resentment, which might be expressed through violent aggression. In this context, it refers to the individual's subjective perception of stress in relation to a set of circumstances, regardless of any "objective" evaluation of those circumstances and an averagely expectable response. Using the example of Zed once again, his loss of employment might, from an outsider's perspective, be regarded as a potentially stressful but reasonably expectable and manageable event. Zed, however, experienced this as highly stressful (or straining), ultimately contributing to his escalating efforts to aggressively control others. Zed's commitment to a narrow, traditional version of masculinity resulted in his jealously guarding the role of "family breadwinner". His experience of employment loss, when combined with Bee's taking up paid work outside the home, led to a sense of belittlement and feelings of resentment. Bee's engagement in the world outside the home, coupled with his sense of insecurity and vulnerability, engendered feelings of possessive preoccupation, and he began to entertain suspicions around Bee's relationships with male colleagues. These responses are portrayed in the literature as common factors in the occurrence of male-to-female perpetrated DFV (Eriksson & Mazerolle, 2013).

Learned helplessness and survivor theory

According to psychologist Martin Seligman (1972), learned helplessness describes the situation where people (in common with other organisms) have "learned" to feel helpless in the face of situations that, while seemingly unpleasant or restrictive, appear to be perfectly "escapable". The explanation for this state is that it occurs as a result of conditioning whereby people have given up trying because they have come to believe, through familiarity with a set of circumstances, that any strategy of escape will not be successful. Such conditioning is the result of a history of attempts to escape from the aversive situation that have consistently resulted in failure. In this way, persons give up on the belief they can have any control over their situation. A classic example from the animal world is the fully grown elephant that is held in captivity chiefly by being tethered to a relatively small stake. The animal has long been physically capable of freeing itself by pulling the stake from the ground, yet it makes no attempt to do so. The reasoning, according to a learned helplessness explanation, is that the elephant has been thus tethered since it was very young. After many early attempts to pull out the stake, it eventually gave up, having "learned" it was incapable of escaping. With the "belief" established over its first years, it has long since stopped trying.

The construct of learned helplessness was adapted to DFV by Walker (1979) to better understand victims' responses, especially related to experiences of prolonged abuse by an intimate partner. At the time, it was observed that women often appeared to take no steps to leave such a relationship. Much conventional thinking held that the reason for this was found in some aspect of the woman's "nature", such as a masochistic urge. Walker (1979), however, maintained that while these women often seemed inactive in response to abuse, they were anything but: victims' apparent passivity in the face of DFV was in fact a learned response shaped to avoid provocation of the abuse. Some research suggests that these victims may try harder to please the abusive partner by becoming compliant and submissive and may have "learned" that the abuse is a response to their lack of "perfection" or obedience (Towns & Adams, 2000; Walker, 1979). Despite victims adjusting and readjusting their responses in such ways, the abuse continues because of the pervasive and powerful presence of the abuser and the continual victimisation. This essentially "teaches" the woman that her past attempts and sacrifices to pacify her partner are ineffective. The ultimate "learning" is that, regardless of what she does or tries, she is unable to end the abuse. As a result, victims may stop trying to behave in expectable ways to put an end to the abuse or to seek help. This presentation might appear to the uninformed observer as passive or helpless.

Experiences of learned helplessness are particularly detrimental for victims because they discourage them from making proactive, help-seeking decisions in the first instance, which can lead to increasing isolation over time. The longer these victims remain in the abusive relationship, the more self-blame they attach and the more shame they experience for not taking action. This, in turn, serves to increase their immobilisation and delays or decreases the likelihood of their disclosing the abuse at any stage.

While learned helplessness initially characterises the victim as "active" in her attempts to avoid abuse, the ultimate picture is one of passivity and helplessness. However, research specifically applied to this matter suggests that most victims in their responses to DFV become increasingly active over time (e.g. Gondolf & Fisher, 1988). Consistent with rational choice theory outlined earlier in this section, victims tend to *actively* contemplate and assess the outcomes of their decisions and subsequent actions. They may remain in or return to abusive relationships, but they tend to be purposeful in goals around harm minimisation.

Symbolically, and perhaps functionally, the term survivor might be preferential to victim because of the latter's erroneous reflection of passive endurance. Gondolf and Fisher's (1988) survivor theory is framed around this survivor construct. Responding to Walker's learned helplessness explanation, it emphasises the active, problem-focused aspects of survival, rather than passive, coping victimhood. Documented victim accounts of escape from abuse (e.g. Hoff, 1990) have added further weight to the survivor theory assertion that victims' responses to DFV are best construed as adaptations in the face of changing dynamics in an abusive relationship. Such responses, it seems, become more active with increasing frequency and severity of abuse and are thought to increase the likelihood of explicit help-seeking over time.

The family violence strand

In contrast to person-level theory strands are sociological explanations of DFV. These explanations can be categorised into two distinct perspectives: feminist and family violence. Both perspectives aim to understand and explain DFV in the broader social interactional context in which it occurs, moving away from a focus on individual traits or characteristics. The feminist perspective considers DFV to be inextricably associated with gender. The other key sociologically oriented explanation, the family violence strand, views DFV primarily as a family conflict issue.

Family conflict and systems theory

Family violence perspectives aim to explain DFV as a manifestation of family conflict, which is considered a universal phenomenon. As such, the unit of analysis is the family, rather than the individual victim or perpetrator, and the problem is viewed through the lens of family interaction. According to such thinking, this type of violence develops out of (normal) family system conflict that has escalated to become increasingly unfettered because of dysfunction in that human system. Since systems operate within wider systems and are cyclical, this theory therefore also claims to be able to account for intergenerational violence stemming from child abuse and neglect.

The family violence strand of theory aligns with the theoretical underpinnings of general systems theory (Bertalanffy, 1968). Using the metaphor of a system, the family is seen as a set of interacting parts essentially functioning to protect, nurture and socialise offspring, and to prepare them for an eventual independent life. Tension and conflict are inevitable by-products of this process (as, for example, the child's desire for independence comes up against the parental priority for protective security) and so these elements are considered both universal and "normal". Explanations of family violence then focus on the particular characteristics of the family unit (system) and the interactions among its members (system parts or subsystems). Such violence is considered to be associated with *cycles* of behaviour. These cycles are predictable and repetitive patterns that change over time. Stemming from an initial individual action that provokes a reaction, followed by a subsequent response in the originator, and so on, a pattern of escalating conflict ensues. Generally, a self-balancing mechanism within the family system will operate to deescalate such patterns, but in some circumstances (or in some family systems) this self-righting mechanism fails and the conflict deteriorates into violence. Contributing factors in DFV include forces for change and mechanisms of stability such as socialisation, conflict resolution competence, stress levels, and the maintenance of the family power structure. Family conflict, seen in this systems-thinking context, can also be used to account for elder abuse, given that this primarily occurs in the family context where adult children act as informal carers for their elderly parents. Family dynamics and system-level stress are said to contribute to occurrences of elder abuse (Ziminski Pickering & Phillips, 2014).

Social control theory

Social control theory has its origins in the functionalist theories of crime (such as Hirschi's social bond theory; 1969) and is linked to rational choice theory. It proposes that, in common with other types of offenders, the DFV perpetrator resorts to violence as a means to achieve a desired outcome, having calculated that the benefits outweigh the risks in doing so. In other words, they believe they can get away with it. DFV is seen as a mechanism used to pursue a certain goal, such as a partner's compliance or submission. So, even though the perpetrator might appreciate their actions as being morally "wrong", they engage in abuse because they believe that repercussions will be absent or negligible. Such a conclusion can be reinforced by subsequent experiences, such as the victim's failure to disclose the abuse, law enforcers accepting the account of the perpetrator over that of the victim, or a court's lenient or delayed formal responses to cases involving DFV. Social policy analysts who subscribe to social control theory then might conclude that the presence of adequate social control mechanisms, such as reliable law enforcement responses, could provide valid responses to the DFV problem. This would work by increasing the likelihood that, in the would-be perpetrator's calculations, potential costs would more likely outweigh potential benefits of DFV as a strategy of goal achievement.

Subsequent revisions of this theory, however, propose that social control and its deterrent mechanisms are only effective in cases where the would-be perpetrator has high stakes in conformity (see, for example, Sherman, Smith, Schmidt, & Rogan, 1992). That is to say, such consequences have sufficient deterrence value only where persons hold a relatively high investment in, and commitment to, conventional reputation and status. In this case, where the individual calculates that they cannot rely on evading the detection of their abusive actions, mechanisms of social control are likely to prevail and therefore be effective in preventing them from going through with acts that would represent such risk. The prospect of the loss of, say, stable employment or the impression of conventional family commitment, might represent a sufficient quantum of deterrence for perpetrators. Where this investment is low, however, the prospect of arrest, conviction, and other criminal consequences are likely to have less inhibitory influence.

Of course, stake in conformity can vary at a group or community level as well as at an individual level. Some communities might place less weight on status investment because they are more concerned with priorities fundamental to day-to-day survival. In addition, the degree of tolerance of DFV along with support for the idea of masculine entitlement may vary across contexts and groups within society, such as "gang culture" settings. Somewhat related to the notion of DFV tolerance is the subculture of violence theory.

Subculture of violence theory

This theory was originally developed to understand the higher prevalence rates of general violence within certain social groups or community settings. It seeks to explain the use of general violence through exposure to social attitudes that tolerate and promote the use of violence (as, for example, a conflict resolution tactic). Communities marked by social marginalisation are said to have higher levels of violence (see, for example, Treadwell & Garland, 2011). Essentially, the subculture of violence theory proposes that frequent exposure to violent norms and attitudes desensitises the individual, normalising violence in their lives. While initially not designed to explain DFV, this theory has the potential to explain why higher levels of intimate partner violence (IPV) tend to be concentrated in neighbourhood or community subcultures where the use of violence is more acceptable in general, such as criminal gangs.

Resource theory

Resource theory suggests that in relationships with traditional gender role distributions, men obtain and maintain status and power through their financial contribution to family life. Relationships where access to resources are reversed by gender – couples where the woman has more success in her career or contributes more to the family income than her male partner – can be problematic where this imbalance challenges male perceptions of superiority. The male partner may feel the need to re-establish his superior social status by drawing on other resources, and the use of violence may be seen as one such resource suitable to achieving this goal. As a result, we tend to see higher levels of DFV in relationships marked by status incompatibility (Kaukinen, 2004).

The feminist strand

While the family violence strand of theorising is characterised by an explanation of DFV as conflict reinforced through individual and community-level factors, feminist theories centre on the role of gender inequality and oppression. Theorists point to the historical legacy of patriarchal norms and institutions, which continue to influence gendered power relations and sustain the oppression of women by men. The unit of analysis here is neither the person nor the family/community, but social structure and institution, and particularly the gendered nature of power relations. The focus is on violence against women, and the family is just one domain where this is expressed.

When taken together, prevalence and crime surveys from around the world suggest that men abuse women in domestic and family settings at a disproportionately damaging rate (World Health Organization [WHO], 2013). The international data on the association between gender inequality and DFV is also strong (WHO, 2013). The very pervasiveness of men's power and status over women globally, and across a wide range of social and economic domains, is compelling evidence in support of the feminist argument that DFV is facilitated, supported, and reinforced by much of the world around us.

Feminist theories relating to the nature of male-perpetrated IPV date back to the late nineteenth century. However, their success in drawing increasing public and policy attention to its patriarchal nature began in the late 1970s (Dobash & Dobash, 1979; Yllö & Bograd, 1988). This movement, led by social activism, was informed by radical feminism and sought to explain the predicament of women in relation to their social identity or status within society. Within this approach, male-perpetrated violence against women is seen as an extension of the historical domination, and even ownership, of women by men. The cultural values and social institutions moulded and generationally transmitted by this history continues to allow men to exercise power and control over their female partners. Feminist theories have traditionally emphasised that DFV in the form of male-to-female perpetrated IPV is substantially different to other forms of family violence (such as child abuse, sibling abuse, IPV between same-sex partners, or perpetrated by women against men). Feminist perspectives strongly reject the notion, portrayed by the family violence theory strand, that IPV may just as likely be perpetrated by women as it is by men (Dobash & Dobash, 1979). Consistent with the family violence perspective, however, feminist theories reject the notion that DFV is the result of individual pathology. DFV is in fact not uncommon, aberrant, or deviant, but instead is common, typical, and normalised. It is not so much individual psychology that causes some to use violence in intimate relationships but rather the socio-structural context of patriarchy that fosters and facilitates violence against women. Such violence encompasses a wide range of exploitive practices applied in combination over time in a setting where women are often presented with few avenues of escape. Viewed through a feminist lens, then, such multifaceted "violence" might be more accurately described as abuse.

Weaving the strands: integrative theories

Polarisation

We mentioned earlier in this chapter that the diversity of views among DFV theories has often been fiercely competitive, as distinct ideological differences between researchers and theorists come to the fore. While family systems theorists, for example, have insisted that their extensive research demonstrates the irrelevance of gender to DFV, feminists counter that such research is invalid because it is based on the measurement of individual behavioural incidents without reference to the context of the aggression or the intentions of the aggressor. Their argument here is that to ignore the importance of the motivation of the aggressor is to miss important indicators of the magnitude of the violence behind any particular incident: whether the intention was, for instance, to reinforce interpersonal domination or to defend oneself (or other family members) from attack. Moreover, feminists argue, research that relies on quantitative measures of violence in isolation is oblivious to features that would reflect a sustained regime of abuse, such as its strategic patterning over time or the power relations involved. Others, taking an individualistic stance, argue that the sociological approaches taken by both the feminist and family violence strands are insufficiently scientifically based or supported to warrant proper consideration. Corvo and Johnson (2013), for instance, argue that the role of psychopathology and neuropsychopathology are far more reliable explanatory concepts than sociological ones, given that these features are much more closely associated with DFV than other factors in empirical investigations. Therefore, such scholars promote an individual (person-level) unit of analysis in research.

While researchers from different camps remain locked in these often bitter debates, they continue to investigate quite different aspects of DFV. The development of DFV theory has been inhibited as a result. For the practitioner, this is problematic. It is important to keep in mind, however, that each of the theories we have outlined can be considered as part of a strand of theory, each with its own strengths and limitations. While interpersonal and sociological theories (such as family conflict theories and feminist theories) help to understand DFV and the social and cultural issues associated with each view, most do not take individual-level factors into consideration. On the other hand, the person-level theories, drawing on individual characteristics and circumstances, help us understand personal experiences of and responses to DFV, but neglect the influence of the social context in which DFV occurs. How, then, does a practitioner choose between these theories while at the same time accommodating the complexities at the level of practice? One response is not to perceive these features in isolation but rather to draw on different theories and aim to integrate them into our understanding of, and responses to, victims and perpetrators of DFV – in other words, to weave the strands.

Ecological theory

Ecological theory weaves these theory strands by combining the individual and interpersonal levels of understanding of DFV with the broader socio-structural level. Individual behaviour is seen as nested within the broader social context. Bronfenbrenner's seminal (1979) ecological systems theory proposed that the experiences and responses of an individual person are informed by their embeddedness in different levels of a broader social context. Each person is inextricably bound into a microsystem, which is most commonly and immediately a family unit. Factors prevalent in this unit of analysis (such as those outlined in the family systems approach), however, are not the only phenomena affecting the dynamics in that family. As well, the family unit experiencing DFV along with its "system" components (child, abusive parent, victimised parent) is influenced by factors shaping the "exosystem". The "exosystem" represents aspects of the general community context (socioeconomic status, poverty, unemployment rates, etc.), along with support services available in that community/neighbourhood. Beyond that, even broader systems bear down and interact with these subsystems in a dynamic relationship. These broader-level systems, with labels such as "exosystem" and "macrosystem" (Bronfenbrenner, 1979), are also each in reciprocal relationships. With respect to DFV, the nature and frequency of media reporting on sensitive topics such as public or domestic violence might be seen to have a desensitising effect on public attitudes and violence may become normalised, especially where a particular neighbourhood is frequently chosen for media reports on violence. At the same time, longstanding patriarchal attitudes and rigid gender role expectations run throughout the lower order systems, influencing female employment opportunities and conditions and creating a semi-tolerance of male aggression in a family setting.

Typologies and categories

Another means of integrating antagonistic theory strands, and perhaps seeking to broker the warring parties, has been to propose distinct types of violence that incorporate both sides of the gender symmetry debate. Johnson and Ferraro (2000) provide a four-category system comprising common couple violence, violent resistance, mutual control, and intimate terrorism. As the labels suggest, these categories form a typology that accounts for symmetrical (equally aggressive), (primarily) female-perpetrated violence, and (primarily male-perpetrated) strategic controlling violence. This latter category is synonymous with the most harmful, highly gendered variant typically portrayed as the core issue in DFV. Drawing on the work of Johnson and colleagues, Stark (2007) developed a three-factor typology that includes the widely cited coercive control type. While not explicitly arguing for a gendered division, such categories as intimate terrorism and coercive control at least hint that gender is a highly influential factor in DFV.

Although these attempts to reconcile competing theory strands appeal to the desire to counter the trend of increasing polarisation in the field, the categorical frameworks they generate have not been well borne out by research. The behaviour and experience of those studied do not fit well into the neat categories and theories that have been generated. Furthermore, the models have struggled to provide answers to the complexity of everyday practice issues. We said at the outset of this chapter that the usefulness of theories to practitioners is in how well they represent the lived experience of workers and their clients in practice. More recent developments in theory-making have brought a post-structuralist lens to bear on this problem.

Post-structural influences and implications for practice

A critique of structuralist and functionalist theory

Post-structural theorising represents perhaps not an additional theoretical strand, or even a way of reconciling the strands, but a different way of reframing the issue. This reframing is based on a different philosophical position. From a post-structuralist perspective, the strands outlined in the previous sections have a common tendency to rely on structuralist and functionalist representations of persons, groups, and societies. That is to say, they are based on grand, overarching, and prescriptive theories (such as Marxism) and positivist notions of social science, such as those held by contemporary psychology. These ideas, while powerful and pervasive, are characterised by post-structuralists as founded on outdated, mechanistic ways of understanding the world of living persons, and on rigid metaphors – such as drives, pressures, stresses, and strains. These metaphors are, it is claimed, derived from nineteenth-century physics. Understanding the multiple shifting intentions, preferences, hopes, and commitments held by people in the groups they live in requires a more human and flexible approach. For DFV practitioners, this is an interesting development. Indeed, rather than trying to impose rigid cause-and-effect explanations that totalise the life situation of those caught up in DFV and assign them and their actions to particular categories, the practitioner is invited to consider the various pressures and drives used to describe the problem not as essential facts and representative of real forces but rather as outmoded social constructions. Alternatively, the practitioner is invited to understand the situation from the ground up: from the perspective of those people who are caught up in DFV. In this, the practitioner engages in speculative curiosity about the person and their hopes, dreams, and wishes for themselves, their children, and their family group. She takes account of these intentions and commitments in relation to the context of powerful expectations that surround them. Post-structuralism helps in responding to the call to hear a wider range of voices and variety of positions from the people we work with and their diversity, plurality, and fluidity. In other words, it is a response to the complexity of this work and a means of reinterpreting persons and families, not as the problem but as actors with the potential to resist the actual problem of DFV, which is itself cast as the common adversary.

The durability of the feminist strand

The feminist strand of DFV theorising has proved remarkably durable and adaptable in the face of the increasing complexity of the field and burgeoning knowledge derived from its research. Feminist thought and activism have pioneered consciousness-raising and practical responses. As such, it has played the lead role in setting the agenda and making the issue visible and public. Agencies and jurisdictions far and wide have tended to use feminist-strand principles, conceptual tools, and practice frameworks (such as the Duluth model; Pence & Paymar, 1993) in their response to the DFV problem.

In terms of its broader development as an activist movement, feminism has evolved in its aspirational endeavours from the political representation of women, to seeking gender equality, to an analysis of gender power relations. More recently, scholarly feminists have led an interrogation of gender in the context of the biographical self, with implications for DFV (Anderson, 2009). In terms of theorising on DFV, feminism has evolved from providing a general definition of women's sexual exploitation to an understanding of gendered experiences in the context of social interaction more broadly.

In these latest manifestations, what has come to be known as post-structural feminism has played a part in resisting the polarising dichotomies of modernist thinking outlined above by reconsidering key issues in the field. These issues include experiences related to power and control, the nature of gender, the nature of family, and the role of patriarchy. Prominent in the reconsiderations of these issues have been diversity, fluidity, and multiplicity. For example, while dominant voices strongly invite men to take up normative masculine roles and women to adopt normative feminine roles, there is increasing recognition among post-structural feminists of personal agency in how one "does" (or "performs"; Butler, 1993) gender. This helps to explain the role of gender in why women are sometimes violent and abusive and how same-sex relationships can become characterised by coercive control. Much of the research that has supported this thinking involves understanding the lived experience of persons who have suffered or perpetrated DFV. This qualitative focus on the flow of events and the experience of them contrasts sharply with studies that have sought to quantify separate, discrete factors such as incidence and frequency. It has been argued, however, that this reductionist way of characterising DFV might in fact serve to reinforce and support ways in which men think about their violence (Kelly & Westmarland, 2016). The more inclusive and less rigid post-structuralist manifestation of feminist thinking on DFV is evident in intersectionality theory, which provides a clear model for practitioners confronted with the complex realities of the field.

Intersectionality

Intersectionality theory helps to make sense of this complexity by describing how not just gender but other layers of disadvantage and discrimination interlock to concentrate and exacerbate the focus of oppression and thereby the relatively high incidence of DFV among particular groups (see Nixon & Humphreys, 2010). While intersectionality has its origins in the feminist (gendered) approaches to understanding DFV, it has moved on from considering gender as the sole unit of analysis. This is based on the acknowledgement that privileging gender in this way has paid insufficient attention to the diversity of women's experiences in relation to other features of their lives. As a result, intersectionality theory seeks to understand the diversity of women's experiences of DFV in the context of other marginalising factors, such as race, culture, religion, sexual orientation, and disability. In particular, it is focused on how these issues tend to interlock and combine in a mutually exacerbating fashion (Crenshaw, 1991). This approach also acknowledges that women's experiences of, and their responses to, DFV are further complicated by factors associated with characteristics of their personal biography or social environments that add additional layers of stigma and social marginalisation. So, for example, the difficulties of a woman living with a disability may be exacerbated by her dependence (e.g. physical and/or financial) on an abusive partner. These victims may experience an even greater level of entrapment than women who do not live with a disability. Furthermore, the intersection between violence and gender with other layers of disadvantage (e.g. class or race) leads to even more egregious experiences of entrapment and restricted access to appropriate resources. We explore several of these elements further in Chapters 7 and 8.

It is clearly helpful to the practitioner to be able to consider the intersection of a range of features when seeking to account for the occurrence of DFV in a particular case. It also helps make sense of the array of factors around a victim's help-seeking inclinations, and how the course of help seeking might differ significantly across a diverse range of settings.

Through an intersectional lens, then, while gender remains the prominent and pervasive variable in understanding DFV, it is considered in relation to a potentially wide range of other factors that combine and intersect with it. This is useful to the practitioner in helping to generate a clear formulation of the case and a well-informed response.

Conclusion

Theory is critical for practice because it helps make sense of the complex array of factors – individual, interpersonal, and social – that are involved in DFV. It also informs practitioners about what to look for in assessing risk and provides guidance in taking action. We conclude that, while other strands of theory, taken separately and together, can be helpful in achieving these practice tasks, when the prevalence and severity of violence against women (and the effects on other family members) is taken account, feminist gender analysis, informed by post-structuralist considerations, provides the most compelling account of DFV.

Throughout the remainder of this book, we return to these strands of theory and in particular to contemporary feminist theory in order to help make sense of the complex circumstances found in practice.

In giving critical consideration to the matter of DFV theory, we have reasoned that it is important to identify explanations that account for the characteristic patterning of DFV in its most pernicious form (coercive control), while also acknowledging the agency and purposes of those involved and affected. Applying this reasoning to those who perpetrate DFV, then, it is important to conceptualise this group and its members in a way that both describes their characteristics and allows for the critical element of choice and responsibility. We take up this challenge in Chapter 4.

References

Agnew, R. (1992). Foundation for a general strain theory. *Criminology, 30*(1), 47–87.

Anderson, K. (2009). Gendering coercive control. *Violence against Women, 15*(12), 1444–1457.

Bandura, A. (1973). *Aggression: A social learning analysis*. Englewood Cliffs: Prentice Hall.

Bertalanffy, L. von. (1968). *General system theory: Foundation, development, application*. New York: George Braziller.

Bronfenbrenner, U. (1979). *The ecology of human development*. Cambridge, MA: Harvard University Press.

Butler, J. (1993). *Bodies that matter: On the discursive limits of "sex"*. London: Routledge.

Corvo, K., & Johnson, P. (2013). Sharpening Ockham's razor: The role of psychopathology and neuropsychopathology in the perpetration of domestic violence. *Aggression and Violent Behavior, 18*(1), 175–182.

Crenshaw, K. W. (1991). Mapping the margins: Intersectionality, identity politics, and violence against women of color. *Stanford Law Review, 43*, 124–299.

Dobash, R. P., & Dobash, R. E. (1979). *Violence against wives: A case against the patriarchy*. New York, NY: Free Press.

Ehrensaft, M. K., Cohen, P., Brown, J., Smailes, E., Chen, H., & Johnson, J. (2003). Intergenerational transmission of partner violence: A 20-year prospective study. *Journal of Consulting and Clinical Psychology, 71*(4), 741–753.

Ellsberg, M., Heise, L., Peña, R., Agurto, S., & Winkvist, A. (2001). Researching domestic violence against women: Methodological and ethical considerations. *Studies in Family Planning, 32*(1), 1–16.

Eriksson, L., & Mazerolle, P. (2013). A general strain theory of intimate partner homicide. *Aggression and Violent Behavior, 18*(5), 462–470.

Gondolf, E. W., & Fisher, E. R. (1988). *Battered women as survivors: An alternative to treating learned helplessness*. Lexington, MA: Lexington Books.

Gottfredson, M. R., & Hirschi, T. (1990). *A general theory of crime*. Stanford, CA: Stanford University Press.

Gracia, E. (2014). Intimate partner violence against women and victim-blaming attitudes among Europeans. *Bulletin of the World Health Organization, 92*, 380–381.

Griffing, S., Fish Ragin, D., Sage, R. E., Madry, L., & Primm, B. J. (2005). Reasons for returning to abusive relationships: Effects of prior victimization. *Journal of Family Violence, 20*(5), 341–348.

Groves, N., & Thomas, T. (2014). *Domestic violence and criminal justice*. Abingdon, UK: Routledge.

Hirschi, T. (1969). *Causes of delinquency*. Berkeley: University of California Press.

Hoff, L. A. (1990). *Battered women as survivors*. London, UK: Routledge.

Johnson, M. P., & Ferraro, K. J. (2000). Research on domestic violence in the 1990s: Making distinctions. *Journal of Marriage and Family, 62*, 948–963.

Kaukinen, C. (2004). Status compatibility, physical violence, and emotional abuse in intimate relationships. *Journal of Marriage and Family, 66*(2), 452–471.

Kelly, L., & Westmarland, N. (2016). Naming and defining "domestic violence": Lessons from research with violent men. *Feminist Review, 112*, 113–127.

Kohlberg, L. (1984). *The psychology of moral development: The nature and validity of moral stages* (1st ed.). San Francisco: Harper Row.

Lawson, J. (2012). Sociological theories of intimate partner violence. *Journal of Human Behavior in the Social Environment, 22*(5), 572–590.

Nixon, J., & Humphreys, C. (2010). Marshalling the evidence: Using intersectionality in the domestic violence frame. *Social Politics, 17*(2), 137–158.

Pence, E., & Paymar, M. (1993). *Education groups for men who batter: The Duluth model.* New York, NY: Springer.

Sabina, C., & Tindale, R. (2008). Abuse characteristics and coping resources as predictors of problem-focused coping strategies among battered women. *Violence against Women, 14*(4), 437–456.

Seligman, M. E. P. (1972). Learned helplessness. *Annual Review of Medicine, 23*, 407–412.

Sherman, L., Smith, D., Schmidt, J., & Rogan, D. (1992). Crime, punishment, and stake in conformity: Legal and informal control of domestic violence. *American Sociological Review, 57*(5), 680–690.

Stark, E. (2007). *Coercive control: How men entrap women in personal life.* Oxford, UK: Oxford University Press.

Towns, A., & Adams, P. (2000). If I really loved him enough, he would be ok: Women's accounts of male partner violence. *Violence against Women, 6*(5), 558–585.

Treadwell, J., & Garland, J. (2011). Masculinity, marginalization and violence: A case study of the English Defence League. *The British Journal of Criminology, 51*(4), 621–634.

VicHealth. (2014). *Australians' attitudes to violence against women: Findings from the 2013 National Community Attitudes towards Violence against Women Survey (NCAS).* Melbourne: Victorian Health Promotion Foundation.

Walker, L. E. (1979). *The battered woman.* New York: Harper & Row.

World Health Organization [WHO]. (2013). *Global and regional estimates of violence against women: Prevalence and health effects of intimate partner violence and non-partner sexual violence.* Geneva: WHO. Retrieved from www.who.int/reproductivehealth/publications/violence/9789241564625/en/

Yllö, K., & Bograd, M. (1988). *Feminist perspective on wife abuse.* Newbury Park, CA: Sage Publications.

Ziminski Pickering, C. E., & Phillips, L. R. (2014). Development of a causal model for elder mistreatment. *Public Health Nursing, 31*(4), 363–372.

Chapter 4

Enacting violence in private spaces
Understanding perpetratorhood

Why practitioners need to understand those who use violence in the home

In Chapter 2, we considered the nature and extent of domestic and family violence (DFV). We described it in terms of an endemic public health problem and a social issue of global proportion. It is an issue of sprawling complexity, with staggering implications. It is, therefore, a priority for law- and policymakers. Responses, however, need to be informed by theory that will take into account the entangled nature of domestic relationships and the enduring centrality of family life. In short, intervention must be informed by a well-developed understanding of the nature of DFV. Because it is a human problem, such knowledge needs to include an appreciation of those who experience it first hand: their circumstances, intentions, and actions. Early responses to this issue were understandably concerned with the primary need to attend to those who had been victimised. However, it has become apparent that, if we are to tackle the problem at its core, then we must – as the oft-told parable implies – go beyond the habitual practice of rescuing bodies from the river and venture upstream to learn who is pushing them in. Once these offenders are identified, we can set about the question of knowing how to approach them. Nevertheless, this next step is not simple. What do we do next when we come face-to-face with the perpetrator? To extend on the metaphor in the parable: after pulling so many from the river, when we encounter this offender upstream, as "the cause" of the bodies in the river, we are likely to feel considerable anger with him. We find that he knows intimately those he has pushed into the river, has shared a life with them, and claims he has loved them. So we expect contrition, regret. Instead, we hear excuses and justifications. Furthermore, he appears sincerely distressed and confused by his "predicament". He appears to believe he is the wronged person. While we remain suspicious of the circumstances and the man's intentions, this situation is more complex than it might have first appeared. If we are going to appropriately assist those he has victimised, and if we seek to prevent reoccurrence, we need a nuanced understanding of the perpetrator's situation vis-à-vis his place in the lives of those he has treated so poorly. Assessing the situation of this man with a view to deciding how to treat him is the subject of this chapter. In short, we intend to review what is known about what we refer to here as per-petratorhood.

We have made the assumption that the offender in the above scenario is male and that the "bodies in the river" are women and children. This assumption is made on the basis of the conclusions from our discussion of debates surrounding gender and violence in Chapter 3. In that chapter, we noted that people use violence for a range of reasons and in order to bring about a variety of outcomes. Sometimes it is used with the intention to deter or to protect, sometimes to con-trol and restrict. We concluded that, regardless of quantitative data concern-ing the incidence of violence and the identity of the initiator, it is the context, pattern, and intention of the violence that are the most persuasive features in understanding DFV as a "wicked" (i.e. deeply concerning and persistent) prob-lem. The sustained and strategic use of violence-based tactics against partner and family, thereby inducing fear and compliance, constitutes a system of oppression that is, predominantly, perpetrated by men over women and their children. Why this should be the case is predicated on a range of explanations and hypotheses. It is important, however, that, from this explanatory literature, we establish clar-ity in order assess, from an informed and insightful perspective, the case that confronts practitioners. As this book is concerned with informing practice, we will concentrate especially here on teasing out those explanations that are best suited to informing intervention. This chapter will look closely at these explana-tions with a view to forming a working hypothesis.

We begin by reviewing the systemic embeddedness of men's dominance and control over women and children. On this basis, we examine theory that best frames the problem, taking into account the diversity and complexity surround-ing the basic scenario of the DFV committed by men. Then we take an in-depth look at gender, and particularly masculinity, as the core issue in determining this kind of abuse. Given the naivety of proposing the simplistic hypothesis that "gender causes DFV", we are left to account for contributing and mediating fac-tors such as the psychology of the man, the circumstances of his community, and the role of personal agency.

Context and history

> Charity and beating begins at home.
> – John Fletcher, *Wit Without Money*, c. 1639

Feminist analysis refers consistently to global gender inequality as the soil in which DFV thrives. Indeed, even those who critique the structural feminist explanation of DFV tend to acknowledge the patriarchal context as at least a significant factor. To achieve a fundamental grasp of the perpetrator's sense of entitlement in using a range of abusive tactics against those he lives with (and professes to care for), we must be deeply aware of the breadth of convention and the depth of institutional bedrock that support this behaviour. This involves understanding his access to privileges and power and the features of society that effectively turn a blind eye to, or are even collusive with, such conduct.

Background

DFV has a longstanding history in Western society. In 1800 BC, the Babylonian king Hammurabi established a code that included the determination that a father and husband could inflict punishment on any member of their household. Under the ancient Roman principle of the *Paterfamilia*, the oldest male of the household was reassured thus:

> If you should discover your wife in adultery, you may with impunity put her to death without a trial, but if you should commit adultery or indecency, she must not presume to lay a finger on you, nor does the law allow it.
>
> (Goldstein, 2002, p. 29)

This notion of the ruling father is the basis of patriarchy, a hierarchical generational concept that centrally empowers men and operates across time and place.

Some 3,500 years later (well into the late nineteenth century), women still had no, or very limited, legal rights. Early Saxon law permitted a wife to inherit property on the death of her husband, but even this law was revoked by the nineteenth-century Dower Acts, whereby husbands were able to will their land away from their wives on their death. In effect, given that women were not able to access independent employment at this time, the year 1832 became a benchmark for removing any remaining economic power women had (McCalman, 1999).

In the traditional English view, an Englishman's home was regarded as his castle and immune from the control or interference of others. Longstanding fear of invasion and violence imposed on the home from outside represented a primary anxiety for homeowners. What happened within the home was the domain of the husband and father. This traditional family structure links gender inequality with violence; and, since the family has a powerful influence over gendered attitudes and conduct, it is widely recognised as a key determinant of DFV (Tur-Prats, 2015).

English Common Law provided the foundation on which the legal systems in the US, Canada, Australia, and New Zealand were founded. In Common Law prior to the 1800s, a husband was permitted to administer corporal punishment towards his wife so long as it did not inflict permanent injury (Siegel, 1996). It was following early agitation by women's rights groups and the suffragette movement that Common Law began to change across Western jurisdictions, although by no means in a consistent fashion. By the late 1800s, physical chastisement was no longer legally sanctioned in England and the US. Nevertheless, such cases continued to be treated differently from other types of violence (Siegel, 1996).

The courts were still loath to intervene, as the privacy of the household was upheld ahead of concerns about violence, and low socioeconomic communities had little recourse to the law (Hafmeister, 2011).

Despite the "physical chastisement" aspect of Common Law being reformed in the 1800s, it was still within the law for husbands to sexually violate their wives well into the late 1900s, with Australia and New Zealand not amending this legislation until the 1980s. Until this time, marital rape immunity was based on the notion that a woman became her husband's property upon marriage, alongside the entrenched expectation that women should not deny their husbands (see the Australian Law Reform Commission [ALRC] report 2010, S24.59).

Given this long history of domestic inequality, it is not surprising that residual beliefs surrounding men's entitlements, including their "ownership" of women and children, have proved difficult to shift and continue to find expression in traditional Christian and other belief systems. This longstanding and pervasive nature of men's hegemony over women and children provides a compelling foundation to a gendered explanation of contemporary DFV – the spine of the structural feminist perspective (see Chapter 3). Nevertheless, even the most strident advocates of this perspective would not claim that this is sufficient to explain DFV in and of itself. The claim, for instance, that patriarchy "causes" a man to engage in DFV is naïve. It is exposed as simplistic when confronted with the facts that not *all* men abuse members of their family and it is not *only* men who engage in such behaviour. Furthermore, it is becoming increasingly apparent that the range of backgrounds of those who use violence in this way, the types of abusive strategies they use, and their motivations for doing so vary quite considerably. Theory drawn on to explain the broad range of problems must be more nuanced or at least supplemented with the consideration of other factors. We next consider ideas for accounting for the differences and diversity surrounding the enacting of DFV, in terms of both person and behaviour.

Framing the issue of perpetration: accounting for diversity of offender and behaviour

Developments in the classification of DFV

The momentum in policy and practice that directs attention towards male perpetrators of DFV was initially shaped by the experiences of women's shelter movements and the compelling nature of feminist analysis. Interventions targeting men and their violence towards women and children correspondingly took the shape of gender-based group psychoeducation programs designed to enlighten and sensitise these men to their exploitation of their position of power and awareness of their engagement with techniques of control through fear and intimidation (Pence & Paymar, 1993). While this educative approach has evolved over time (e.g. Pence & Paymar, 2003), the paradigm has proved enormously influential, winning favour with policymakers across jurisdictions (e.g. Maiuro & Eberle, 2008). Nevertheless, there has been increasingly shrill opposition to it. Critics draw attention to the mixed outcomes from evaluation research into the effectiveness of such programs (e.g. Dutton & Corvo, 2006). One reason proposed for the uncertainty in terms of outcome is that this kind of intervention tends to consider the DFV perpetrator to be a particular and uniform type of abuser, when in fact there are a range of motivations and strategies for engaging in violent behaviour, not only among individuals but also between couples, within family systems, and across different cultural settings and social groups. According to this counterargument, the monolithic image of the serially offending, abusive, and controlling man has dominated because this type of violence and those seen to be responsible for it have most commonly been brought to public attention (Holtzworth-Munroe & Meehan, 2004). Such men therefore are the most likely to be arrested, convicted, and mandated to attend treatment, chiefly because, in these cases, the abuse has become extreme over a prolonged period. These critics say that it is not that this classification is unimportant but rather the identified needs of this particular type of aggressor might be quite different from those whose violence is more typically related to, say, unrestrained, explosive anger. These two presentations – one a calculated regime of control by means of threat-based fear, the other characterised by outbursts of out-of-control temper – represent a bifurcation in the typology of DFV aggressors. They are sometimes referred to respectively as "instrumental" violence and "expressive" violence. These two aggressor types can be broken down into subtypes, which have been proposed to inform assessment tools by providing more precision and tailoring by intervention programs (Boxall, Rosevear, & Payne, 2015).

This subtyping around intimate partner violence (IPV) has excited debate – and indeed tension – within the field (see Johnson, 2011), resulting in challenges to the feminist orthodoxy, which has persistently characterised such abuse as uniformly based on power and control. With theoretically informed research suggesting diversity within DFV (and especially IPV), some have criticised the conventional construal of this kind of violence as being predominantly male-to-female perpetrated and have subsequently argued that the phenomenon in fact leans towards a balance in perpetration by males and females ("gender symmetry"; Straus, 2011). Nevertheless, as we concluded in Chapter 2, the forms of violence that result in severe and lasting harm tend to result from a pattern of sustained, strategic, and controlling behaviour. Given the exploitive and dominating intentions underlying it, this pattern of violence is perhaps more aptly characterised as *abuse* and might be contrasted with less predictable outbreaks of domestic conflict in which violence is used by one or the other or both partners. The key point here is that abuse, defined in this way, is overwhelmingly perpetrated by men against the women and children with whom they share living arrangements. The causes of such abuse seem rooted in gendered power differentials that are consistent with and supported by broader social structures that promote the dominance of men over women across a wide range of social indicators. Stark (2007) presents a compelling political and analytical representation of this picture with his construct of coercive control. Given the emphasis by policymakers on targeting this pernicious form of violent behaviour and the incontrovertible nature of gender inequality as a context for it, it might reasonably be argued that even apparently "expressive" violence, when conducted in a context of coercive control, might be seen to have a severe and sustained impact on women and children. This conclusion has the effect of blurring the conceptual boundaries between distinct "types" of perpetrator. Indeed, Gondolf (2012) calls into question the usefulness of such typologies and suggests that variation among "batterers" might be better presented in terms of dimensions along continua of severity of abuse on the one hand and the psychopathology of those who perpetrate it on the other.

As aforementioned, for a theoretical conceptualisation to be useful in formulating a coherent response, it must be capable of informing practice. It should provide guidance to the practitioner in how to work. While structural feminist theory emerges as the single most useful explanatory framework for understanding the perpetrator and perpetration, the focus for the practitioner is on responding to any and all real-world cases. One example that confounds the notion that even the most severe (abusive) forms of DFV are exclusively about men as perpetrators and women as victims is that of IPV in same-sex relationships. IPV in these relationships is of similar prevalence to heterosexual cases (e.g. Blosnich & Bossarte, 2009). To resolve this apparent discrepancy, and at the same time, to advance our understanding of the dynamics of DFV, it is useful to have a clear grasp of the construct of gender.

Masculinities and vulnerable populations

Responses to DFV uniformly demand of perpetrators that they are held accountable for their violence. Explanations that propose causes of DFV in the absence of accounting for the personal agency and intentions of the perpetrator in their abusive practices are therefore insufficient. Given the centrality of gender roles in the domestic and family setting, and given that there is considerable evidence that gender is powerfully implicated in DFV, we now turn to consider the role of gender, and particularly masculinity, in accounting for this phenomenon.

Explaining men: cultures of masculinity

Across global crime statistics, men and violence are inextricably connected (e.g. Krug, Dahlberg, Mercy, Zwi, & Lozano, 2002). In the public realm (outside the "home"), they are significantly overrepresented in violence statistics, both as victims and as perpetrators. Criminologist Steve Hall goes as far as to assert that "the claim that men commit most acts of physical violence is possibly the nearest that criminology has come to producing an indisputable fact" (Hall, 2002, p. 36). It should come as no surprise, then, that, regarding the incidence and degree of violence in the circumscribed setting of the heterosexual family, the picture is very plainly one of men as perpetrators and women and children as victims.

So, what is it about men? Or is it about men per se? One reasonable hypothesis is that men are "constitutionally" the violent sex. That is to say, there is something inherently violent about being male. To examine what constitutes these inherent differences, it might be considered that higher dosages of, say, testosterone available in the male biological system increase the likelihood that, among other things, men are more likely to employ violence as a way of attempting to meet their needs, respond to desires, or solve problems. This hypothesis supports conservative moral views, such as that men are the "naturally" dominant sex, are helpless in the face of their aggressive and sexual "drives", and are dependent upon women to moderate and direct these appetites. Such conservative reasoning supports status quo patriarchal power structures. However, such explanations cannot stand alone. Logically, they presuppose some sort of mediating interaction with the environment – such as provocation or opportunity – for violence to be motivated and enacted. But these accounts are also deficient in that they undermine any understanding of the ethical agency of men in acting responsibly and accountably to regulate their own behaviour. Considerable empirical evidence supports the idea that the critical element in explaining men's violence is gender norming (see Fleming, Gruskin, Rojo, & Dworkin, 2015). Norming is a process of social construction, suggesting that a propensity to violence in men cannot be adequately explained by their "nature" but by a function of identity formation, which takes place in an interpersonal setting.

More plausible and more current accounts of this tendency of men to resort to violence then emerge from holistic explanations, which incorporate sociological, psychological, feminist, gay, and queer analyses. These are then biopsychosocial explanations. That is to say, while biology is seen to play a part in men's violence, it is an insufficient explanation out of context. In this view, violence is to do with cultures of masculinity (Ray, 2011). We are using a broad definition of culture here to denote a shared system of meanings. The boundaries of such a system of meanings relate to a group at some level, whether it is societal, ethnic, or even family. Cultures help us make sense of the world and provide norms for behaviour that relate to the identity of the group and help us feel part of the group. Traditional indigenous New Zealand Maori society, for instance, valorises the norm of reciprocal welfare across family, extended family, and tribe. Playing one's part in such reciprocity both confirms identity and confers a sense of belonging. So, for instance, to "be a man" in any particular wider culture requires certain ways of presenting and conducting oneself in order to hold one's place and receive the benefits of that membership. In this sense, masculinity is not conferred but has to be actively *performed* through one's attitudes and conduct in alignment with local prescriptions (Anderson, 2009).

Gender inequalities and violence

Among policymakers, appreciation of this broader context of oppression has been slow. Despite some 30 years of mainstream political acknowledgement of the problem of men's violence in the home and attempts to address it through policy, feminists point out that gender relations continue to be characterised by the dynamics of dominance and subordination. The underrepresentation of women in positive statistics, such as income, social status, management, and directorship, is well documented internationally (United Nations, 2018). Under these circumstances, women are more readily objectified, subjugated, and exploited by men who themselves are attempting, sometimes desperately, to conform to the demands of highly prescriptive blueprints for masculinity. Especially in contexts of disadvantage and trauma, arguably such demands often outstrip coping resources and responses that would allow for non-violent outcomes. The full picture, however, is more complex. Between groups of men there exist hierarchies of masculinity in terms of signifiers such as employment, sexuality, and status. Competition for places on these hierarchies breeds anxiety and socially mandated conflict. In her chapter "Masculinity matters: Super-capitalism, men and violence", Carrington (2014) refers to a study of the behaviour of men in frontier Australian mining towns that illustrates the heightening of these tensions emerging from the context of threatened masculinity.

Having imported, imposed, and, over time, developed such hierarchies, what does a contemporary blueprint for masculinity look like? Carrington (2014) paints some vivid pictures, based somewhat on her research into psychosocial contexts in contemporary regional Australia. In part, she concludes, the current blueprint is based around attributes and ideals, such as risk-taking, bravery, and physical prowess. These ideals can be perceived as underpinned by individualism, self-sufficiency, power, and influence. Where such qualities are assured and apparent to others, masculine status is affirmed and requires only maintenance by those in this privileged position. To achieve and maintain membership of masculine culture, and thereby to secure its privileges, a man must engage in performances that advertise that he is both in control *and* unlike a woman. In order to claim this version of masculine identity, he must have access to the forums where it can be performed. Ideally, these are based in positions of power in the workforce, in traditional male sporting arenas, and so on. They should at least allow access to commensurate levels of wealth or appropriate employment. Where such access is poor or threatened, however, men are more likely to resort to aggressive or violent means of establishing or recovering it. In these circumstances, domestic and family settings offer opportunities to perform and establish masculine identity. Here we see men use explicit violence, or – more commonly – resort to other techniques of power (restriction, intimidation, subjugation) in order to gain or restore the prescribed identity. Where this mode of performance has become entrenched, the man may only need to resort to threats to sustain the abusive regime. Over time, such threats might be signalled in the form of subtle acts or implied intimidation, such as reversion to a particular tone of voice, opening a can of beer, sharpening a knife, or engaging in "accidental" barging. Because of their experiential association with violence in the minds of victims, such precursor acts have the effect of efficiently drawing women and children into line. Fearfully motivated to avoid his wrath, they anticipate his wishes and revert to compliance and obedience in his presence.

Contemporary contexts

The traditional blueprint for being a man could be characterised as reflecting principles of individualism and exploitation. In terms of providing a social identity, however, it is narrow and limiting. Unsurprisingly, then, this version of masculinity is widely considered in the literature to be a significant factor in precipitating and maintaining DFV. Furthermore, the more constrained the possibilities are for attaining the preferred markers of manhood, the more anxious men become to attain them. So, for instance, the traditional forms of performing masculinity – through power, material possession, status within the family, and dominion over property – are severely compromised or threatened by social contingencies such as underemployment. From across wide-ranging and global studies, a report based on World Health Organization (WHO) data established a list of very common "triggers" to DFV that are remarkably consistent across nations and cultures (Krug et al., 2002). This list includes items that WHO has labelled: "not obeying the husband", "arguing back", "not having food ready on time", "going out without permission", "refusing sex", and "pregnancy". While this paints a bleak picture of the concept of traditional masculinity, it does at least provide some clues to a way forward. Given that gender is increasingly considered a fluid element of identity and that contemporary masculinity is modelled in increasingly diverse ways, there is optimism that those who have perpetrated DFV might be invited to consider other, more mutually respectful and generous, ways of "doing" gender as a means of expressing that part of their identity (see Jenkins, 2009). We return to consider these possibilities in Chapter 10.

Cultural requirements for manhood vary from community to community and through history, and this is why we can speak of "masculinities" – the noun in its plural form. As such, context (time and place) makes a difference. We can consider the influence of a global context of masculinity, but local notions of masculinity are also influenced by local history. In Australia, in common with a number of similar countries, the impact of history (e.g. colonisation and systematic dispossession) and global influences (e.g. "super-capitalism"; see Carrington, 2014) are evident. In countries that have a history of colonisation, indigenous cultures, which had previously lived according to principles of collectivism and reciprocity with the natural world, became subject to imported and alien ethics of exploitation and extraction and a presumed status hierarchy of existence (Foucault, 1970). These ethics subverted traditional meanings and alienated people and communities from established forms of welfare and wellbeing. This colonising process has had a devastating effect on indigenous populations. Among its impact on a range of negative outcomes, colonisation has resulted in the disproportionate levels and severity of DFV in these communities, wrought by its destruction of traditional welfare structure. For this reason, indigenous responses to the problem have tended to be sceptical of modernist feminism that has focused more on the "problem of men" and less on the broader oppressive context.

Incorporating agency

As well as considering factors influencing the occurrence of DFV, such as (masculine) identity imperatives, we need to account for the perpetrator as a choice-maker. A theoretically informed guide to intervention must incorporate the volitional aspects of the person and not just characterise him as a complicit component in a system of biological drives and social influences. Furthermore, from the perspective of program intervention, merely confronting the perpetrator with a list of directives for how he needs to change his life in order to help realise an abstracted set of ideals (around, say, human rights) is unlikely to constitute a successful initial strategy to inspire and empower him in a process of change. Moreover, a treatment strategy that is based on an appeal to righteous authority risks mirroring the mechanisms of abuse itself (Jenkins, 2009). Theory that supports persons to enact changes in their lives and asserts that the person is responsible for that change cannot merely be about external causal factors acting on them but must also incorporate the person's felt sense of personal agency within a particular context. How can the perpetrator be held personally accountable for changing the course of his relationships while adhering to his commitments and identity preferences around a masculine identity?

A desistance paradigm

The thinking that has predominated in the general field of offender rehabilitation since the 1990s (evidence-based practice, the psychology of criminal conduct) reflects an orientation that has come to be known by the generic label of "what works" (see, for example, Sarre, 2001). Advocates have proudly proclaimed this approach to be scientifically superior. This involves addressing the range of behavioural and psychological factors associated with the individual and that have been assessed as functionally related to their offending. This orientation tends to construe the client as someone to be *treated*, and his offending as something to be *managed*. In its application to DFV perpetrators, the violent behaviour, along with the thoughts and feelings associated with it and the power structures that inform and support it, are typically construed as events impelled by various forces and drivers (such as cognitions and emotions), or environmental influences (such as patriarchal conditioning).

In order to incorporate a more responsible role for the perpetrator/client, some writers have proposed an alternative position to the "what works" position – arguably an alternative paradigm. This alternative is more concerned with the subjectivity and lived experience of the client, particularly the client's experience of the change process itself. Maruna (2001) has suggested that the stance taken by advocates of this alternative paradigm is less characterised by asking *what* works and more by enquiring into *how* it works. Following McNeill (2006), then, we refer to this collection of practice responses as the desistance paradigm. The "science" of the desistance paradigm is based more around observations of the "natural" inclination of offenders over time to desist from offending, a process which is based around their reconnecting with kin and community. It represents a less rigid class of thinking, less influenced by the disciplines of psychology and sociology and more by anthropology, criminology, and social work. The desistance paradigm is associated less with quantitative research and positivist science and more with qualitative research and social constructionist principles.

Reformulating the task

In articulating this paradigm, we refer particularly to the work of Shadd Maruna (2001) and colleagues, who explore the role of self-narrative in the desistance process. Those who subscribe to this desistance paradigm point to the importance of the personal agency of the man undertaking the program and the context of his struggle to do with personal transformation – in embracing and resisting change. Significantly, desistance from offending is considered not an event or a stage but a *process*. This process has been revealed through research investigation into DFV perpetrators as not straightforward or linear but having a to-and-fro or spiralling (Walker, Bowen, Brown, & Sleath, 2015) dynamic to it. In other words, the successful desistor is likely to relapse or falter a number of times on the way to long-term desistance. This is consistent with outcomes from Maruna's original research, which points to two classes of desistance – primary and secondary. Primary desistance here refers to the initial and faltering attempts of the person to cease offending, whereas secondary desistance refers to an enduring "lifestyle" pattern change. Not only is successful desistance empirically confirmed as a nonlinear process, but also as a process that must be "owned" by the desistor. That is to say, unless the commitment to desistance is made and authentically embraced by the desistor himself, it is unlikely to endure. It is not something that can be imposed. Research confirms that a criminal offending propensity decays with age (Bottoms, Costello, Holmes, Muir, & Shapland, 2004). In this sense, the assumed naturally occurring progress towards desistance by way of maturation is something to be *supported* by intervention; enforcement might only serve to harden resistance and further entrench habits.

Another distinguishing feature of the desistance paradigm, as characterised here, is an insistence that the person is not the problem; it is "the problem that is the problem" (see White, 2001) – in this case, the problem of DFV. It is the person's alignment with certain ways of being that are tolerant of violence, and the circumstances that reproduce that violence is seen as problematic. With respect to DFV, these might centre on the performance of traditional blueprints for masculinity. It is the perpetrator's reflection on the usefulness of this blueprint and his resistance to it that supports change. Alan Jenkins (2009) proposes that, in a practice setting, the man might be invited to reflect on the value of his subscribing to misogynistic attitudes and claims to male privilege in relation to the hopes, dreams, and wishes he has for his life and commitments. In a clinical sense, this separation of the person from the problem allows the person to take up a position of agency in resisting the counter-invitations of violent habits and practices and the cultural narratives that support them (Jenkins, 1990, 2009).

In his seminal research into criminal persisters versus successful desistors, Maruna (2001) found the latter group were distinguished by a narrative identity that supported their move away from offending. That is, the group who managed to leave criminal offending behind tended to have an enduring belief that they were the sort of person who would, at some point, turn away from crime – a belief that preceded their behavioural attempts to do so. This notion of identity construction as a fluid process is also central to Jenkins' (1990, 2009) theorising. Jenkins proposes the use of a "theory of restraint" and its concern with what holds the man back (i.e. restrains him) from living a non-abusive and respectful lifestyle. This is pertinent to the current context in that the desistance paradigm is concerned with bringing attention to evidence of honourable (non-abusive) intentions and preferences. The presence of these, while absent in much of the man's current lifestyle, is revealed as implicit in his expressed desires, wishes, and commitments. For instance, the man's underlying wish to be a good father might become revealed in the pain and sadness evident in his recounting of his own adverse experiences as a son. In this way, like an archaeological dig, evidence of desistance might be uncovered in a careful excavation around these artefacts of the man's hopes, intentions, and commitments.

In this section, we discussed the importance of incorporating personal agency and intention as necessary components of understanding the perpetration of DFV. While this aspect of theory is necessary, it alone is not sufficient. As discussed earlier, there are clearly psychological circumstances that might exacerbate or in other ways mediate the use of this kind of violence. There is a plainly social structural backdrop to the perpetration of DFV. If the strategy of posing questions around what *caused* this man to use violence against his family is problematic in intervention practice, and insistence that the man consciously and by way of preference set out on a regime of terror against his family is also plainly not helpful in terms of motivating men to change, we are left with the task of developing a more sophisticated question. To pursue this, we next consider contexts and settings that have explanatory value in accounting for DFV.

DFV as an intergenerational issue

DFV might well be considered heritable. Adults, as perpetrator or victim, come disproportionately from family backgrounds characterised by such violence. The intergenerational transmission of violence has been a concern in the study of DFV since the 1970s (Becker-Blease & Frey, 2005). Children exposed to DFV appear to be at increased risk for a wide range of emotional and behavioural difficulties. What comes to manifest as a "disorder of conduct", in particular, may be implicated in the perpetration of violence in adulthood. Exposure to violence in family-of-origin has, in this way, consistently been linked to IPV in adulthood. The key linking factors offered in the literature involve constructs such as trauma (particularly complex trauma), behavioural learning, the absorption of certain attitudes and beliefs, and the general harm to self and relationships that results from adverse circumstances for growth and development (Siegel, 2013).

While the link between adverse childhood experiences and a range of poor outcomes is empirically strong retrospectively, it is not so strong prospectively. That is to say, for our purposes here, although a high proportion of those involved as adults in IPV have a family-of-origin background of DFV, the majority of those children experiencing DFV (directly and indirectly) do not themselves go on to become victims or perpetrators (Johnson & Ferraro, 2000). The simple relationship between childhood experiences of violence and adult experience requires a supplementary explanation by way of reference to other things that are going on. In other words, there is a need to identify mediating factors that help account for an increased likelihood of perpetrating domestic abuse as an adult. Of course, from the perspective of practice, it would be also very useful to be able to identify those resources, events, and actions that might subvert the pathway into perpetratorhood (or victimhood). These features of resilience are referred to in the literature as protective factors (cf. risk factors; Fortune & Ward, 2017), and we examine this aspect of practice in Chapter 10.

In view of what we have argued about the place of patriarchal culture and gender inequity, it would seem clear that this is what lays the foundation and opportunity for perpetratorhood. On the other hand, because not all men (or anyone engaging in performances of masculinity) resort to DFV, it remains to account for what might incline some to resort to violent means as a mechanism for achieving a sense of masculine identity. In this final section of this chapter, we briefly consider factors that mediate and intersect with gender in DFV. Specifically, we refer to both the early experiences of individuals and to the influence of community adversity experienced by disadvantaged groups.

Early family experience as a mediating factor

As we have suggested, IPV is used as a way of achieving masculine gender identity when other means are perceived as unavailable. In this way of thinking, the pathway to masculinity might be hampered or constrained, for instance, by circumstances associated with adverse early childhood experiences. The trauma associated with these circumstances is often in the form of emotional troubles and adverse mental health outcomes. These outcomes can interact with gender relational issues in a variety of ways that might result in DFV (for a useful summary of the influence and interaction of such mediating features, see Devaney & Lazenbatt, 2016). For example, in response to distress, persons typically use intoxicants such as alcohol as a self-administered emotional "medication" (Crum et al., 2013). The intoxication that results can have a disinhibitory or destabilising influence on the intention to act respectfully and non-abusively, thereby apparently increasing the attractiveness of violence as an option to gain or restore a compensatory sense of "masculine" dominance. Adverse circumstances, however, can apply not just to individuals but to entire groups.

Intersectionality and perpetratorhood

> Gender inequality is the problem, but it is not the only problem. Gender intersects with other forms of social difference, such as race and ethnicity, class and sexuality. In turn, gender inequalities intersect with other forms of inequality associated with race and ethnicity, class and sexuality.
>
> (Flood, 2016, p. 24)

As we have seen, structural feminist orthodoxy has successfully promoted and led theory around DFV perpetrators, widely influencing policy and practice. Nevertheless, its insistence on the primacy of gender over other sorts of oppression, along with a tendency to dismiss factors relating to personal history as simplistic psychological individualism, has attracted trenchant criticism. Such criticism has been increasingly supported by research. This critique has coalesced into a challenge to the conventional feminist claim that a common set of risk factors applies to all groups of perpetrators equally. A more inclusive and convincing understanding of those who use DFV then requires that the structural feminist explanation incorporates more nuanced conceptual theory to better characterise the complexity of this topic. Intersectionality theory (Crenshaw, 1991; described in Chapter 3) has been proposed as a means of bridging this conceptual gap. This theory seeks to account for how multiple systems of domination and gender patterning interlock with other forms of discrimination and disadvantage, to explain why some individuals, families, groups, and communities might be more vulnerable to DFV than others. Incorporating an intersectional lens into theorising on perpetratorhood advances structuralist forms of feminism and reflects a *post*-structuralist position (Cannon, Lauve-Moon, & Buttell, 2015). In this way, gender inequality intersects in dynamic relationships with race, ethnicity, class, and sexualities to combine and manifest in the life of a man in diverse ways (Nixon & Humphreys, 2010; Stubbs, 2015). Chronic underemployment in industries traditionally occupied by men, enduring discrimination, and other "threats" to their claim to masculinity in the absence of access to other sites for its performance might help account for an increased prevalence of DFV among men in certain groups (Hunnicutt, 2009). As well, particular individual problematic issues in a man's life – addiction, intoxication, poor psychological functioning, and so on – can, as we have seen, intervene to exacerbate external factors to influence, or to act as restraints on, his intentions to conduct his domestic relationships in more respectful, equitable ways.

A helpful question for practice

Placing these mediating and intersectional features in the context of a post-structuralist account of DFV provides a resulting multifactorial means of conceptualising perpetratorhood. This helps to frame our approach at a practice level in a way that is broadly encompassing. Arguably, it also promotes perpetrator accountability rather than diminishing it. So, rather than posing the question "what caused this man to behave violently towards his family?", we might more helpfully ask "what were the circumstances in which this man chose to enact abuse?"

The next chapter seeks to extend these ideas around context and personal agency to the situation of victims and to a practically useful understanding of victimhood. It does so with reference to acts of resistance to DFV..

References

Anderson, K. (2009). Gendering coercive control. *Violence against Women*, 15(12), 1444–1457.

Australian Law Reform Commission [ALRC]. (2010). *Family violence: A national legal response* (Final report 114). Canberra, ACT: Australian Government Publishing Service.

Becker-Blease, K. A., & Frey, J. J. (2005). Beyond PTSD: An evolving relationship between trauma theory and family violence research. *Journal of Interpersonal Violence*, 20(4), 403–411.

Blosnich, J. R., & Bossarte, R. M. (2009). Comparisons of intimate partner violence among partners in same-sex and opposite-sex relationships in the United States. *American Journal of Public Health*, 99, 2182–2184.

Bottoms, A., Costello, A., Holmes, D., Muir, G., & Shapland, J. (2004). Towards desistance: Theoretical underpinnings for an empirical study. *Howard Journal of Criminal Justice*, 43(4), 368–389.

Boxall, H., Rosevear, L., & Payne, J. (2015). Domestic violence typologies: What value to practice? *Trends and Issues in Crime and Criminal Justice*, (494), 1–9.

Cannon, C., Lauve-Moon, K., & Buttell, F. (2015). Re-theorizing intimate partner violence through post-structural feminism, queer theory, and the sociology of gender. *Social Sciences*, 4(3), 668–687.

Carrington, K. (2014). *Feminism and global justice*. Hoboken: Taylor & Francis.

Crenshaw, K. (1991). Mapping the margins: Intersectionality, identity politics, and violence against women of color. *Stanford Law Review*, 43(6), 1241–1299.

Crum, R., Mojtabai, R., Lazareck, S., Bolton, J., Robinson, J., Sareen, J., . . ., Storr, C. (2013). A prospective assessment of reports of drinking to self-medicate mood symptoms with the incidence and persistence of alcohol dependence. *JAMA Psychiatry*, 70(7), 718–726.

Devaney, J., & Lazenbatt, A. (2016). *Domestic violence perpetrators: Evidence-informed responses*. London: Routledge.

Dutton, D., & Corvo, K. (2006). Transforming a flawed policy: A call to revive psychology and science in domestic violence research and practice. *Aggression and Violent Behavior*, 11(5), 457–483.

Fleming, P. J., Gruskin, S., Rojo, F., & Dworkin, S. L. (2015). Men's violence against women and men are inter-related: Recommendations for simultaneous intervention. *Social Science & Medicine, 146*, 249–256.

Flood, M. (2016). Involving men in ending violence against women: Facing challenges and making change. *Graduate Journal of Social Science, 12*(3), 12–29.

Fortune, C., & Ward, T. (2017). Problems in protective factors research and practice. *Aggression and Violent Behavior, 32*, 1–3.

Foucault, M. (1970). *The order of things: An archaeology of the human sciences.* New Yok: Vintage Books.

Goldstein, M. A. (2002). The biological roots of heat-of-passion crimes and honor killings. *Politics and the Life Sciences, 21*(2), 28–37.

Gondolf, E. G. (2012). *The future of batterer programs: Reassessing evidence-based practice.* Boston, MA: Northeastern University Press.

Hafmeister, T. L. (2011). If all you have is a hammer: Society's ineffective response to intimate partner violence. *Catholic University Law Review, 60*(4), 919–1002.

Hall, S. (2002). Daubing the drudges of fury: Men, violence and the piety of the "hegemonic masculinity" thesis. *Theoretical Criminology, 6*(1), 35–61.

Holtzworth-Munroe, A., & Meehan, J. (2004). Typologies of men who are maritally violent: Scientific and clinical implications. *Journal of Interpersonal Violence, 19*(12), 1369–1389.

Hunnicutt, G. (2009). Varieties of patriarchy and violence against women: Resurrecting "patriarchy" as a theoretical tool. *Violence against Women, 15*(5), 553–573.

Jenkins, A. (1990). *Invitations to responsibility: The therapeutic engagement of men who are violent and abusive.* Adelaide, SA: Dulwich Centre Publications.

Jenkins, A. (2009). *Becoming ethical: A parallel, political journey with men who have abused.* Lyme Regis, UK: Russel House.

Johnson, M. P. (2011). Gender and types of intimate partner violence: A response to an anti-feminist literature review. *Aggression and Violent Behavior, 16*, 289–296.

Johnson, M. P., & Ferraro, K. J. (2000). Research on domestic violence in the 1990s: Making distinctions. *Journal of Marriage and Family, 62*, 948–963.

Krug, E. G., Dahlberg, L. L., Mercy, J. A., Zwi, A. B., & Lozano, R. (2002). World report on violence and health. *The Lancet, 360*(9339), 1083–1088.

Maiuro, R. D., & Eberle, J A. (2008). State standards for domestic violence perpetrator treatment: Current status, trends, and recommendations. *Violence and Victims, 23*(2), 133–155.

Maruna, S. (2001). *Making good: How ex-convicts reform and rebuild their lives.* Washington, DC: American Psychological Association.

McCalman, I. (Ed.). (1999). *An Oxford companion to the Romantic Age.* Oxford, UK: Oxford University Press.

McNeill, F. (2006). A desistance paradigm for offender management. *Criminology and Criminal Justice, 6*(1), 39–62.

Nixon, J., & Humphreys, C. (2010). Marshalling the evidence: Using intersectionality in the domestic violence frame. *Social Politics, 17*(2), 137–158.

Pence, E., & Paymar, M. (1993). *Education groups for men who batter: The Duluth model.* New York: Springer.

Pence, E., & Paymar, M. (2003). *Creating a process of change for men who batter: An education curriculum.* Duluth, MN: Domestic Abuse Intervention Project.

Ray, L. (2011). *Violence and society.* London, UK: Sage Publications.

Sarre, R. (2001). Beyond "what works?" A 25 year jubilee retrospective of Robert Martinson's famous article. *Australian and New Zealand Journal of Criminology*, 34(1), 38–46.

Siegel, J. (2013). Breaking the links in intergenerational violence: An emotional regulation perspective. *Family Process*, 52(2), 163–178.

Siegel, R. B. (1996). *"The rule of love": Wife beating as prerogative and privacy* (Faculty Scholarship Series Paper No. 1092). Retrieved from http://digitalcommons.law.yale.edu/fss_papers/1092

Stark, E. (2007). *Coercive control: How men entrap women in personal life*. Oxford, UK: Oxford University Press.

Straus, M. (2011). Gender symmetry and mutuality in perpetration of clinical-level partner violence: Empirical evidence and implications for prevention and treatment. *Aggression and Violent Behavior*, 16(4), 279–288.

Stubbs, J. (2015). Gendered violence, intersectionalities and resisting gender neutrality. *Oñati Socio-Legal Series*, 5(6), 1433–1451.

Tur-Prats, A. (2015). *Family types and intimate-partner violence: A historical perspective*. Retrieved from http://hdl.handle.net/10230/23809

United Nations. (2018). *The millennium development goals report*. New York: United Nations Publications.

Walker, K., Bowen, E., Brown, S., & Sleath, E. (2015). Desistance from intimate partner violence: A conceptual framework for practitioners for managing the process of change. *Journal of Interpersonal Violence*, 30(15), 2726–2750.

White, M. (2001). Narrative practice and the unpacking of identity conclusions. *Gecko: A Journal of Deconstruction and Narrative Ideas in Therapeutic Practice*, 1, 28–55.

Chapter 5

Resisting violence in private spaces

Understanding victimhood

Theoretical approaches to understanding victims' agency in resisting violence in private settings

We start with two theoretical approaches that have been used to explore and understand victims' experiences of DFV and their associated decision-making and agency. Both approaches set the scene for our subsequent exploration of victimhood versus survivorhood, along with some of the individual and social perceptions attached to each term. We use the term "victim" throughout this chapter, while acknowledging that our readers may have a different preference. After addressing the victim–survivor dichotomy, we unpack the social construction of victimhood more broadly to better understand how victims are "made". That is, we explore how someone is labelled a victim, how and why this label may be applied differently across different types of victims, and where victims of DFV fit into this rhetoric. This chapter concludes with an illustration of victims' diverse strategies of resistance and thus agency when exposed to DFV.

Early work by Lenore Walker (1979), examining the experiences of battered women, framed victims' responses to DFV (especially after prolonged abuse at the hands of an intimate partner) as a learned behaviour that is often unsuccessful in resolving the experience of abuse. Walker (1979) developed her theory to counter existing beliefs that battered women remain silent about experiences of abuse due to their "masochistic" nature. She argued that while victims who endure violence and remain silent about such experiences may appear passive, they exercise agency, which is often invisible to outsiders. Within this theoretical framework, victims' responses to DFV – or apparent lack thereof – are seen as a learned behaviour displayed around the abusive partner to avoid his rage and abuse. Some research has suggested that these victims may try harder to please the abusive partner by becoming compliant and submissive to avoid situations where they feel the abuse is a response to their lack of "perfection" or obedience (Towns & Adams, 2000; Walker, 1979). Despite adjusting their behaviour, victims tend to be continuously victimised by their intimate partner, which teaches them that all their past attempts and sacrifices to pacify their abuser are ineffective. As a result, these victims develop an experience of "learned helplessness";

that is, their experiences have taught them that regardless of what they do or try, they seem to be unable to end the abuse. Therefore, victims may stop trying to behave in a way that is expected to put an end to the abuse or may refrain from seeking help. To an outsider, this can appear passive or helpless.

Experiences of learned helplessness are particularly detrimental for victims because they can have a deterrent effect on potential proactive help-seeking decisions (i.e. reaching out for external support in the absence of an ability to control the internal situation). This can lead to increasing isolation over time. The longer the victim remains in the abusive relationship, the more self-blame and shame the victim develops for not taking action, which in turn increases immobilisation and decreases the likelihood of disclosing the abuse to external sources at an even later stage.

Walker's theory of "learned helplessness" has repeatedly been criticised since its development in the late 1970s. While it initially describes victims as "active" in their behaviour modifications to avoid subsequent violence, it ultimately paints victims as passive and helpless. Although many victims may be able to identify with the feeling of isolation and helplessness, contemporary research shows that most become active and resilient in their responses to DFV over time (Hamby, 2014; Meyer, 2015; Moe, 2007). Resistance to violence is part of a common process for many victims. Active contemplation of decisions and subsequent action frequently informs victims' responses to DFV (Hamby, 2014; Meyer, 2012, 2016). While many may remain in or return to an abusive relationship, at least temporarily, they tend to be active agents in their decision-making aimed at harm minimisation (Kim & Gray, 2008; Meyer, 2012). As such, some prefer the term survivor over victim, because it suggests resilience and active responses rather than passive endurance of DFV.

Survivor theory and a change towards problem-focused coping strategies

One particular theory framed around the survivor concept is Gondolf and Fisher's (1988) early survivor theory. Initially developed in response to Walker's concept of "learned helplessness", it incorporates important perspectives of the theoretical approaches of active and problem-focused coping. Within this theoretical framework, victims' responses to DFV are said to change with the changing dynamics of the abusive relationship. Gondolf and Fisher (1988) argued that victims' responses to DFV are likely to become more active as the problem of victimisation increases in frequency and severity. Put plainly, victims may be willing to endure (or excuse) minor and early incidents of DFV but will become increasingly proactive in their responses once an escalation in the frequency and/or severity of abuse occurs (Brown, 1997). Under this theoretical explanation, the increased severity of violence is said to push victims into the "visible" field of help seekers instead of isolating them in their private and "invisible" abusive environment. In the next section, we unpack the victim–survivor dichotomy, before further exploring how victims may resist experiences of abuse in private settings, including through help seeking and other forms of agency.

Terminology: the victim–survivor dichotomy

The victim–survivor dichotomy has received attention from academics as well as practitioners for a number of decades (Gondolf & Fisher, 1988; Gupta, 2014; Walker, 1979). The term "survivor" was borne out of the politicised debate around the resilience and recovery of women who experienced sexual violence in the 1980s (see for example Kelly, 1988). Around this time, the feminist movement inspired a general shift towards defining female victims of male violence as survivors rather than victims during their journey to recovery. The term "victim" was associated with the initial experience of violence and vulnerability. Transitioning from being a victim to a survivor was seen as a process of empowerment and recovery. However, the terms, along with their implications, have raised some controversies (Gupta, 2014).

Some may have a personal, professional, or ideological preference for one term over the other. Some see the term "survivor" as more aligned with a strength-based approach to working with victims. From a feminist perspective, this term aligns with the notion of empowerment and rejects attributes of weakness and vulnerability (Gupta, 2014). It aims to highlight the resilience of those who have endured – and essentially survived – different forms of DFV, sometimes against all odds (Moe, 2007). Others prefer the term victim, partly to emphasise the wrongdoing inherent to the behaviours that the person has been exposed to. Where there is a victim, there usually is a perpetrator. By removing this label, attention may be diverted away from perpetrator accountability as well as the responsibility of the state to acknowledge and respond to the issue of victimisation (Gupta, 2014).

Essentially, it may be up to the victim or survivor, who may have a preference for one "label" over the other. It is therefore important to be aware of the different nuances associated with the terminology and implications this may have for engaging with victims. Some victims may prefer to be addressed as survivors (e.g. in information pamphlets) due to the implication of strength and resilience and the empowerment that can arise from this term. Others may prefer being referred to as victims based on how it clearly contrasts with and sets them apart from perpetrator behaviour and accountability. In addition, some victims may prefer this term because once they overcome the abusive experiences and rebuild a violence-free future, they can be fully removed from any label. Being a survivor, on the other hand, continues to connect people to a past marked by victimisation and trauma. For some, this may remind them of their strength and resilience, but for others, it may remind them of their loss and trauma and they may wish to remove themselves from that identity. The primary message here is that there is no one-size-fits-all "label" for those affected by DFV. It may best be left up to the person who has experienced this kind of abuse to choose the term s/he feels most comfortable with. For the purpose of the book, we continue to refer to those affected by DFV as victims and those responsible for the harmful behaviours as perpetrators for ease and consistency.

Victimhood and DFV

Violent victimisation is a complex phenomenon that affects many victims from all walks of life. While men most commonly experience violence at the hands of male acquaintances or strangers, women most commonly experience violence within interpersonal and intimate relationships with the opposite sex. As you will recall from Chapter 2, national and international surveys reveal that between one in three and one in four women experience victimisation by an intimate partner at some stage in their life (World Health Organization [WHO], 2013). DFV can have severe short- and long-term consequences, and women and children are the ones who suffer the most adverse outcomes (Devries et al., 2013). Victims' needs are often complex and require a range of different services to ensure protection and recovery, ranging from crisis to long-term support (Meyer, 2014; Stark, 2007).

Despite the various achievements of the feminist movement in its attempts to change social attitudes and empower women in general and victims of DFV in particular (Barrett Meyering, 2010; Ofstehage, Gandhi, Sholk, Radday, & Stanzler, 2011), victims of DFV still face a range of victim-blaming attitudes when disclosing their experiences. Research continues to reveal that many help-seeking victims of DFV continue to experience a lack of empathy and support. These attributes often seem to be reserved for victims of other offences that are seen as innocent and vulnerable in the process of their victimisation (Carpenter, 2005; Dignan, 2005; Kogut, 2011).

Public perceptions of innocence tend to vary greatly in relation to different types of victims and victimisation (Dunn, 2010; Fattah, 1989; Kogut, 2011). Those regarded as weak, shy, and vulnerable, and those who suffer victimisation at the hands of a stranger, are more likely to be seen as the "ideal victim" worthy of empathy and support. Conversely, those engaging in behaviours that are seen as risky or morally questionable are often seen as contributing to their experiences of victimisation (Carpenter, 2005; Christie, 1986; Strobl, 2004). In order to better understand how the experiences of victims of DFV may differ from those of other crime victims, we need to start by examining how society constructs the ideal or worthy victim in the first place.

The concept of the "ideal victim"

The concept of the "ideal victim" has generated much interest in victimology and other disciplines. Formal and informal responses to victims of crime tend to be affected by a perceived degree of victim innocence and vulnerability. While underlying beliefs around innocence or blameworthiness of a victim have always played into these responses, Nils Christie was the first to introduce the concept of the "ideal victim" and examine its rhetoric and implications in the mid-1980s. Since then, the concept has been re-examined and reapplied in various research contexts, especially relating to how victim status is constructed from a social and health science perspective (Dignan, 2005; Strobl, 2004; van Wijk, 2013).

When Christie first developed his concept of the "ideal victim", he proposed five key attributes that victims needed to meet in order to fall into this category. Christie (1986, p. 19) argued that the "ideal victim" has to be seen as:

- weak or vulnerable,
- involved in a respectable activity at the time of victimisation,
- blameless in the circumstances of his/her victimisation, and
- having been victimized by a big bad offender,
- who is unknown to him/her.

Victims meeting these criteria tend to be seen as innocent and thus worthy of support, compensation, empathy, and where applicable, protection (Christie, 1986; Strobl, 2004). In addition, little is expected of these victims to ensure they do not fall victim to the same or another perpetrator in the future. The responsibility of preventing or avoiding future crimes and victimisation lies with the perpetrator (if known) and, to a certain extent, the state. Criminal justice and victim support agencies have made it their responsibility to prevent future violent crimes through interventions, including deterrence and punishment, and situational forms of crime prevention, generally targeting the potential or known perpetrator (Davis, Guthrie, Ross, & O'Sullivan, 2006).

Christie's conceptualisation of the "ideal victim" is the "little old lady". His argument is that social reactions towards victims of crime are more likely to be supportive towards those seen as innocent, helpless, or vulnerable and whose harm is inflicted by someone who is bigger, stronger, or otherwise more powerful and takes advantage of that power imbalance (Christie, 1986). The example of "the little old lady" is based on the idea of the elderly female victim who gets robbed on her way to the store by a younger, stronger (male) offender, who uses his physical strength to take advantage of the victim's vulnerability (e.g. lack of strength required to fight back or chase after him). While this example is most commonly illustrated by contrasting the elderly female victim with a younger, stronger, male offender, it could also be applied to a female perpetrator.

Criminological research shows that young women are becoming increasingly engaged in a number of crimes, including violent crimes and theft (Schwartz & Steffensmeier, 2011). In this scenario, the victim could equally be an elderly male who is assaulted or robbed by a young female. Under Christie's concept, the key focus is on the vulnerability and innocence of the victim, the blameworthiness and "badness" of the perpetrator, and no existing relationship between the two. These attributes are easiest to apply where the roles are clear-cut, like in the example of "the little old lady". Unfortunately, when working with victims of certain crimes (such as DFV and sexual assault), these roles are often not as definitive as the ones defined by Christie.

Why are some victims constructed as different from others?

The level of innocence ascribed to a victim is affected by a number of factors, including the victim–offender relationship, victims' behaviours, and the location of the crime. Victims of DFV are not the only group of victims that do not fit the "ideal victim" concept. Sex workers are frequently exposed to victim-blaming attitudes when reporting physical or sexual assault (Menaker & Franklin, 2015). This is due to an underlying assumption that sex workers deliberately expose themselves to high-risk scenarios and are thus not completely innocent in their victimisation as it is defined by Christie. Another example is women who report sexual assault by strangers when walking home after dark instead of taking a taxi or taking short cuts (e.g. through parklands) instead of walking along well-lit and busy streets. Women assaulted by an acquaintance after a night out face similar challenges, where their innocence is questioned due to the established "relationship" prior to the incident; their innocence is further diminished if the victim was intoxicated. These types of crimes seem to attract social responses marked by a shift from focusing on perpetrator behaviour and accountability to focusing on victim behaviour and whether s/he has taken sufficient precaution to avoid the harm s/he has suffered (Menaker & Franklin, 2015; Meyer, 2016).

How do we construct the victim of DFV?

The research evidence on victims' help-seeking experiences suggests victims of DFV do not seem to fit the concept of the "ideal victim" and thus do not always enjoy the sympathy and support associated with responses to victims perceived as innocent. This raises the question: what it is about victims of DFV that excludes them from the categories Christie originally put forward under his concept of the "ideal victim"?

When examining key characteristics of DFV and its victims, the prominent gendered nature of the phenomenon (Devries et al., 2013) suggests that most victims are likely to be physically weaker and more vulnerable in comparison to their "big bad" abusive partner. One could further argue that victims of DFV meet Christie's category of "carrying out a respectable role at the time of victimisation". Research shows that victimisation by an intimate partner usually takes place within the victim's (or the couple's mutual) home (Mouzos & Makkai, 2004). In this context, one can argue that the victim was most likely carrying out a respectable role, for example the role of wife, partner, and/or mother. The victim-blaming attitudes reported by victims of DFV in different studies (e.g. Gillis et al., 2006; Meyer, 2010, 2016), however, suggest that victims of DFV are not seen as completely blameless in their victimisation, despite the fact that accountability should clearly lie with the abuser, not the abused (Meyer, 2016).

While meeting most of Christie's categories of the "ideal victim", there is one aspect where victims of DFV differ significantly from victims of most other types of violent crimes. That is, the existing relationship between victim and offender. This raises the question of whether the existing relationship is seen as a choice where victims are not taking the necessary precautionary measures to avoid victimisation (recall the expectations of victims of stranger violence when walking home after dark or sexual victims as sex workers who are seen as repeatedly placing themselves in highly vulnerable situations). Recent findings derived from population-based surveys on attitudes and beliefs around DFV conducted in a number of countries, including Australia and a range of European Union (EU) member states, support this victim-blaming notion. In the Australian survey, one in three respondents stated that women who remain in an abusive relationship are partly to blame for their victimisation experiences. One in six survey respondents further believed that leaving an abusive relationship is not as hard as people say it is (Australia's National Research Organisation for Women's Safety [ANROWS], 2017a). Similar observations have been made in the EU. In 2010, 27 EU member states participated in a survey on attitudes and beliefs around DFV. Victim-blaming attitudes varied greatly across countries. In some countries (for example Spain), about one-third of survey respondents stated that victims of DFV were at least partly to blame for their victimisation. In other countries, including new member states (such as Latvia and Lithuania) as well as economically advanced original member states (such as Finland and Denmark), these victim-blaming attitudes were shared by between 71% and 86% of respondents. In addition to high prevalence rates of victim-blaming attitudes, respondents in the EU survey who held victim-blaming attitudes were also less likely to be empathetic towards or supportive of someone experiencing DFV (Gracia, 2014).

The attitudes observed in a number of international settings suggest that the construction of the victim of DFV has a lot to do with their relationship with the perpetrator and the fact that remaining in an abusive relationship – if only temporarily – is seen as exposing oneself to unnecessary harm and therefore contributing to one's ongoing risk of revictimisation. This suggests that victims of DFV are being stigmatised as blameworthy, or even complicit in their victimisation, a perception that is most likely the result of a lack of understanding of the complexities associated with victims' experiences of and responses to DFV.

The stigma associated with being a victim of DFV

In the context of social responses to human behaviour, stigma is often associated with socially undesirable personality traits and choices of different social actors. These range from mental illnesses and disabilities through to addictions, criminal behaviours, and sexual orientation (LeBel, 2008; Link & Phelan, 2001; Winnick & Bodkin, 2008). Where individuals are seen as having character blemishes or engaging in morally questionable and unconventional behaviour (take for example the stigma and victim-blaming attitudes associated with the experiences of sex workers), they are more likely to receive stigmatising, unsupportive responses from informal and formal support sources alike (Gracia, 2014; Kogut, 2011).

The victim-blaming attitudes associated with the nature of the relationship between victims and perpetrators of DFV may explain the role of stigma here. Many victims receive victim-blaming attitudes at one point or another when reaching out for support. This applies, in particular, to those experiencing DFV in the form of intimate partner violence (IPV). Support sources may question what the victim did or did not do to incite or avoid the abuse and why s/he does not simply remove him/herself from the risk of repeat victimisation by ending the relationship (Anderson et al., 2003; Meyer, 2012). Despite research and practice accounts suggesting that victims of DFV are everything but weak or helpless (see for example Hamby, 2014; Meyer, 2012; Moe, 2007), it is essentially the approached support source's decision as to how they label the victim and whether this affects their level of empathy and support offered. In order to overcome stereotypical, victim-blaming attitudes that construct the victim as blameworthy, support sources therefore require an understanding of the complexities associated with victims' experiences and the implications this has for working with victims. Otherwise, victims of DFV will continue to be constructed as persons who have to redeem themselves by proving to their supporters that they have done everything they can to minimise their risk of revictimisation (Meyer, 2016).

Victims' experiences of stigma and blame

In the following section, we draw on some of our own research findings around victims' responses to and experiences of DFV. Women interviewed for a research project on the help-seeking experiences of female DFV victims frequently talked about perceptions of not being worth the time and effort of supporters where support sources saw them as contributing to their own victimisation by returning to or remaining with the abusive partner. A mother of three young children, for example, talked about how her family blamed her for her experiences of DFV because she had previously left her abusive partner and initially stayed with immediate family. She later returned to the abusive partner when staying with family became unsustainable with her children, and after the abusive partner made repeat promises to not hurt her again. This mother described her family's responses as follows:

> they [family] told me the whole time it's going to happen again, it's going to happen again, it's going to happen again, it's your own fault [for staying].

When this mother subsequently approached her family for a place to stay after another episode of violence, they refused to offer further support based on her perceived past "failures":

I rang dad and I said this is what happened, I've left him, can I come and stay at your place? [. . .] His partner said "she's not coming here. She went back before, it's her own fault, she got what she deserved".

Perceptions of victims as contributing to their victimisation was a common theme that emerged from a number of our research interviews. Another mother of a 9-year-old son recalled how the police turned her away because she had previously called them for help but then decided against leaving or pressing charges:

> I felt like I was being blamed or held responsible or accountable in some way. I went to the police station and said "help". The young copper that was on the desk was one of the cops that had been to the house before and he said, "You won't do anything about it anyway. I'm not going to help you today". It really fulfilled that prophecy that I was worthless.

These common themes have emerged from a number of studies over time (see for example Koss, 2000; Lempert, 1997; Moe, 2007) and illustrate that responses from both formal and informal supports can be marked by victim-blaming attitudes. Whereas victims of other types of crime are primarily seen as vulnerable and innocent in their victimisation experiences (Dignan, 2005; Strobl, 2004), community attitude surveys suggest that the same does not necessarily apply to victims of DFV (see for example ANROWS, 2017a). These observations are concerning in a social landscape where up to one in three women experience DFV at some point over the life course. Access to relevant support and protection may be delayed, which has adverse effects on victims' ability to overcome the trauma associated with severe and prolonged experiences of DFV. In addition, victim perceptions of having to redeem themselves as worthy of empathy and support by proving that they are innocent in their victimisation experiences can have a negative effect on future help-seeking decisions. As a result, victims may experience prolonged abuse. It is therefore important to grow public and professional awareness of factors influencing how victims respond to – and therefore resist – experiences of violence in private settings.

Other factors influencing victims' responses to DFV

A range of other factors, beyond shame, self-blame, and the wider stigma associated with the social construction of the victim of DFV, influence victims' responses to experiences of DFV, including their informal and formal help-seeking decisions (Koepsell, Kernic, & Holt, 2006; Stark, 2007; Meyer, 2011a, 2016). These factors include the interplay of emotional attachment and the hope for change (Griffing et al., 2005; Koepsell et al., 2006; Meyer, 2016), along with situational factors, such as social isolation of the victim (Hamberger,

Larsen, & Lehmer, 2017; Stark, 2007; Meyer, 2016). The nature and extent of experienced abuse (Gondolf & Fisher, 1988; Meyer, 2010), and the fear for the safety and wellbeing of children residing with the victim and/or abuser (Meyer, 2014), further play a crucial role here. While it is beyond the scope of this chapter to unpack the variety of help-seeking options along with their enabling and disabling factors, it is important to understand victims' attempts to resist violent victimisation in private settings in the context of their individual and situational circumstances (Hamby, 2014). Further, it is crucial to recognise that perpetrators of DFV frequently make concerted efforts to disable victims' resistance through the strategic manipulation of the victim's circumstances, including access to finances, social support, and children (Hamberger et al., 2017).

Perpetrators of DFV frequently use children as a tool to control or manipulate their victims. This includes threats to harm the children, taking the children away into hiding, or ensuring the victim is restricted in his/her access to the children via family law court decisions (Hamby, 2014; Meyer, 2011b). Many mothers therefore contemplate the pros and cons of disclosing abuse, leaving the abusive relationship, and the risk of retaliatory violence against the victim and/or children (Meyer, 2014; Nixon, Tutty, Radtke, Ateah, & Ursel, 2016). At times, the threats made towards children's safety and wellbeing can outweigh the perceived benefits associated with reaching out for support and leaving an abusive partner (Meyer, 2011a, 2015). Financial abuse equally complicates victims' experience of DFV in general, but disproportionately so, where the decision to leave the abusive relationship affects more than one person to house, feed, and support financially. While many victims of DFV have supportive family members behind them initially, perpetrators often strategically minimise contact with these support networks by actively undermining the victim's relationships with family, friends, and co-workers through frequent interference in those relationships (i.e. coercive control; Stark, 2007). This pattern of non-physical abuse is strategically employed by perpetrators with the aim of isolating the victim from potential support sources before the victim starts to recognise their relevance in coping with and ending the abusive experiences. Once victims realise the need for external support to successfully resist their experiences of victimisation, most perpetrators have successfully isolated their victims from their previously available sources of support. Further, while formal sources of support, such as police, remain available to all victims of DFV, research indicates that many victims prefer to rely on informal sources of support, at least initially (Moe, 2007; Meyer, 2010; Sabina & Tindale, 2008).

"Why doesn't she just leave?"

Despite the outlined challenges faced by many victims of DFV when trying to cope with and respond to their experiences, we continue to hear the question "why doesn't she just leave?" This is a question raised by many, including the public, as well as some of the support sources victims approach – for example family, friends, and service providers (Anderson et al., 2003; Meyer, 2012). As discussed earlier in this chapter, a number of population-based surveys conducted in recent years have revealed that the majority of the general public believes that victims of DFV could leave the abusive relationship if they really wanted to (Gracia, 2014; ANROWS, 2017a). The research evidence relating to enabling and hindering factors associated with victims' resistance of DFV presented throughout this chapter highlights the need to rephrase the question of "why doesn't she just leave?" as "how do victims manage to leave despite the systemic barriers and the strategic control implemented by the abuser?" and "how do they survive in the meantime?" While earlier literature often focused on the deficit model of why victims stay if "things are as bad as they say", more recent work has focused on the reasons why women stay, at least temporarily, and how they survive, often against all odds (Hamby, 2014; Meyer, 2012; Moe, 2007).

To an outside observer, it can be difficult to comprehend why victims remain in or return to an abusive relationship despite the risks of harm involved. It is therefore important to understand the factors that inform the decision-making processes around leaving versus staying in an abusive relationship, and the rational choice processes that inform either option (Kim & Gray, 2008; Koepsell et al., 2006; Meyer, 2012). Victims of DFV need to be understood as rational individuals who make decisions to the best of their knowledge, and this knowledge generally involves an actual or perceived awareness of any efforts or risks involved in different responses to the abuse, including seeking help or separating from the abusive partner. While leading a violence-free life is a benefit many outsiders believe outweighs any costs involved in seeking help, many victims never seek the support they need to terminate the violence, and those who do often endure years of abuse before taking that step (Hamby, 2014; Sabina & Tindale, 2008; Stark, 2007). It therefore appears that the cost–benefit analysis involved in resisting violent victimisation in private settings is much more complex than outsiders perceive it to be.

As discussed earlier in this chapter, many victims are exposed to manipulation, strategic control, and threats of harm throughout their abusive relationship. Those who have previously left temporarily or decided to seek help are aware that the abuse often escalates around these points in time. Perpetrators can become more violent in order to maintain control, and victims suffer the repercussions of having disclosed the abuse to a third party. In addition to the risk of increased levels of violence, victims face other risk factors, including the risk of harm to their children, the risk of financial instability, and the risk of homelessness should they decide to leave permanently (Hamby, 2014; Meyer, 2014). Within the cost–benefit analysis of victims considering separation from an abusive partner, these risks (or costs) often outweigh the anticipated benefits of separation unless victims are convinced that seeking help and leaving the abuser will offer the desired relief from their violent experiences in both the short and, maybe more importantly, the long term. As a result, many victims remain in or return to an abusive relationship, at least temporarily.

Essentially, the factors influencing a victim's decision to leave are very similar to those influencing initial help-seeking decisions because disclosure of abuse forms part of the process of resisting violence in private settings and potentially ending the abusive relationship. While some victims may separate without ever seeking informal or formal support, this scenario is rare. Nationally representative survey data shows that the vast majority of women affected by DFV disclose these experiences at some point or another (ANROWS, 2017b; Mouzos & Makkai, 2004). For some, this may be after having endured DFV for many months or even years. For the many, surviving DFV requires informal and formal support.

Summary

In this chapter, we examined victims' experiences of DFV from a gendered lens, acknowledging that resisting violence in private settings disproportionately affects women and children. We further explore children's involvement in DFV in the following chapter and unpack victims' experiences beyond the gendered intimate partner paradigm in Chapter 7. Here, however, we focused on how victims may experience as well as resist victimisation in private settings. We explored underpinning theories that inform the construction of those affected by DFV as victims versus survivors and unpacked the social construction of victimhood more broadly. Understanding how victimhood is constructed is crucial to understanding the implication it raises for victims' experiences of and responses to violent victimisation in private settings. Our exploration of passive endurance of violence versus agency in managing and surviving abuse highlights the predominantly proactive nature of victims' resistance in the face of DFV. However, this chapter also illustrates prevailing misconceptions around victims' experiences of and responses to DFV, highlighting the crucial role of ongoing public awareness raising and education around the complex nature of DFV and the various effects it can have on different aspects of victims' lives.

References

Anderson, M. A., Gillig, P. M., Sitaker, M., McCloskey, K., Malloy, K., & Grigsby, N. (2003). Why doesn't she just leave? A descriptive study of victim reported impediments to her safety. *Journal of Family Violence, 18*(3), 151–155.

Australia's National Research Organisation for Women's Safety (ANROWS). (2017a). *Are we there yet? Australians' attitudes towards violence against women & gender equality: Summary findings from the 2017 National Community Attitudes towards Violence against Women Survey (NCAS)*. Retrieved from https://ncas.anrows.org.au/wp-content/uploads/2018/12/ANROWS_NCAS_Summary_Report.pdf

Australia's National Research Organisation for Women's Safety (ANROWS). (2017b). *Personal Safety Survey 2016 fact sheet*. Retrieved from http://anrowsnationalconference.org.au/fact-sheet-personal-safety-survey-2016/

Barrett Meyering, I. (2010). *Victim compensation and domestic violence: A national overview* (Stakeholder Paper 8). Sydney, Australia: Australian Domestic & Family Violence Clearinghouse.

Brown, J. (1997). Working toward freedom from violence: The process of change in battered women. *Violence against Women*, 3(1), 5–26.

Carpenter, R. C. (2005). "Women, children and other vulnerable groups": Gender, strategic frames and the protection of civilians as a transnational issue. *International Studies Quarterly*, 49(2), 295–334.

Christie, N. (1986). The ideal victim. In E. Fattah (Ed.), *From crime policy to victim policy* (pp. 17–30). Basingstoke: MacMillan.

Davis, R., Guthrie, P., Ross, T., & O'Sullivan, C. (2006). *Reducing sexual revictimization: A field test with an urban sample* (Document No. 216002). Report to the US Department of Justice. Retrieved from www.ncjrs.gov/pdffiles1/nij/grants/216002.pdf

Devries, K. M., Mak, J. Y. T., Garcia-Moreno, C., Petzold, M., Child, J. C., Falder, G. F., . . ., Watts, C. H. (2013). The global prevalence of intimate partner violence against women. *Science*, 340(6140), 1527–1528.

Dignan, J. (2005). *Understanding victims and restorative justice*. New York: Open University Press.

Dunn, J. L. (2010). *Judging victims: Why we stigmatize survivors, and how they reclaim respect*. Boulder, CO: Lynne Rienner.

Fattah, E. (1989). Victims and victimology: The facts and the rhetoric. *International Review of Victimology*, 1(1), 43–66.

Gillis, J. R., Diamond, S. L., Jebely, P., Orekhovsky, V., Ostovich, E. M., & MacIsaac, K. (2006). Systemic obstacles to battered women's participation in the judicial system: When will the status quo change? *Violence against Women*, 12(12), 1150–1168.

Gondolf, E. W., & Fisher, E. R. (1988). *Battered women as survivors: An alternative to treating learned helplessness*. Lexington, MA: Lexington Books.

Gracia, E. (2014). Intimate partner violence against women and victim-blaming attitudes among Europeans. *Bulletin of the World Health Organization*, 92, 380–381.

Griffing, S., Ragin, D. F., Morrison, S. M., Sage, R. E., Madry, L., & Primm, B. J. (2005). Reasons for returning to abusive relationships: Effects of prior victimization. *Journal of Family Violence*, 20(5), 341–348.

Gupta, Rahila (2014). 'Victim' vs. 'Survivor': Feminism and Language. Retrieved from: https://www.opendemocracy.net/5050/rahila-gupta/victim-vs-survivor-feminism-and-language.

Hamberger, K., Larsen, S., & Lehmer, A. (2017). Coercive control in intimate partner violence. *Aggression and Violent Behavior*, 37, 1–11.

Hamby, S. (2014). *Battered women's protective strategies: Stronger than you know*. New York, NY: Oxford University Press.

Kim, J., & Gray, K. (2008). Leave or stay? Battered women's decision after intimate partner violence. *Journal of Interpersonal Violence*, 23(10): 1465–1482.

Kelly, L. (1988). *Surviving sexual violence*. Cambridge: Polity Press.

Koepsell, J. K., Kernic, M. A., & Holt, V. L. (2006). Factors that influence battered women to leave their abusive relationships. *Violence and Victims*, 21(2), 131–147.

Kogut, T. (2011). Someone to blame: When identifying a victim decreases helping. *Journal of Experimental Social Psychology*, 47(4), 748–755.

Koss, M. P. (2000). Blame, shame, and community: Justice responses to violence against women. *The American Psychologist*, 55(11): 1332–1343.

LeBel, T. P. (2008). Perceptions of and responses to stigma. *Sociology Compass*, 2(2), 409–432.

Lempert, L. B. (1997). The other side of help: Negative effects in the help-seeking processes of abused women. *Qualitative Sociology*, 20(2): 289–309.

Link, B. G., & Phelan, J. C. (2001). Conceptualizing stigma. *Annual Review of Sociology*, 27(1), 363–385.

Menaker, T. A., & Franklin, C. A. (2015). Gendered violence and victim blame: Subject perceptions of blame and the appropriateness of services for survivors of domestic sex trafficking, sexual assault, and intimate partner violence. *Journal of Crime and Justice*, 38(3), 395–413.

Meyer, S. (2010). *Responding to intimate partner violence victimization: Effective options for help-seeking* (Trends & Issues in Crime and Criminal Justice Series, No. 389). Canberra: Australian Institute of Criminology.

Meyer, S. (2011a). Seeking help for intimate partner violence: Victims' experiences when approaching the criminal justice system for IPV-related support and protection in an Australian jurisdiction. *Feminist Criminology*, 6(4), 268–290.

Meyer, S. (2011b). Acting in the children's best interest? Examining victims' responses to intimate partner violence. *Journal of Child and Family Studies*, 20(4): 436–443.

Meyer, S. (2012). Why women stay: A theoretical examination of rational choice and moral reasoning in the context of intimate partner violence. *Australian & New Zealand Journal of Criminology*, 45(2), 179–193.

Meyer, S. (2014). *Victims' experiences of short- and long-term safety and wellbeing: Findings from an examination of an integrated response to domestic violence* (Trends & Issues in Crime and Criminal Justice Series, No. 478). Canberra: Australian Institute of Criminology.

Meyer, S. (2015). Examining women's agency in managing intimate partner violence and the related risk of homelessness: The role of harm minimisation. *Global Public Health*, 11(1–2), 198–201.

Meyer, S. (2016). Still blaming the victim of intimate partner violence? Women's narratives of victim desistance and redemption when seeking support. *Theoretical Criminology*, 20(1), 75–90.

Moe, A. M. (2007). Silenced voices and structured survival: Battered women's help seeking. *Violence against Women*, 13(7), 676–699.

Mouzos, J., & Makkai, T. (2004). *Women's experiences of male violence: Findings from the Australian component of the International Violence against Women Survey (IVAWS)* (Research and Public Policy Series No. 56). Canberra: Australian Institute of Criminology.

Nixon, K., Tutty, L., Radtke, H., Ateah, C., & Ursel, J. (2016). Protective strategies of mothers abused by intimate partners: Rethinking the deficit model. *Violence against Women*, 23(11), 1271–1292.

Ofstehage, A., Gandhi, A., Sholk, J., Radday, A., & Stanzler, C. (2011). *Empowering victims of domestic violence* (Social Issues Report). Boston, MA: RootCAUSE.

Sabina, C., & Tindale, R. S. (2008). Abuse characteristics and coping resources as predictors of problem-focused coping strategies among battered women. *Violence against Women*, 14(4), 437–456.

Schwartz, J., & Steffensmeier, D. (2011). Stability and change in girls' delinquency and the gender gap: Trends in violence and alcohol offending across multiple sources of evidence. In S. Miller, L. Leve, & P. Kerrig (Eds.), *Delinquent girls: Contexts, relationships and adaptation* (pp. 3–23). New York: Springer.

Stark, E. (2007). *Coercive control: How men entrap women in personal life*. New York, NY: Oxford University Press.

Strobl, R. (2004). Constructing the victim: Theoretical reflections and empirical examples. *International Review of Victimology*, 11(2–3), 295–311.

Towns, A., & Adams, P. (2000). "If I really loved him enough, he would be okay": Women's accounts of male partner violence. *Violence against Women, 6*(6), 558–585.

van Wijk, J. (2013). Who is the "little old lady" of international crimes? Nils Christie's concept of the ideal victim reinterpreted. *International Review of Victimology, 19*(2), 159–179.

Walker, L. E. (1979). *The battered woman.* New York: Harper & Row.

Winnick, T. A., & Bodkin, M. (2008). Anticipated stigma and stigma management among those to be labeled "ex-con". *Deviant Behavior, 29*(4), 295–333.

World Health Organization (WHO). (2013). *Global and regional estimates of violence against women: Prevalence and health effects of intimate partner violence and non-partner sexual violence.* Department of Reproductive Health and Research, London School of Hygiene and Tropical Medicine, South African Medical Research Council. Retrieved from www.who.int/reproductivehealth/publications/violence/9789241564625/en/

Chapter 6

The burden on children

Children's involvement in DFV

> I grew up witnessing domestic abuse. My mum would get beaten by my father. When she wasn't there he would turn to me and my brothers. I used to sit in my room and hear them fighting then I'd hear my mum scream and I'd know he'd have hit her. To be honest, at the age I was at, I actually thought it was normal. I thought that many families were like this but now when I think about it I was in denial because I never mentioned it to my friends or teachers.
>
> – Jay's story, Hidden Hurt[1]

Research suggests that one in four children have been exposed to DFV by the age of 18 (Humphreys & Bradbury-Jones, 2015). Children's involvement in DFV can take various forms. Sometimes they indirectly witness parental abuse from another room, whereas other times they are in the same room, directly exposed to the harm inflicted on the non-abusive parent (Edleson, Mbilinyi, Beeman, & Hagemeister, 2003). Sometimes children silently witness the abuse, whereas other times they may become a direct target (Devaney, 2008; McGuigan & Pratt, 2001). Children exposed to DFV also often take on various duties beyond their age or level of maturity, referred to as "developmental overload" by some (see for example Jenkins, 1990). Research based on parents' accounts of children's exposure to DFV as well as children's own accounts shows that in addition to witnessing and intervening in abusive incidents, older children especially often take on "carer" or "protector" roles for younger siblings and/or the non-abusive parent. Some intuitively know to take younger siblings into a separate room and turn on music or the TV to distract them from witnessing the abuse and to keep them out of the "firing line". Others are instructed to call for help or send "coded" messages to neighbours or friends when violence escalates (Edleson et al., 2003; Edleson, Nguyen, & Kimball, 2011).

In addition, older children frequently take on "parenting responsibilities", often referred to as the "parentification of children" (Edleson et al., 2011, p. 12). For some, this may mean looking after younger children while the non-abusive parent is emotionally or physically unavailable (e.g. due to injuries, trauma, or mental health issues), and for others, this may entail care for the non-abusive parent after incidents of severe physical abuse. This involvement of children beyond witnessing DFV places an additional burden on their own ability to cope with the experiences. Given the diverse nature of exposure and involvement of many children, responses to DFV need not only to focus on victims and perpetrators but also further to incorporate a child-focused and child-centred approach.

Children's involvement in DFV-related homicide

As well as children's widespread exposure to non-lethal DFV, research identifies an increased risk of lethal violence directed at children in families affected by DFV (Dobash & Dobash, 2012; Hazel, Hamilton, Jaffe, & Campbell, 2013; Jaffe, Campbell, Olszowy, Hazel, & Hamilton, 2014; Olszowy, Jaffe, Campbell, & Hamilton, 2013). As we discuss earlier in this book, the gendered nature of DFV becomes even more prominent at the most severe and lethal end of DFV. International statistics suggest that at least four in five intimate partner homicides are male-to-female perpetrated (Bundeskriminalamt, 2017; Home Office, 2016; Queensland Domestic and Family Violence Death Review and Advisory Board, 2018). As a result, children involved in parental domestic homicide most commonly face the loss of their mother.

As illustrated in the previous section, children's involvement in parental DFV takes various forms, ranging from witnessing the abuse while waiting in a different room for a particular incident to pass, to getting hurt in an attempt to intervene and protect the non-abusive parent (Edleson et al., 2003). Similar observations are true in the context of DFV-related homicide. A study by Katz (2014) examined children's observations and perceptions of their father killing their mother and offers a rare insight into the traumatic nature of children's involvement in parental domestic homicide. Children's perceptions of the incident differed depending on their involvement, level of maturity, and history of exposure to DFV.

In some cases, children were directed or knew from experience to go into another room when the situation started to escalate. Others directly witnessed their father killing their mother. What stands out from this study is the level of exposure to trauma and the fact that many were too young to comprehend the impact of what they witnessed. Some of the children had witnessed injuries to their mother and damage to the property on multiple previous occasions and assumed their mother was going to be okay because she always cleaned up and would be okay after past escalations of violence (Katz, 2014). Others said that something was different this time because their mother would not respond when they tried to talk to her or she looked different this time. Often, these children were too young to fully comprehend the fact that their father had just killed their mother. Aside from the severe trauma associated with witnessing a parent being killed, this study further highlights children's repeated exposure to parental DFV leading up to a domestic homicide. It is therefore not surprising that children with extensive exposure to parental violence often know what to do when violence escalates in the home but in the aftermath struggle to distinguish a fatal event and its consequences from the many non-fatal ones they have witnessed previously (Katz, 2014).

Children may be targeted as a form of revenge

In addition to children experiencing the loss of a parent where DFV escalates and becomes fatal, children are further at risk of becoming the target of such fatal violence. While child deaths in the context of DFV are less common than adult deaths, they still account for a significant proportion of domestic homicides. Research based on DFV death review data reveals that the proportion of child deaths ranges from 7% to 16% of all domestic homicide victims. If only including domestic homicides where children are present in the relationship, child victims make up around one-third of homicide victims (Hazel et al., 2013). When children die in the context of DFV, it is often because they have been targeted as a form of revenge by the perpetrator. Primarily male perpetrated, this type of domestic homicide uses children as the ultimate "tool" of power and control over the original victim of DFV (Hazel et al., 2013; Olszowy et al., 2013). This type of domestic homicide disproportionately occurs in the context of recent or impending parental separation. Here, an almost exclusively male perpetrator population murders mutual children with the (soon to be) ex-partner as a form of revenge for the initiated separation and/or the limited access to their children post-separation.

DFV, child exposure, and child protection

The evidence around children's frequent and diverse exposure to and involvement in parental DFV has generated increasing attention to child welfare concerns in the context of DFV from research, policy, and practice perspectives. The growing awareness of the various detrimental impacts that childhood exposure to DFV can have on victims' safety, development, and wellbeing has led to a philosophical shift in the way child protection agencies approach families affected by DFV (Nixon, Tutty, Weaver-Dunlop, & Walsh, 2007). While mothers were traditionally encouraged to keep the family together and to protect the children by maintaining the adult relationship, the 1990s saw a shift towards expectations of victims to remove children from the abusive environment (Humphreys & Absler, 2011). Exposure to DFV started to be framed as a form of child maltreatment due to its equivalence – in terms of seriousness – to other forms of maltreatment and its impact on children's development and wellbeing. Policy and practice responses became increasingly "protective", taking a child-centred rights-based approach (Ewen, 2007; Nixon et al., 2007).

At the core of this approach were children in need of protection from ongoing exposure to harmful parental behaviour. On the margins were mothers who – while victims themselves – were held responsible for the protection of their children from exposure to their own victimisation. This approach made the intersection of DFV and child safety contentious (Nixon et al., 2007). Situated on the one side were child protection agencies which followed a "failure to protect" principle where mothers "failed" to separate from the abusive partner or avoid children's exposure. On the other side were victim support services, which lobbied for more holistic approaches that treat mothers and children as equally vulnerable and in need of support and protection in the context of DFV (Ewen, 2007).

The "protective" child protection approach was in many ways punitive towards the non-abusive parent. In many jurisdictions, statutory interventions are warranted where children are known or believed to be at risk of harm and where the child is lacking a parent that is *able* or *willing* to protect them (see for example Ewen, 2007; Nixon et al., 2007). Research shows that mothers affected by DFV engage in various protective strategies to minimise its adverse impact on their children's safety and wellbeing (Meyer, 2011; Nixon, Tutty, Radtke, Ateah, & Ursel, 2017). However, mothers' *ability* and *willingness* to adequately protect their children is often only recognised where victims follow the advice of removing themselves and their children (through separation) from the risk of subsequent victimisation (Douglas & Walsh, 2010; Ewen, 2007; Meyer, 2011). This policy approach left many mothers unsupported due to a lack of focus and understanding on how DFV affects victims' ability to parent. In addition, it left many children subject to regulatory interventions that were often counterproductive to what they were designed to achieve. This was especially true where interventions that involved the separation of children from the non-abusive parent failed to hold the perpetrator accountable in their role as a parent (Featherstone & Peckover, 2007; Nixon et al., 2007). These traditionally regulatory and, in part, punitive responses to DFV at the intersection with child safety contributed to an increasing number of children at all levels of the child protection system (James, 1994; Trepiccione, 2001).

Defining exposure to DFV as a form of child maltreatment

The growing body of knowledge around the multifaceted impacts of DFV on children has shaped policy and practice reforms in Australia, Canada, the US, and beyond (Kaukinen, Powers, & Meyer, 2016; Nixon et al., 2007; Richards, 2011). However, policy and legislative responses vary greatly. Some jurisdictions have made reforms to directly address children's exposure to DFV as a form of child maltreatment. Others have broadened their legislative definitions to capture exposure to DFV and associated harm under sections addressing issues around emotional abuse or neglect. Further, some address children's need for protection in the context of DFV under their existing legislation, that is, where exposure to DFV substantially affects the child's wellbeing as covered under the legislative definition of harm (Nixon et al., 2007).

An examination of child protection legislation in five Western countries by Nixon and colleagues (2007) showed that policies and legislation not only vary across but also within countries. For example, Australia, like Canada, has no federal child safety legislation. Instead, child protection legislation is developed, implemented, and exercised at the state and territory (or province) level. While some states and territories have incorporated a definition of exposure to DFV as child maltreatment, this appears to be more common in Canada than Australia. In Canada, over half of all jurisdictions specifically define exposure to parental DFV as a form of maltreatment. In Australia, New South Wales is in the minority in this sense, as most states address child exposure to DFV under their broad definitions of what constitutes risk of harm (Children and Young Persons (Care and Protection Act), 1998 (NSW); Nixon et al., 2007).

The UK moved towards the inclusion of exposure to DFV as a specific child protection concern in 2002. However, exposure is not defined as a form of maltreatment as such. Instead, child safety concerns arising from DFV are addressed through establishing whether children have suffered or are likely to suffer harm from witnessing DFV. Where a child is considered to be at "significant" risk of harm in the context of DFV, they are seen as in need of protection, and exposure to DFV warrants a child protection intervention (Nixon et al., 2007). The different national and international policies and legislation demonstrate that, while child exposure to DFV has received increasing policy attention over the last two decades, the way in which it is addressed varies across jurisdictions. Some have taken the approach of reforming existing policies towards underpinning principles that clearly identify exposure as child maltreatment, whereas others aim to address the issue under broadened, existing definitions.

Summarily, national and international policy and law reforms to better address child exposure to DFV are based on good intentions, where the safety and wellbeing of children is seen as paramount. In an attempt to better address the need for protection of children exposed to severe and often repeated episodes of parental violence, some jurisdictions underwent reforms to warrant child protection interventions in cases of DFV where the abuse was not directed at the children but where children were nevertheless perceived as "at risk" (Nixon et al., 2007). Such reforms had a number of objectives, including:

- Acknowledging that DFV not only affects its direct victims (e.g. mothers) but further has severe impacts on its "indirect" victims (i.e. children)
- Sending a strong message of social accountability, i.e. DFV is unacceptable and will have consequences for parents who fail to protect their children from such exposure
- Offering a "straightforward" means of intervening for workers in the child safety and wellbeing space without having to identify and demonstrate actual harm suffered by a relevant child
- Facilitating identification and awareness of children's exposure to DFV among child protection frontline workers

- Extending awareness and opportunities for intervention to other professionals through the inclusion of children's exposure to DFV in mandatory reporting policies

While well intended in their origins, these reforms had a number of unintended consequences. Nixon and colleagues (2007) found that the lack of clear definitions around which forms of DFV warrant a child protection intervention meant that in some jurisdictions, child protection services found themselves inundated with referrals and notifications relating to children's exposure to any form of parental DFV, regardless of severity. Many notifications did not meet the threshold for warranting child safety investigations but had to undergo an initial assessment (Nixon et al., 2007). As a result, an already overburdened system was further slowed down by numerous notifications that varied greatly in severity. This issue is further exacerbated by mandatory reporting policies.

The contentious issue of mandatory reporting

Mandatory reporting laws define the requirements of different groups or professions to report knowledge or suspicions of children at risk of harm. The underlying objective of mandatory reporting is to address a social issue that otherwise frequently remains largely hidden. Proponents of mandatory reporting argue that it raises awareness and moral consciousness among the general population as well as particular professions (Australian Institute of Family Studies [AIFS], 2017). Opponents, on the other hand, warn that it can lead to an over-reporting of cases that do not meet the threshold for child protection (AIFS, 2017); child welfare organisations may also become overburdened with notifications where the behaviour and circumstances warranting mandatory reporting are not clearly defined. Further, opponents argue that mandatory reporting has a deterrent effect on parents' help-seeking behaviours where parents fear statutory child protection interventions (Nixon et al., 2007). Victims of DFV who have dependent children residing with them at least some of the time may, for example, become increasingly reluctant to disclose their experiences, anxieties, and need for support to professionals who are subject to mandatory reporting laws, such as their family doctor or the police.

One example of where mandatory reporting can lead to overburdening for child welfare organisations can be found in the 1999 child protection reforms passed in Minnesota in the US (Edleson, Gassman-Pines, & Hill, 2006 as cited in Nixon et al., 2007). Exposure to DFV was adopted into the state's child protection statute as a form of neglect. The statute failed to provide a sufficiently circumscribed definition of DFV cases to be covered under the new reforms, meaning that professionals working with children, parents, and/or families were mandated to report nearly all forms of exposure, leading to a 100% increase in child safety notifications within the first year of the reforms (Nixon et al., 2007). Since no additional funding had been allocated in line with the reforms, the child protection system was unable to respond to this level of increase. As a result, Minnesota repealed the legislation changes in 2000 (Edleson et al., 2006).

A similar unintended consequence could be observed in Queensland, Australia in 2013. In an attempt to acknowledge the often detrimental impact of DFV on children, reformed law enforcement policies mandated police officers to notify child protection agencies of all attended DFV incidents in which children were residing with either or both parties (i.e. victims and perpetrators) at the time of the incident (Queensland Government, 2013). As a result, child safety offices across the jurisdiction became inundated with police-initiated child safety notifications relating to all forms of DFV, regardless of severity or whether children were present at the time of the incident. Due to the substantial backlog caused by this mandatory procedure, child safety agencies were unable to identify and investigate relevant notifications within the crucial period of initial crisis and safety concerns. This policy has since been revoked, and police notification processes have been realigned with the definition that a child "has suffered, is suffering [. . .] or is at unacceptable risk of suffering significant harm" (Child Protection Act, 1999, S10(a); Queensland Government, 2013, p. 3).

These examples highlight that mandatory reporting is only useful where the organisation expected to investigate and address relevant concerns has the capacity to respond in a timely manner. Clearly defined behaviours and circumstances are therefore vital to avoid overburdening child welfare agencies with a wide range of notifications that prevent them from identifying children most in need of protection within critical timeframes.

Impact on children's development and wellbeing

As alerted to in the beginning of this chapter, the impact of childhood exposure to DFV has received increasing attention over the last two decades. A meta-analysis of 118 empirical studies on outcomes observed in children exposed to parental DFV, for example, showed that two-thirds of these children experience developmental, cognitive, and behavioural problems, including lower academic achievement and poor mental health and wellbeing (Dube, Anda, Felitti, Edwards, & Williamson, 2002; Kitzman, Gaylord, Holt, & Kenny, 2003).

Most research has examined childhood exposure to DFV from a sociological, criminological, or victimological perspective. This research has shown that exposure to DFV can affect children's immediate safety and wellbeing (such as physical injuries and emotional trauma; Edleson, 1999), as well as long-term academic performance and adult relationships (Kitzman et al., 2003; Whitfield, Anda, Dube, & Felitti, 2003). More recently, studies have further highlighted the impact of exposure to DFV on children's neurobiological development, linking the sociological "how" with the neurobiological "why" (Schafran, 2014; Perry, 2001). This means that where sociological enquiry has identified how exposure to DFV may affect children's behaviour, development, and wellbeing, the neurological examination explains why. This provides the missing link by explaining what exactly happens "underneath the surface" (i.e. in a child's neurological system) that leads to some of the concerning outcomes observed in sociological research, such as substance misuse, academic performance problems, risk of victimisation, and mental health problems (Dube et al., 2002; Schafran, 2014).

Emotional and psychological trauma

Research shows that many children exposed to DFV suffer various forms of trauma due to the way in which they experience the abuse. Some may witness it by listening from another room, some may watch the abusive acts directly, and others may become directly involved by verbally or physically intervening in the abusive incidents (Edleson et al., 2003). While the risk of physical injuries is higher for those who are present in the same room, especially when intervening in the abusive incidents to protect the non-abusive parent, emotional and psychological trauma is also observed in children who do not suffer any physical harm (Edleson, 1999; Whitfield et al., 2003; Levendosky, Bogat, & Martinez-Torteya, 2013). Common symptoms of trauma exposure observed in children affected by DFV include depression, anxiety and post-traumatic stress disorder (PTSD) (Holt, Buckley, & Whelan, 2008; Perry, 2001). Exposure may manifest in a variety of other symptoms, such as night terrors, bed-wetting, emotional withdrawal, and a lack of progress in children's development. As a result, children may not be able to sleep and rest well, which leads to further adverse effects on their growth and development. Young children who are in their formative years of language development may show a regression in language and communication skills. Some further disassociate with the traumatic experiences as a form of coping (Burgess Chamberlain, 2008).

Emotional and psychological impacts are problematic in themselves but become even more challenging for children when they start to accumulate as complex trauma (Holt et al., 2008). As a result, children exposed to DFV often require early and skilled interventions that help them to recover long-term. Below, we examine examples of the nature and accumulation of adverse experiences and outcomes for children exposed to DFV.

Neurobiological impacts

Recent research on the impact of childhood exposure to DFV has identified concerning outcomes for children's brain development. Young children are especially susceptible to adverse neurobiological outcomes because their brains are more vulnerable to the impact of trauma (Burgess Chamberlain, 2008; Schafran, 2014). While very young children and babies may not actively remember exposure to traumatic experiences, their developing brain does. Research shows that loving, nurturing interactions with babies are crucial because they foster healthy neurobiological, emotional, and cognitive development (Maggi, Irwin, Siddiqi, & Hertzman, 2010). Frightening or threatening experiences, on the other hand, have the opposite effect. Burgess Chamberlain (2008) describes a baby's brain as a flower that is ready to blossom when stimulated with the right input. When exposed to adverse childhood experiences, such as parental neglect, childhood abuse, or parental DFV, the brain cannot flourish. This is partly due to the highly unpredictable and often dangerous nature of the child's life, and as such, the young brain struggles to adapt to everyday scenarios of risk and survival (Burgess Chamberlain, 2008; Perry, 2001).

Especially early trauma can leave a permanent imprint on a child's brain. Children growing up in safe and nurturing environments are able to focus on bonding with their carer and acquire new developmental skills, such as social interaction and communication with others. Conversely, children growing up in an unsafe home environment spend a significant amount of time responding and adjusting to potential threats of harm (Schafran, 2014; Perry, 2001). Burgess Chamberlain (2008) describes the brain in two parts: the "lower building blocks" and the "upper building blocks". Lower building blocks develop first and form the foundation for later development of social, emotional, and cognitive skills. They are also particularly sensitive to the impact of trauma. As a result, the constant exposure to stress and potential harm that is associated with exposure to DFV negatively affects foundational and subsequent brain development. Consequences can include delayed or limited upper brain development, an overall smaller brain size, and a disruption of brain connections (Burgess Chamberlain, 2008; Delima & Vimpani, 2011).

Academic achievement

The neurobiological impact of childhood exposure to DFV is closely linked with other areas of adverse outcomes for children, such as poor academic achievement. This outcome area is complex because it is associated with a number of risk factors that tend to accumulate for children exposed to DFV. As discussed earlier, exposure to DFV can have an adverse impact on children's brain development, which in return adversely affects cognitive development. Delayed speech, poor communication and/or social interaction skills, and short attention spans are all known risk factors for poor school performance, including lower academic achievement, higher rates of absenteeism, and higher rates of withdrawal from school (O'Donnell, Hawkins, Catalano, Abbott, & Day, 1995; Walker & Sprague, 1999). This is partly because these risk factors can create learning difficulties for children and partly because they are associated with behavioural problems. While some children affected by DFV become withdrawn, others start to externalise their violent observations and experiences by displaying anger and aggression in their social interactions. Aggressive behaviour towards other children and/or primary carers, early childhood educators, and teachers is not uncommon in children exposed to DFV and can create further problems for them, such as social exclusion and/or expulsion from school (Evans, Davies, & DiLillo, 2008; Kiesel, Piescher, & Edleson, 2016).

These outcomes are problematic for children (and their parents) in two ways. While they create immediate concerns about academic achievement and social engagement, failure in those areas leads to an accumulation of further risk factors. School failure is associated with lower employability in adulthood. Aggression and violent behaviour during childhood is associated with a greater risk of engagement in other troublesome and potentially harmful behaviour during adolescence and adulthood, including substance misuse and criminality (Moffitt & Caspi, 2001; Walker & Sprague, 1999). It is therefore extremely important to identify the adverse effects of DFV early and to facilitate access to age-appropriate interventions.

Aggressive behaviour towards (non-abusive) parent

Research alerts to an increase in parents reporting abuse at the hands of their dependent children, predominantly during adolescence, after exposure to parental DFV during childhood (Condry & Miles, 2014; Ibabe, Jaureguizar, & Bentler, 2013). This phenomenon has also been identified as a gendered one, with sons showing a greater likelihood than daughters to behave abusively towards their mothers (Fitz-Gibbon, Elliott, & Maher, 2018). While the role of social learning has traditionally been applied to explain the increased risk of men's use of violence in adult relationships when exposed to parental DFV in their own upbringing, it applies in the same sense to teenage sons using violence against their already victimised mothers. When applying Bandura's (1973, 1978) social learning theory, this can be attributed to the social learning effect associated with observation and role modelling. While girls who grow up witnessing parental DFV are said to have an increased risk of becoming victims in their own adult relationships, boys learn through observation that their father or father figure is entitled to certain privileges and often ensures these through the use of violence (verbal, physical, or otherwise). From a social learning theory perspective, there are two key ingredients here:

- The witnessing of someone using violence as a tool to get their way (e.g. in order to maintain control over the victim, get the victim to comply, get the victim to act in line with the perpetrator's expectations), and
- The witnessing of this use of violence as being successful (e.g. because the perpetrator gets his way and the victim is perceived as "not fighting back" or seems unable to stop the abuse despite various efforts)

This observation can translate into the social learning outcome. Children may observe and learn that the use of violence is a legitimate tool to get one's way. They may further come to realise that they can take advantage of the fact that the victim is likely to comply (e.g. out of fear, because the victim may be physically weaker than the perpetrator, or because the victim can empathise with the underlying reasons for the perpetrator's behaviour). The latter is not uncommon in mothers who become exposed to their own children's abusive behaviour because they often blame themselves for having exposed their children to DFV in the first place. Below, we share some unpublished extracts from our own research projects to help illustrate children's experiences of social learning and mothers' self-blame and empathy for their abusive behaviour:

> He used to wake up [our son] in our fights and sit him on his lap and make [him] stare at me and call me a c***. That was when [our son] was two and when he was three I'd have [him] call me a c*** for days. I couldn't crack at him because he didn't know what he was saying.
>
> – Mother of two

> There was lots of violence. It was continually and in the last 12 years it was horrific and it really impacted on the children. The 18 year old still talks about it. [The second eldest] has been profoundly affected and is a very aggressive boy and is very aggressive towards me. He's a lovely boy but he's very aggressive. So much behaviour was modelled to him that that's how you got your needs met. [. . .] Part of the domestic violence was he abused the children as a tool and a lever to hurt me so those boys were encouraged to call me [names]. I can't believe I allowed my children to go through this.
>
> – Mother of two

> My babies have seen a lot of stuff that they shouldn't have seen. They've been involved in it. Even to this day they still disrespect me because of the way their father did, because of the way he showed them and told them to do what they do.
>
> – Mother of three

These three examples are an indication of how children may be exposed and the impact this can have on their relationship with the non-abusive parent. In some cases, children may literally be "taught to be abusive, as in the extracts where the abusive parent forced the children to be verbally abusive towards their mothers. In other examples, perpetrator behaviour may solely be directed at the victim, but the ongoing exposure to this behaviour can have enough of a social learning impact for children to essentially "step into the perpetrator's footsteps". This pattern of social learning and role modelling requires skilled interventions for many children. These range from therapeutic play all the way to cognitive behavioural and trauma therapy, depending on the timing, nature, and extent of childhood exposure.

The impact on children's short- and long-term safety, development, and wellbeing outlined here highlights the need for child-centred approaches when responding to families affected by DFV.

Taking a child-centred approach when responding to families affected by DFV

The importance of child-centred approaches has received increasing attention in research and practice over the past decade (Alderson, Westmarland, & Kelly, 2013; Baker, 2005; Ermentrout, Rizo, & Macy, 2014). Rather than relying on parent-focused interventions to address the problem, children have increasingly become the target population. This is partly due to a cultural shift from viewing children as passive dependants towards acknowledging them as active agents or social actors (Edleson et al., 2011; Morris, Hegarty, & Humphreys, 2012) who share views and experiences that are often distinct from those of their parents. The shift has led to the realisation that many children have the desire to express how they feel and have their voices considered in adult decision-making, and want to be heard.

Historically, the social status of the child was associated with the perception that adults know best what is in a child's best interest. As a result, decisions are often made *for* rather than *with* them. However, upon being asked, many children express very strong feelings and clear ideas about the decisions they would like to see made (Alderson et al., 2013; Edleson et al., 2011; Ermentrout et al., 2014; Morris et al., 2012). Indeed, while younger children may not fully grasp the complexities and risks associated with living with an abusive parent, their voices need to be considered. Research and practice evidence suggests that children as young as 5 years old are able to clearly voice their concerns around things that happen in the family home (see www.honourourvoices.com for children's accounts of DFV by age group). Children younger than 5 may not always be able to articulate their desires or concerns verbally but are able to express emotions through drawings or creative play, for example (Ermentrout et al., 2014).

Not all service responses can offer a specific child-centred response. Depending on their service mandate, the primary client is often the adult victim (e.g. where the victim presents to a police station, the family doctor, or the emergency room). The focus here is therefore not on ensuring that every agency or organisation offers specific child-centred interventions. Instead, the argument informed by the evidence base on child-centred practice is that any response to DFV should incorporate considerations relating to the presence of children, their imminent risk and general support needs, and the options for suitable referral pathways (Edleson et al., 2011). This is particularly important when considering that research evidence suggests children often do not have access to relevant service responses until the victim decides to leave (Devaney, 2009). It is often at this "pointy end" of DFV where victims' help seeking becomes more proactive and where service responses become more holistic. Given the evidence that many victims do not separate, at least not immediately, after the onset of DFV, the lack of early access to child-centred interventions often leaves children exposed to DFV and its detrimental impacts for an extended period.

Traditionally, children's needs for safety and protection have been addressed by responding to the support needs of the adult victim, and by doing so, achieving safety and protection for any dependent children. This may be true to some extent (e.g. by arresting the perpetrator, temporary relief and safety can be achieved for victims and children and long-term protection may be granted through a protection order [also referred to as restraining orders in some jurisdictions]). However, some limitations apply, for instance, where victim and perpetrator may not separate (at least initially), or where perpetrators remain in contact with their children despite parental separation. It is therefore important to consider children in their own right and to consider *if and how* their needs can be best addressed by an adult-focused intervention.

Challenges around taking a child-centred approach

While the social shift towards treating children in their experiences of DFV as social actors (rather than dependants) has generated an increase in child-centred practice (Baker, 2005; Morris et al., 2012), implementing such approaches is not without challenges. There are several ethical and legal hurdles attached to working with children and including their voices in research evidence. As a result, most of the evidence base around children's exposure to DFV and their related service needs remains based on parents' accounts captured by adult-focused research projects (Baker, 2005).

Parental consent

One of the main challenges associated with offering child-centred interventions in the context of DFV is the role of parental consent. As noted previously, some argue that children should be treated as social actors who are capable of articulating their lived experiences and should therefore not be spoken for (Baker, 2005). Others disagree, arguing that children are immature and thus incompetent in terms of giving consent for participation in relevant interventions unless supported in their decision by a parent or guardian (Brannan, 1999). This proves to be problematic in cases of DFV as well as child abuse because those expected to speak on behalf of minor children may have a vested interest in silencing them. While sometimes this is carried out with the best intentions (e.g. where a parent believes that talking about the abuse may be re-traumatising for the child), other times the vested interest is to keep the abusive family life a secret. Explaining the benefits of interventions and being transparent with parents about what will be involved in relevant practice with children can be useful in overcoming some of these challenges – at least with the non-abusive parent (Ermentrout et al., 2014).

Another challenge in this area can arise from court orders that may stipulate whether both parents are required to give consent for children's involvement in certain activities (such as participation in research, counselling, parent–child interventions; Ermentrout et al., 2014; Morris et al., 2012). In the case of DFV, the abusive parent may engage in manipulating behaviours to avoid children's disclosure of details around the abusive incidents. Research on perpetrator behaviour during and post-family law court proceedings has shown that manipulation and abuse of power are common tools used by the abusive parent to restrict children's participation in a variety of activities (Bagshaw & Hart, 2008), including counselling for DFV. Parental consent can therefore create a barrier for researchers and practitioners when attempting to include children affected by DFV.

Risk of ongoing harm

While consent can be a hurdle in providing children with relevant support mechanisms, having obtained parental and child consent is not necessarily the end to all considerations. As mentioned earlier, a significant number of minor children remain in contact with the abusive parent. Some continue to live with the perpetrator where parents do not separate or where shared contact arrangements are in place. Others continue to see the abusive parent during a number of different visitation arrangements. Although consent for participation in counselling or other child-centred interventions may not be required from the abusive parent in all cases, children's participation in the aforementioned scenarios may place them at risk during contact with the abusive parent. Perpetrators either may not recognise or admit to the wrongfulness of their behaviour, or may have a vested interest in children remaining silent about their experiences. Once the abusive parent realises that his (or her) children are discussing the abusive behaviour with "outsiders", this can have repercussions for both children and the non-abusive parent (Alderson et al., 2013; Ermentrout et al., 2014).

Practitioners, especially, therefore often consider this risk and reassess its prevalence throughout an intervention. In many cases, child-centred interventions involve repeated contact over a matter of weeks or months. This offers an opportunity for practitioners to "check in" on a regular basis with both the non-abusive parent and the child to ensure participation in an intervention does not cause any adverse effects on children's safety and wellbeing with regard to contact with the abusive parent (Ermentrout et al., 2014). Overall, it is important to consider necessary safeguards prior to commencing work with children affected by DFV to ensure their participation is both voluntary and in their best interest.

Considerations specific to safety planning with children

In addition to child-centred interventions around DFV, safety planning with victims who are mothers also requires a number of child-centred considerations. A lot of the safety planning with mothers is informed by the broader evidence base around safety planning for victims, regardless of their parental status. However, specific considerations apply to safety planning when children are involved. Similar to any other child-focused interventions, safety planning is guided by the child's age. Incorporating those old enough to understand the risk and role of safety has been described as important because it has the potential to empower children in an otherwise often disempowering and unpredictable experience (Ministry of Justice, 2011; The National Domestic Violence Hotline, n.d.).

For very young children, it is often sufficient to explain who to listen to and follow in the event of a crisis. Research and practice guidelines recommend more detailed safety planning with children aged 3 and older, although it is important to keep instructions short. Children in a pre-school age group (around 3 to 5 years old) are curious, often have the capacity to understand what is going on at a basic level, and need to know why certain things are happening around them (Ministry of Justice, 2011). In this age group, it can be suitable to teach children how to use the phone and call emergency services. Safety planning may also include the incorporation of age-appropriate safety planning games or drawings (Ministry of Justice, 2011; The National Domestic Violence Hotline, n.d.). Practice guidelines in this area further recommend that practitioners teach children about different signs of danger and explain where they can go if leaving the family home is required. Children exposed to DFV already experience a number of unpredictable factors in their everyday life. Using brief and basic terms to explain what to expect may help with children's adjustment to change if/once this change occurs (Ministry of Justice, 2011). This may include preparing children for a potential shelter stay or a stay with family or friends. When discussing a safety plan with children in this age group, it is recommended to do so in the presence of the "safe parent" (i.e. the non-abusive parent who is part of the safety plan).

When safety planning with young children following parental separation, it is important to consider whether children have contact with the abusive parent and what type of information they may be sharing on such occasions. Sharing less rather than more information can assist in improving safety. Where children have no contact with the abusive parent, it is important to incorporate further safety considerations, such as advising schools and childcare providers about who is allowed to pick up the children (Western Integrated Family Violence Partnership, n.d.). Overall, it is important to avoid talking negatively about the abusive parent in front of the children. Safety planning should focus on explaining to children why the perpetrator's behaviour is dangerous and that it requires certain safety strategies rather than applying labels to the abusive parent. Despite the harmful behaviour of an abusive parent, many children are attached to them and may find themselves in a loyalty conflict between wanting to support the non-abusive parent and still wanting to see the abusive one (Peled, 2000). Talking in critical terms about the abusive parent as a person rather than in relation to their behaviour can therefore add to this inner conflict for some children.

Safety planning may become somewhat easier with older children. Pre-teens and teens have a greater capacity to understand arguments and reasoning around risk and safety. They are capable of following instructions, especially if they have been involved in the safety planning in a collaborative way. They may wish to have a say in where they would like to go in case of an emergency (e.g. they may be old enough to stay with friends if they wish to do so; Ministry of Justice,

2011). When working with older children and teens around safety planning, it is important to reiterate that they are at risk of injury if they get involved in physical attacks against the non-abusive parent and that it may be safer to call for help instead. Older children can be more involved in the safety planning, for example through instructions around when to call emergency services, when to get a neighbour to come over for help, or where to seek safety (e.g. in a room where they can lock themselves in until help arrives or by seeking refuge at a neighbour's place via an escape route). For younger children, it is, however, important to explain to them that leaving the house without the non-abusive parent or an older sibling is not a safe option (Ministry of Justice, 2011).

For further readings around safety planning with victims and children affected by DFV, we recommend the following publicly available resources:

- A comprehensive guide in safety planning with victims and children produced by the Ministry of Justice in British Columbia, Canada: www2.gov. bc.ca/assets/gov/law-crime-and-justice/criminal-justice/victims-of-crime/vs-info-for-professionals/training/child-youth-safety-toolkit.pdf
- A number of resources around safety planning provided by the National Centre on Domestic and Sexual Violence (US): www.ncdsv.org/publications_safetyplans.html
- A number of resources on safety planning for victims who co-reside, have separated, have children in their care, have pets, or are pregnant provided by the National Domestic Violence Hotline (US): www.thehotline.org/help/path-to-safety/#types
- A safety plan brochure produced by the Western Integrated Family Violence Partnership as part of the Victorian *Staying Home, Leaving Violence* scheme: http://whwest.org.au/wp-content/uploads/2012/05/Safety_Plan2.pdf

Summary

In this chapter, we examined the complex nature of children's exposure to DFV and its impact on short- and long-term child safety and wellbeing along with the implications this raises for practice. We unpacked the various ways in which children may be involved in and affected by parental DFV, including through witnessing the abuse, protecting younger siblings, intervening to defend an abused parent, and in some instances becoming a direct target of the abuse. The complex nature of children's experiences of DFV has gained increasing attention in research, policy, and practice and has informed a number of policy and legislation changes, as discussed in this chapter. Drawing on research evidence around the diverse nature of the impact of children's exposure to DFV, we addressed the role of trauma-informed and child-centred approaches to working with children exposed to DFV. In addition, specific considerations arising in the safety planning with victims who have dependent children in their care have been discussed and links to relevant resources have been provided for those new to safety planning.

Note

1 For more information on Hidden Hurt, visit www.hiddenhurt.co.uk/jay_child_abuse_and_domestic_violence.html.

References

Alderson, S., Westmarland, N., & Kelly, L. (2013). The need for accountability to, and support for, children of men on domestic violence perpetrator programmes. *Child Abuse Review, 22*(3), 182–193.

Australian Institute for Family Studies (AIFS). (2017). *Mandatory reporting of child abuse and neglect: Child family community Australia resource sheet, September 2017.* Retrieved from https://aifs.gov.au/cfca/publications/mandatory-reporting-child-abuse-and-neglect

Bagshaw, D., & Hart, A. (2008). The idealised post-separation family in Australian family law: A dangerous paradigm in cases of domestic violence. *Journal of Family Studies, 14*(2–3), 291–309.

Baker, H. (2005). Involving children and young people in research on domestic violence and housing. *Journal of Social Welfare & Family Law, 27*(3/4), 281–297.

Bandura, A. (1973). *Aggression: A social learning analysis.* Oxford, England: Prentice Hall.

Bandura, A. (1978). *Social learning theory.* Oxford, England: Prentice Hall.

Brannan, J. (1999). Reconsidering children and childhood: Sociological and policy perspectives. In E. B. Silva & C. Smart (Eds.), *The new family?* (pp. 143–158). London: Sage Publications.

Bundeskriminalamt. (2018). *Partnerschaftsgewalt: Kriminalstatistische Auswertung – Berichtsjahr 2017.* Wiesbaden: Bundeskriminalamt. Retrieved from www.bka.de/Shared Docs/Downloads/DE/Publikationen/JahresberichteUndLagebilder/Partnerschaftsgewalt/Partnerschaftsgewalt_2017.pdf

Burgess Chamberlain, L. (2008). *The amazing brain: Trauma and the potential for healing.* Retrieved from www.instituteforsafefamilies.org/sites/default/files/isfFiles/The_Amazing_Brain-2.pdf

Child Protection Act 1999 (QLD). Retrieved from www.legislation.qld.gov.au/view/pdf/inforce/2018-10-29/act-1999-010

Children and Young Persons (Care and Protection) Act 1998 (NSW). Retrieved from www8.austlii.edu.au/cgi-bin/viewdb/au/legis/nsw/consol_act/caypapa1998442/

Condry, R., & Miles, C. (2014). Adolescent to parent violence: Framing and mapping a hidden problem. *Criminology & Criminal Justice, 14*(3), 257–275.

Delima, J., & Vimpani, G. (2011). The neurobiological effects of childhood maltreatment: An often overlooked narrative related to the long-term effects of early childhood trauma? *Family Matters, 89,* 42–52.

Devaney, J. (2008). Chronic child abuse and domestic violence: Children and families with long-term and complex needs. *Child & Family Social Work, 13*(4), 443–453.

Devaney, J. (2009). Children's exposure to domestic violence: Holding men to account. *Political Quarterly, 80*(4), 569–574.

Dobash, R. P., & Dobash, R. E. (2012). Who died? The murder of collaterals related to intimate partner conflict. *Violence against Women, 18*(6), 662–671.

Douglas, H., & Walsh, T. (2010). Mothers, domestic violence and child protection. *Violence against Women, 16*(5), 489–508.

Dube, S. R., Anda, R. F., Felitti, V. J., Edwards, V. J., & Williamson, D. F. (2002). Exposure to abuse, neglect, and household dysfunction among adults who witnessed intimate partner violence as children: Implications for health and social services. *Violence and Victims, 17*(1), 3–17.

Edleson, J. L. (1999). Children's witnessing of adult domestic violence. *Journal of Interpersonal Violence, 14*(8), 839–870.

Edleson, J. L., Gassman-Pines, J., & Hill, M. B. (2006). Defining child exposure to domestic violence as neglect: Minnesota's difficult experience. *Social Work, 51*(2), 167–174.

Edleson, J. L., Mbilinyi, L., Beeman, S., & Hagemeister, A. (2003). How children are involved in adult domestic violence: Results from a four-city telephone survey. *Journal of Interpersonal Violence, 18*(1), 18–32.

Edleson, J. L., Nguyen, H. T., & Kimball, E. (2011). *Honor our voices: A guide for practice when responding to children exposed to domestic violence.* Minneapolis, MN: Minnesota Center against Violence and Abuse (MINCAVA). Retrieved from www.honorour-voices.org/docs/GuideforPractice.pdf

Ermentrout, D. M., Rizo, C. F., & Macy, R. J. (2014). "This is about me": Feasibility findings from the children's component of an IPV intervention for justice-involved families. *Violence against Women, 20*(6), 653–676.

Evans, S. E., Davies, C., & DiLillo, D. (2008). Exposure to domestic violence: A meta-analysis of child and adolescent outcomes. *Aggression and Violent Behavior, 13*(2), 131–140.

Ewen, B. M. (2007). Failure to protect laws: Protecting children or punishing mothers? *Journal of Forensic Nursing, 3*(2), 84–86.

Featherstone, B., & Peckover, S. (2007). Letting them get away with it: Fathers, domestic violence and child welfare. *Critical Social Policy, 27*(2), 181–202.

Fitz-Gibbon, K., Elliott, K., & Maher, J. (2018). *Investigating adolescent family violence in Victoria: Understanding experiences and practitioner perspectives.* Melbourne, Australia: Monash Gender and Family Violence Research Program, Faculty of Arts, Monash University. Retrieved from https://arts.monash.edu/gender-and-family-violence/wp-content/uploads/sites/11/2018/07/Adolescent-Family-Violence-in-Victoria-Final-Report.pdf

Hazel, L., Hamilton, A., Jaffe, P., & Campbell, M. (2013). Assessing children's risk for homicide in the context of domestic violence. *Journal of Family Violence, 28*(2), 179–189.

Holt, S., Buckley, H., & Whelan, S. (2008). The impact of exposure to domestic violence on children and young people: A review of the literature. *Child Abuse & Neglect, 32*(8), 797–810.

Home Office (2016). *Domestic homicide reviews: Key findings from an analysis of domestic homicide reviews.* Retrieved from: https://assets.publishing.service.gov.uk/government/uploads/system/uploads/attachment_data/file/575232/HO-Domestic-Homicide-Review-Analysis-161206.pdf

Humphreys, C., & Absler, D. (2011). History repeating: Child protection responses to domestic violence. *Child & Family Social Work, 16*(4), 464–473.

Humphreys, C., & Bradbury-Jones, C. (2015). Domestic abuse and safeguarding children: Focus, response and intervention. *Child Abuse Review, 24*, 231–234.

Ibabe, I., Jaureguizar, J., & Bentler, P. M. (2013). Risk factors for child-to-parent violence. *Journal of Family Violence, 28*(5), 523–534.

Jaffe, P., Campbell, M., Olszowy, L., Hazel, L., & Hamilton, A. (2014). Paternal filicide in the context of domestic violence: Challenges in risk assessment and risk management for community and justice professionals. *Child Abuse Review, 23*, 142–153.

James, M. P. (1994). *Domestic violence as form of child abuse: Identification and prevention.* New South Wales: Australian Domestic & Family Violence Clearinghouse.

Jenkins, A. (1990). Invitations to responsibility: The therapeutic engagement of men who are violent and abusive. *Australian and New Zealand Journal of Family Therapy, 11*(2), 74–74.

Katz, C. (2014). The dead end of domestic violence: Spotlight on children's narratives during forensic investigations following domestic homicide. *Child Abuse & Neglect, 38*(12), 1976–1984.

Kaukinen, C., Powers, R., & Meyer, S. (2016). Estimating Canadian childhood exposure to intimate partner violence and other risky parental behaviours. *Journal of Child Custody, 13*(2–3), 199–218.

Kiesel, L. R., Piescher, K. N., & Edleson, J. L. (2016). The relationship between child maltreatment, intimate partner violence exposure, and academic performance. *Journal of Public Child Welfare, 10*(4), 434–456.

Kitzman, K. M., Gaylord, N. K., Holt, A. R., & Kenny, E. D. (2003). Child witness to domestic violence: A meta-analytic review. *Journal of Consulting and Clinical Psychology, 71*(2), 339–352.

Levendosky, A. A., Bogat, G. A., & Martinez-Torteya, C. (2013). PTSD symptoms in young children exposed to intimate partner violence. *Violence against Women, 19*(2), 187–201.

Maggi, S., Irwin, L. J., Siddiqi, A., & Hertzman, C. (2010). The social determinants of early child development: An overview. *Journal of Paediatrics and Child Health, 46*(11), 627–635.

McGuigan, W. M., & Pratt, C. C. (2001). The predictive impact of domestic violence on three types of child maltreatment. *Child Abuse & Neglect, 25*(7), 869–883.

Meyer, S. (2011). "Acting in the children's best interest?": Examining victims' responses to intimate partner violence. *Journal of Child and Family Studies, 20*(4), 436–443.

Ministry of Justice. (2011). *Safety planning with children and youth: A toolkit for working with children and youth exposed to domestic violence.* British Columbia: Ministry of Justice. Retrieved from www2.gov.bc.ca/assets/gov/law-crime-and-justice/criminal-justice/victims-of-crime/vs-info-for-professionals/training/child-youth-safety-toolkit.pdf

Moffitt, T. E., & Caspi, A. (2001). Childhood predictors differentiate life-course persistent and adolescence-limited antisocial pathways among males and females. *Development and Psychopathology, 13*(2), 355–375.

Morris, A., Hegarty, K., & Humphreys, C. (2012). Ethical and safe: Research with children about domestic violence. *Research Ethics, 8*(2), 125–139.

The National Domestic Violence Hotline (USA). (n.d.). *What is a safety plan?* Retrieved from www.thehotline.org/help/path-to-safety/#types

Nixon, K. L., Tutty, L. M., Radtke, H. L., Ateah, C. A., & Ursel, E. J. (2017). Protective strategies of mothers abused by intimate partners: Rethinking the deficit model. *Violence against Women, 23*(11), 1271–1292.

Nixon, K. L., Tutty, L. M., Weaver-Dunlop, G., & Walsh, C. A. (2007). Do good intentions beget good policy? A review of child protection policies to address intimate partner violence. *Children and Youth Services Review, 29*(12), 1469–1486.

O'Donnell, J., Hawkins, J. D., Catalano, R. F., Abbott, R. D., & Day, L. E. (1995). Preventing school failure, drug use, and delinquency among low-income children: Long-term intervention in elementary schools. *American Journal of Orthopsychiatry*, 65(1), 87–100.

Olszowy, L., Jaffe, P. G., Campbell, M., & Hamilton, L. H. A. (2013). Effectiveness of risk assessment tools in differentiating child homicides from other domestic homicide cases. *Journal of Child Custody*, 10(2), 185–206.

Peled, E. (2000). Parenting by men who abuse women: Issues and dilemmas. *British Journal of Social Work*, 30(1), 25–36.

Perry, B. D. (2001). The neurodevelopmental impact of violence in childhood. In D. Schetky & E. P. Benedek (Eds.), *Textbook of child and adolescent forensic psychiatry* (pp. 221–238). Washington, DC: American Psychiatric Press, Inc.

Queensland Domestic and Family Violence Death Review and Advisory Board. (2018). *Annual report 2017–2018*. Retrieved from www.courts.qld.gov.au/__data/assets/pdf_file/0003/586182/domestic-and-family-violence-death-review-and-advisory-board-annual-report-2017-18.pdf

Queensland Government. (2013). *Taking responsibility: A roadmap for Queensland Child Protection, Queensland Government response to the Queensland Child Protection Commission of Inquiry final report*. Retrieved from www.cabinet.qld.gov.au/documents/2013/Dec/Response%20cpcoi/Attachments/Response.pdf

Richards, K. (2011). *Children's exposure to domestic violence in Australia* (Trends and Issues in Crime and Criminal Justice Series, No 419). Canberra: Australian Institute of Criminology. Retrieved from www.aic.gov.au/media_library/publications/tandi_pdf/tandi419.pdf

Schafran, L. H. (2014). Domestic violence, developing brains, and the lifespan: New knowledge from neuroscience. *The Judges Journal*, 53(3), 32–37.

Trepiccione, M. A. (2001). At the crossroads of law and social science: Is charging a battered mother with failure to protect her child an acceptable solution when her child witnesses domestic violence? *Fordham Law Review*, 69, 1487–1523.

Walker, H., & Sprague, J. (1999). The path to school failure, delinquency, and violence: Causal factors and some potential solutions. *Intervention in School & Clinic*, 35(2), 67–73.

Western Integrated Family Violence Partnership. (n.d.). *My safety plan*. Retrieved from http://whwest.org.au/wp-content/uploads/2012/05/Safety_Plan2.pdf

Whitfield, C., Anda, R., Dube, S., & Felitti, V. (2003). Violent childhood experiences and the risk of intimate partner violence in adults: Assessment in a large health maintenance organization. *Journal of Interpersonal Violence*, 18(2), 166–185.

Chapter 7

Not just a heterosexual, intimate relationship problem

Introduction

As raised earlier in this book, you will notice that the prevalent focus of knowledge and research evidence around DFV is on intimate partner violence (IPV), and that research addressing the diverse nature of DFV in terms of the relationships it affects is still emerging in many areas. A number of national and international studies have examined the experiences of different subgroups of victims and perpetrators in most recent years (Dank, Lachman, Zweig, & Yahner, 2014; Drijber, Reijnders, & Manon, 2013; Fitz-Gibbon, Elliot, & Maher, 2018; Hague, Thiara, Magowan, & Mullender, 2008; Frohmader, 2014). Yet research addressing the particular experiences of diverse victim populations defined by age, sexual orientation, disabilities, or the nature of their relationship with the perpetrator remains scarce compared to the extensive evidence surrounding the experiences of female victims of IPV perpetrated in heterosexual relationships. While women with disabilities have been the focus of advocacy for some time, they remain an under-researched at-risk population; limited data are available on the experiences of and responses to victims with disabilities (Frohmader, 2014). The same applies to the experiences of victims of elder abuse or adolescent family violence. Further, victims identifying as lesbian, gay, bisexual, transgender, intersex, or queer (LGBTIQ) are probably the least understood at-risk population in terms of their experiences and service needs due to the relatively recent empirical attention paid to these communities and the high level of diversity among them. You will notice that up until recently, most national and international prevalence studies did not capture (or at least did not identify) the experiences of LGBTIQ communities with regards to DFV (University of New South Wales [UNSW], 2014; Walters, Chen, & Breiding, 2013). After considering the range of aspects of vulnerability associated with sexual identity and orientation, the final part of this chapter examines the under-researched and often contested issues of male victimisation in the context of IPV.

Defining "domestic relationships": the role of legislation in help seeking and service delivery

Before we unpack the different types of relationships in which individuals may experience DFV, it is useful to consider how DFV and relevant relationships are defined and the implications this raises for victims' help-seeking decisions and opportunities for protection. Globally, DFV protection legislations vary greatly in scope (Buzawa & Buzawa, 2017a). A number of jurisdictions cover intimate and family (both immediate and extended) relationships under legislation designed to offer legal protection for victims and families from DFV (Buzawa & Buzawa, 2017b; Phillips & Vandenbroek, 2014). Some further include protection for victims experiencing violence within informal care relationships (Phillips & Vandenbroek, 2014). While by no means exhaustive, these three overarching categories (intimate, family, and informal care relationships) are fairly inclusive, reflecting contemporary forms of relationships and living/caring arrangements.

Intimate relationships tend to include dating, cohabiting/de facto and marital relationships for same-sex and opposite-sex couples. While not all jurisdictions cover adolescent dating relationships under relevant protection acts, protection offered for adult victims of IPV is fairly inclusive. Other family relationships are further covered by family violence legislation, offering protection for victims of violence and abuse experienced at the hands of immediate and extended family. This offers protection for a range of individuals who may be experiencing abuse, intimidation, or harassment by a family member. However, the definition of family relationships has its limitations and often varies across jurisdictions. While some laws may cover any family member – including extended family networks in diverse cultural settings – others may be limited to protection from abuse perpetrated by an intimate (ex-)partner only (Buzawa & Buzawa, 2017b; Phillips & Vandenbroek, 2014). Less consistency prevails around parent–child relationships. While some jurisdictions offer parents protection from violence perpetrated by adolescent children (see for example Family Violence Protection Act 2008 [Victoria]), others only cover child-to-parent abuse where the perpetrator is an adult child (see for example Domestic and Family Violence Protection Act 2012 [Queensland]).

The category of informal care relationships offers protection for elderly parents or other family members. With many elderly people cared for by their adult children or under other informal carer arrangements, rather than relying on nursing homes or paid in-home care, the inclusion of this relationship type under a number of DFV protection laws (see for example Buzawa & Buzawa, 2017a) acknowledges the particularly vulnerable position of these victims. Where covered under relevant laws, this relationship category offers protection for the growing number of identified victims of elder abuse but often restricts protection to perpetrators who provide informal care to the victim. As an example, depending on the jurisdiction, abuse and exploitation perpetrated by someone receiving remuneration for his or her caretaker role may not always fall under this category, despite the abuse occurring within a domestic setting. The same limitation applies to the protection of victims with disabilities. While abuse perpetrated by an intimate (ex-)partner or a family member providing informal care for victims is often covered under relevant legislation, abuse perpetrated by a professional carer or a housemate in a group home setting may not be. Available protection therefore depends on the definition of relationship categories included in different juris-dictions under relevant legislation (see for example Buzawa & Buzawa, 2017b; Phillips & Vandenbroek, 2014).

The differences surrounding relationship definitions across national and inter-national protection legislation highlight the limitations that can arise for victims in need of protection and service providers responding to diverse client popula-tions. While protection legislation is increasingly recognising the need to protect victims beyond traditional intimate partner relationships, gaps remain for vic-tims who do not fit the prescriptive categories of some legislation. Throughout the subsequent sections, we will examine the experiences and service needs of victims affected by DFV at the intersection of diversity and related vulnerability.

Victims with disabilities

Experiences of DFV affecting victims with disabilities has primarily been docu-mented for female victims (VicHealth, 2016; Frohmader, 2014; Hague et al., 2008; Mays, 2006). Indeed, women with disabilities are disproportionately affected by DFV. While women with disabilities make up around 20% of Australia's female population, they are said to be 40% more likely to experience DFV than abled women. This overrepresentation with regards to experiences of abuse becomes even more substantial when looking at sexual abuse. Women with disabilities are four to ten times more likely to experience sexual violence at some point over the life course (Frohmader, 2014). Neither experiences of emotional and physical DFV, nor experiences of sexual violence, are limited to intimate rela-tionships. Women with intellectual disabilities especially are at significant risk of experiencing various forms of abuse in a range of family and other carer rela-tionships (VicHealth, 2017), with two-thirds of intellectually disabled women in Australia reporting experiences of sexual abuse commencing during childhood or adolescence (Australian Law Reform Commission, 2010; Frohmader, 2014).

Australian research has found that abuse perpetrated in an intimate, family, or informal carer relationship makes up around 88% of abusive incidents expe-rienced by women with disabilities overall (VicHealth, 2016). The remaining 12% were reportedly perpetrated mainly by neighbours, family friends, and for-mal carers. Only on rare occasions were the perpetrators strangers. This study found over half (54%) of the incidents falling under the definition of DFV were experienced at the hands of an intimate partner, with 43% involving a male intimate partner and a further 11% involving a female intimate partner. The remaining 34% of DFV-related incidents were perpetrated by parents, followed by other relatives, the victims' children, and informal carers (VicHealth, 2016). International research reveals that women with disabilities often report repeat experiences of abuse by more than one perpetrator over the life course (Hague et al., 2008).

Research identifying the nature and extent of DFV affecting women with disabilities remains scarce at an international level. This gap has repeatedly been criticised (Briding & Armour, 2015; Salthouse & Frohmader, 2004; Shah, Tsitsou, & Woodin, 2016). In addition to the lack of comprehensive data reflecting the diverse experiences of people with disabilities, variations in definitions, legislation, and service delivery across different jurisdictions further complicates the experiences of women with disabilities already subjected to multi-layered vulnerability (Briding & Armour, 2015; Shah et al., 2016). While some jurisdictions offer protection for victims in a range of domestic relationships, others limit protection for victims with disabilities to DFV experienced in intimate and family relationships only.

In addition to challenges posed by legal definitions of DFV and relevant relationships in some jurisdictions, victims with disabilities face a number of other barriers when attempting to report and/or escape the abuse, including physical, emotional, social, and financial dependence on the abuser (Shah et al., 2016). This is particularly prominent where the abuser is also the victim's carer. In addition to common forms of abuse experienced by victims regardless of level of ability or disability (such as physical, sexual, emotional, verbal, financial, and social abuse along with elements of ongoing control and manipulation), victims with disabilities often experience types of abuse arising from their disability-related dependence. This can include withholding medication, withholding or destruction of disability aids (such as walking frames or wheelchairs), and the destruction of other possessions while the victim has to watch helplessly (VicHealth, 2016; Hague et al., 2008). As alerted to previously, victims with intellectual disabilities are particularly vulnerable to sexual abuse and financial abuse, for example, due to particularly sensitive issues around consent in the case of intellectual disability. Perpetrators may subject their victims to unwanted – and at times humiliating – sexual practices by taking advantage of the victim's limited capacity to consent. Perpetrators may further take over control of finances and property, making decisions on the victim's behalf without consent, and may also isolate the victim from family and friends and other external support sources to evade detection (VicHealth, 2016; Shah et al., 2016).

The increased vulnerability of victims with disabilities raises significant challenges for policy and practice. Consistent legislation covering a broader range of domestic relationships relevant to the experiences of victims with disabilities is crucial to facilitate comprehensive practice responses that offer protection and interventions for this at-risk population. In addition, it is important for practitioners to understand the specific challenges associated with experiencing DFV as a disabled victim, including the role of abuse suffered by someone acting as a carer for a victim with intellectual disabilities and potentially exploiting the victim's inability to give informed consent across a range of matters. It is important to understand the inner conflict faced by victims reporting abuse by someone who acts as a carer while simultaneously reinforcing feelings of shame and self-blame by repeatedly telling the victim s/he needs to be grateful that someone is looking after them instead of placing them in institutionalised care (Hague et al., 2008). Services should also consider the provision of information that specifically relates to the experiences of victims with disabilities and their needs. This can open doors and encourage help seeking by those who may otherwise feel discouraged by mainstream service approaches due to a perceived lack of understanding and/or acknowledgement of their particular needs arising from their experiences at the intersection of disability and DFV.

Victims of elder abuse

While not a new phenomenon, elder abuse remains a relatively under-researched area of DFV. Recent scoping and systematic reviews provide an emerging picture of the broader issue of elder abuse along with implications for policy and practice (Dong, 2015; Pillemer, Burnes, Riffin, & Lachs, 2016). However, there remains a paucity of data relating to intervention models for elder abuse and their effectiveness (Mills, 2015). Elder abuse often occurs within informal care relationships, which further complicates this type of abuse beyond the victim's vulnerability associated with age. Victims and perpetrators are often related, with perpetrators frequently being adult children providing informal care for the victim (Cooper, Selwood, & Livingstone, 2008; Ziminski Pickering & Phillips, 2014). These factors create additional layers of complexity, including shame, gratitude for receiving care, and fear of losing this care if the abuse is disclosed. Financial abuse is said to be the most common form of elder abuse, although emotional and physical abuse along with neglect are not uncommon, either (Oh et al., 2006).

Elderly victims of DFV experience a number of barriers to help seeking that are similar to victims of DFV more broadly as well as those unique to their specific victim characteristics. Similar challenges include financial dependence, emotional attachment to the abuser, concerns for their housing stability or alternative living arrangements should they disclose the abuse, and fear of retaliatory violence if the abuse is disclosed and no adequate protection is offered (Mills, 2015; Wolfe, 2003). Challenges unique to this population are vulnerabilities relating to their age and the particular relationship in which many incidents of elder abuse occur. Especially where elder abuse occurs within an informal care relationship (provided by either adult children or an intimate partner), the victim tends to be dependent on the abuser beyond assumptions of financial dependence. Being the carer can provide perpetrators with an additional level of power and control over victims' finances, support with everyday tasks and activities, access to social support, and access to more formal forms of support if needed (Mills, 2015). The nature of this relationship complicates help seeking for many victims of elder abuse because the perpetrator/informal carer often accompanies the victim during contact with the outside world (Dong, 2015; Wolfe, 2003).

Intervening in cases of elder abuse can be particularly challenging due to victims' isolation, their frequent dependence on the abuser, and the associated issue of underreporting (Dong, 2015; Mills, 2015). For many victims of elder abuse, visits to their family doctor or other healthcare providers can be the only time they leave their home and gain access to potential sources of support. If accompanied by the abuser – who, in many cases, is also the primary carer – victims face similar challenges to disclosing the abuse to those described by victims of IPV presenting for medical treatment in the presence of their abusive partner (Wolfe, 2003). Fear of retaliatory abuse or neglect can constitute a substantial barrier here and, as a result, often leads to prolonged exposure to neglect and abuse (Dong, 2015; Pillemer et al., 2016).

In many ways, interventions relevant to addressing experiences of elder abuse are similar to those provided to victims of other types of DFV, such as IPV. Primary interventions include applying for a protection order (also referred to as restraining orders in some jurisdictions), removing the victim from the abusive care setting if necessary, or admitting the elderly victim to hospital where medical treatment is required (Mills, 2015). If intervening in a way that involves relocating the victim into medical or another type of care facility, releasing the victim back into their home can pose other challenges. In some cases, this may require the victim to provide informed consent to return to the environment where the abuse initially took place. Where informed consent to be released cannot be obtained from the victim him/herself (for example, due to ongoing mental health issues), the victim's carer or guardian may be asked to give consent. This is problematic where the carer is also the abuser and where the victim is unwilling or unable to disclose abuse. A referral to social services and/or a specialised DFV support service will become a relevant avenue of support here if it has not been established already (Mills, 2015).

Other types of interventions for victims of elder abuse include crisis care (such as respite care in a nursing home facility), long-term respite care (such as in the form of formal in-home carer support), and counselling (including DFV-specific trauma counselling addressing issues such as PTSD or, where suitable, family therapy). In addition, perpetrator accountability and their need for support and intervention must be addressed. Research has repeatedly linked elder abuse to carer stress and strained family relationships between victim and perpetrator (Cooper et al., 2008; Ziminski Pickering & Phillips, 2014). Counselling and specialised interventions for the perpetrator to identify the potential for eliminating the abusive behaviour without ending the victim–carer relationship is crucial in establishing victims' long-term safety and wellbeing.

In the context of service delivery, it is therefore important to understand the complex challenges faced by victims of elder abuse and create opportunities for disclosure in a safe environment, such as during one-on-one contact between the victim and healthcare professionals. Such opportunities need to be created in a supportive, nonthreatening way that does not raise any suspicions among perpetrators. Here, healthcare responses to elderly patients would benefit from drawing on women's health practice guidelines relating to pre- and post-natal appointments, for example, where one-on-one contact is to be ensured between patients and healthcare practitioners to ensure safe and confidential opportunities for disclosure of victimisation experiences. This would allow practitioners to screen for potential risk or presence of DFV when responding to potential victims of elder abuse in a safe space that centres on healthcare (or other service provision) rather than obvious screening for DFV (Dong, 2015).

Young people's experiences of dating violence

In this section, we focus on the experiences and service needs of young people facing DFV in the form of dating violence. While not as frequently researched as adult IPV, adolescent dating violence along with suitable intervention strategies have received increasing research attention since the 1990s (Foshee et al., 1998; Levy, 1990; O'Keefe, 1997; Wekerle & Wolfe, 1999). Estimations of the prevalence of adolescent dating violence are subject to similar limitations as estimations of adult IPV. Clinical samples (such as those derived from community health clinics or support programs for at-risk youths) show higher rates than do population-based samples (such as representative youth surveys conducted in high schools; Martin, Houston, Mmari, & Decker, 2012; O'Keefe & Aldridge, 2005).

Other factors associated with varying prevalence rates of adolescent dating violence include the method of data collection (e.g. anonymous surveys versus face-to-face interviews) and the definitions used to capture dating violence. Studies including emotional, verbal, and cyber abuse generally reveal higher prevalence rates, whereas studies focusing on physical and sexual abuse tend to reveal lower rates (O'Keefe & Aldridge, 2005). As a result, prevalence estimates range from 10 to over 50% depending on the definition of dating violence and the sample targeted to capture this information (O'Keefe & Aldridge, 2005).

In addition to some of the commonalities shared with adult IPV, there are some noteworthy differences. To start with, the evidence base around adolescent dating violence incorporates a much greater understanding of both victimisation and perpetration of abuse. Whereas adult-focused studies tend to focus on experiences of victimisation, a number of studies focusing on adolescent dating violence have captured both young persons' likelihood of experiencing *and* perpetrating dating violence (Dank, Lachman, Zweig, & Yahner, 2014; Malik, Sorenson, & Aneshensel, 1997; Niolon et al., 2015; Zweig, Dank, Yahner, & Lachman, 2013). Unlike the gendered pattern of DFV observed in adult populations, examinations of adolescent dating violence in school-based populations suggest similar rates of DFV perpetrated by girls and boys in their dating relationships – at least in terms of overall prevalence rates. A clear gendered pattern – similar to that observed in adult samples – exists around sexual abuse, which disproportionately affects girls and is predominantly perpetrated by males (Niolon et al., 2015; Zweig et al., 2013). However, verbal and emotional abuse have been identified at similar rates for adolescent boys and girls. Some studies further reveal higher perpetration rates of physical violence for girls than for boys (Malik et al., 1997; Niolon et al., 2015; O'Keefe, 1997; Zweig et al., 2013). The controversial argument of gender symmetry (Kimmel, 2002; Straus, 2007) examined in Chapter 2 seems to be more accurate for the perpetration and experience of certain types of adolescent dating violence, excluding sexual violence (O'Keefe & Aldridge, 2005).

With regard to the experiences of young LGBTIQ victims, we can observe tendencies similar to LGBTIQ adult populations. Research on adolescent dating violence shows that LGBTIQ adolescents are significantly more vulnerable to dating violence than heterosexual adolescents, both in terms of victimisation and perpetration (Dank et al., 2014). With increasing maturity, the risk of perpetration decreases, especially for women. However, the overrepresentation in victimisation statistics for LGBTIQ people remains across the life course, highlighting the persistence in increased risk of IPV victimisation for this diverse population (Dank et al., 2014). We discuss the experiences of adult LGBTIQ populations in greater detail later on in this chapter.

Aside from revealing higher prevalence rates for adolescent dating violence compared to adult IPV more broadly, research identifies that young people are less likely to seek help for their experiences of victimisation as well as perpetration (Martin et al., 2012). In other words, young people are more likely than adults to experience IPV but substantially less likely to seek support. There may be different reasons for this observation. Firstly, scholars and practitioners have repeatedly argued that young people tend to struggle with defining what constitutes abusive behaviour (Johnson et al., 2005; Martin et al., 2012; Wekerle & Wolfe, 1999). In addition, they may not wish to discuss their dating relationship with informal sources of support (such as parents) and may not feel that the more formal avenues of support available to adult victims of DFV (such as law enforcement and victim support services) are suitable to their needs. Barriers to informal help seeking are particularly significant where parents may be unaware that their children are dating and/or sexually active. If it is the young person's intentions to hide their dating relationship, they can find themselves without any family support to rely on, especially in cases where disclosing the abuse may create additional problems such as family tension and alienation (Dank et al., 2014; Martin et al., 2012).

Where victims have chosen to keep their intimate relationship a secret from family or friends due to fears of rejection or tension, this avenue of support is often unavailable once help is needed to deal with the abusive nature of the relationship. This is particularly problematic when we consider that family and friends are often the first point of contact for help-seeking victims. They tend to have a validating and informative function with regard to victims' experiences. As addressed earlier in the book, understanding and supportive reactions from family and friends are said to facilitate victims' access to further support (if needed), whereas responses marked by disbelief, judgement or victim-blaming can isolate victims further (Liang, Goodman, Tummala-Narra, & Weintraub, 2005). One of the best ways to facilitate parental support is a strong and honest relationship between children and parents to ensure children feel they confide in their parents when experiencing dating violence. However, this may be easier said than done during the period of adolescence where family becomes less important to the young person and peers start to be the primary source of information and support (Haynie & Osgood, 2005).

Other "vulnerability factors" identified in research around adolescent dating violence include culture and race. US-based research reveals that dating violence disproportionately affects African American adolescents (Martin et al., 2012). Similar observations have been made for Canadian Indigenous youth (Hautala, Hartshorn, Armenta, & Whitbeck, 2017). In addition to an increased risk identified for adolescents belonging to different racial minority groups, research further reveals individual-level risk factors for experiences of dating violence. These risk factors are similar to those identified in the broader literature on at-risk youths and deviant behaviour, such as school problems, family problems, and substance misuse (Martin et al., 2012). Young people exposed to family violence within the home, those with a record of truancy, and young people engaging in excessive drinking or illicit substance use all have an increased risk of experiencing and perpetrating dating violence (Niolon et al., 2015). These observations raise implications for practice, with service providers needing to be aware of the correlation between exposure and perpetration of dating violence and other risk factors affecting young people. Interventions for young people displaying multiple risk factors can benefit from screening for experiences of dating violence along with early interventions focusing on education around recognising abusive relationships and establishing respectful ones (Flood, Fergus, & Heenan, 2009; Silverman, Raj, Mucci, & Hathaway, 2001).

Adolescent family violence

Aside from their role as victims and perpetrators in their adolescent dating relationships, emerging research further identifies young people as perpetrators of DFV against other family members (Condry & Miles, 2014; Ibabe, Jaureguizar, & Bentler, 2013; Fitz-Gibbon et al., 2018). Consistent with other forms of DFV outside of IPV, research on family violence perpetrated by young people against other family members remains scarce. This paucity is particularly surprising, however, given the known social learning effect of children's exposure to parental DFV on their own risk of developing aggressive and abusive behaviours towards others (Bandura, 1973; Condry & Miles, 2014; Ibabe et al., 2013). The limited research available alerts us to an increased risk of affected children resorting to aggressive and abusive practices towards their parents or carers and – at times – also other siblings in the household (Condry & Miles, 2014; Ibabe et al., 2013; Fitz-Gibbon et al., 2018). This phenomenon has been observed in particular for sons who become abusive towards their mothers. While adolescent family violence is not solely male-to-female perpetrated, sons tend to be the primary perpetrator group and mothers the primary targets of this type of DFV. Further, research reveals that where mothers are the primary target, the adolescent perpetrators have previously been exposed to parental DFV, often perpetrated by their father or male carer against the mother (Fitz-Gibbon et al., 2018). This intergenerational transmission of violence forms part of the intergenerational trauma and impact of childhood exposure to DFV examined in Chapter 6.

Social learning theory (see Chapter 3) offers a useful framework to understanding how control, manipulation, and violence can be role-modelled by some young people. While this idea has traditionally been applied to explain the increased risk of men's use of violence in adult relationships when exposed to parental DFV in their own upbringing, it applies in the same sense to adolescent sons using violence against their already victimised mothers. As discussed in Chapter 6, Bandura's (1973) social learning theory offers a suitable framework for understanding the social learning effect associated with observing and role modelling abusive behaviours. For a discussion of the gendered impact of witnessing abuse during childhood, please refer back to Chapter 6.

Children adopting violence as a legitimate tool to impose one's will on the victimised parent may perceive the victim as likely to comply out of fear, weakness, or empathy. In addition, most recent research has revealed that DFV perpetrated by an adolescent child remains mostly unreported by parents – particularly mothers as the primary victims (Fitz-Gibbon et al., 2018). Often, calling the police is the only available source of support at the time when violence escalates. However, parents report a reluctance to report their own children to police, often fearing the welfare and justice responses this can trigger. As a result, many parents experiencing adolescent-perpetrated family violence endure the abuse in order to protect their children. Feelings of shame and self-blame further complicate parents' help seeking. Mothers, especially those who have previously experienced DFV by an intimate partner, report feelings of shame and self-blame for the children's exposure to these experiences.

The challenges observed around parental help seeking where children become perpetrators of DFV raise important implications for child and family welfare practice. Given parents' reluctance to report children's violence to police, early interventions are crucial in supporting families affected by DFV (Fitz-Gibbon et al., 2018). Family support and child protection services especially are well placed to identify children's exposure to parental DFV early and assist in breaking the intergenerational cycle of DFV through early interventions and referrals to child-focused support services.

Victims identifying as LGBTIQ

Victims identifying as LGBTIQ are another under-researched population which experience DFV at the intersection of other factors that elevate their level of vulnerability. Despite a longstanding history of advocacy around LGBTIQ rights and other matters, DFV-related experiences of victims who identify as LGBTIQ have only recently received increasing attention (UNSW, 2014; Walters et al., 2013). Recent Australian and US examinations of the experiences of people identifying as LGBTIQ compared to the experiences of those identifying as heterosexual have revealed that gender and sexuality diverse people are significantly more likely to experience various forms of violence, including DFV and lifetime prevalence of sexual abuse (UNSW, 2014; Walters et al., 2013). It is important here that the limited research available predominantly sheds light on the inter-section of DFV experiences and sexual identity. While a recent Australian preva-lence study captured gender identity and intersex status, the number of survey respondents identifying as intersex or transgender was small (1.4% and 4.4% respectively) (UNSW, 2014). A recent US prevalence study based on second-ary survey data was limited by the information captured in the original National Violence Against Women Survey (NVAWS), which did not capture information on intersex or transgender status (Walters et al., 2013). The findings discussed hereafter therefore predominantly relate to the experiences of gay, lesbian, and bisexual men and women.

The Australian prevalence study captured 813 Australian survey respon-dents identifying as LGBTIQ. Over half of these people reported experiences of DFV in a previous relationship. This is significantly higher than the nation-ally and internationally identified prevalence rates, which indicate that one in four to one in three women have experienced DFV in heterosexual relationships (Australia's National Research Organisation for Women's Safety [ANROWS], 2017; European Union Agency for Fundamental Rights [FRA], 2014; Mouzos & Makkai, 2004; Tjaden & Thoennes, 2000).

When examining these experiences by sexual identity and orientation, it becomes obvious that people identifying as LGBTIQ are significantly more likely to experience various forms of victimisation across the life course. The subgroup identified as most vulnerable were victims who described themselves as bisexual. Almost two-thirds (63.5%) of respondents identifying as bisexual reported lifetime experiences of DFV, compared to 57.3% of respondents iden-tifying as lesbian and 50.2% identifying as gay (UNSW, 2014). These findings align with recent observations made in the US using the National Violence Against Women Survey (NVAWS). Findings from the NVAWS confirmed the commonly observed lifetime prevalence rate of one in four women reporting experiences of severe physical DFV in a heterosexual relationship (Walters et al., 2013). The prevalence of DFV for lesbian women, on the other hand, was one in three, and a staggering one in two bisexual women (Walters et al., 2013). Bisexual women were overall more likely to experience abuse across the life course, including physical, sexual, and emotional abuse by an intimate partner as well as sexual abuse during childhood and adolescence (Walters et al., 2013). Further, bisexual women were more likely to have experienced DFV by more than one partner over the life course (39.8%), followed by heterosexual (28.4%) and lesbian women (21.1%).

Some similarities were observed for male victims captured by the NVAWS. Concerning lifetime prevalence of sexual abuse, bisexual men were similarly vul-nerable to bisexual women, with 47.4% reporting experiences of sexual abuse at some point in their life, compared to 40.2% of gay men and 20.8% of hetero-sexual men. Similar to bisexual women, bisexual men were most likely to report experiences of sexual abuse as a minor, compared to gay and heterosexual men, further highlighting the vulnerability of people identifying as bisexual. Bisexual men (37.3%) were furthermore likely to experience different forms of DFV, including physical and sexual abuse along with stalking behaviour, compared to their heterosexual (29.0%) and gay (26.0%) counterparts. However, the differences were less substantial across some of the subcategories of abuse and sexual orientation compared to those observed for female victims (Walters et al., 2013).

In terms of perpetrator sex, perpetrators are primarily of the opposite sex for reports of DFV by bisexual men and women (Walters et al., 2013). For bisexual women, perpetrators were overwhelmingly male, with 10.5% of bisexual women reporting they had only experienced DFV by a female partner. Bisexual men, on the other hand, have a slightly higher likelihood of experiencing DFV by a same-sex partner, with 21.5% of bisexual men reporting that they had only experienced DFV at the hand of another male (Walters et al., 2013). However, statistical identification of perpetrator sex needs to be regarded with care, as no information is provided on the frequency of partnering with the same or opposite sex for bisexual men and women in this study. Without knowing whether bisexual men or women have primarily shared intimate relationships with one or the other sex, it is difficult to establish whether same or opposite sex partners are more likely to perpetrate DFV against bisexual victims.

Despite their limitations, the recent Australian and US studies of the experiences of DFV among people identifying as LGBTIQ address a significant knowledge gap, one that is frequently raised by LGBTIQ communities. These findings show that DFV is as much (if not more) an LGBTIQ issue as it is a heterosexual or general social issue. Both studies reveal that gay men and lesbian women experience DFV at similar or higher rates than heterosexual men and women. Furthermore, both studies identify bisexual women and men as the most vulnerable of the compared groups in relation to experiences of DFV as well as other forms of sexual abuse, especially as a minor. These findings have important implications for practice responses to LGBTIQ victims. Practitioners responding to bisexual victims in particular need to be aware of the accumulation of risk and trauma over the life course. Acknowledging this risk and trauma needs to be reflected in practice responses that are sensitive to the experiences of bisexual victims (along with other vulnerable populations), including the need for protection as much as the need for trauma counselling to help victims break the cycle of violence and recover from the multi-layered trauma suffered over time.

In addition, it is important for practitioners to understand the general barriers to seeking help and accessing services among victims identifying as LGBTIQ. This diverse population has an increased risk of enduring prolonged and repeated experiences of DFV (and other types of victimisation) due to the social stigma that remains attached to sexual diversity. In addition to the various forms of DFV and related control exercised by perpetrators in heterosexual relationships, LGBTIQ victims frequently report additional barriers, including the fear of being outed against their will to their family, friends, or employer (UNSW, 2014).

Aside from having specialised support services, it is important for mainstream services and their practitioners to understand the intersection of DFV and sexual diversity and to offer inclusive service models (e.g. through the provision of information material tailored towards diverse populations and subgroups of victims and promotion via their websites). Awareness-raising campaigns and/ or information provided in hard copy at potential points of contact for victims identifying as LGBTIQ, such as medical practices, hospitals, community and welfare organisations, law enforcement agencies, and educational institutions, can further help to break down barriers towards help seeking.

Working with male victims

The previous section drew attention to some of the experiences of male victims, specific to their sexual orientation. In this section, we will expand on the experiences of male victims of DFV more broadly and address some of their support needs. Some of the challenges experienced by gay and bisexual men affected by DFV are very similar to the ones reported by men experiencing DFV in heterosexual relationships. However, while issues faced by gay and bisexual men may be primarily associated with barriers arising from discrimination relating to sexual orientation, challenges for heterosexual men tend to be associated with traditional perceptions of masculinities. These include the notion that men should be able to solve their problems – especially those of a personal nature – without the need for external support (Drijber et al., 2013; Martin et al., 2012). As highlighted throughout the discussion of DFV as a gendered issue in Chapters 2 and 3, male victimisation in the context of DFV is a complex issue and frequently sparks a debate around gender symmetry in DFV. It is therefore important to understand the circumstances and social context of female-to-male perpetrated DFV.

Research arguing there is gender symmetry in DFV tends to count abusive incidents rather than appreciate the context of intention and the pattern over time. Critics have frequently highlighted that without understanding the context in which violence occurs (i.e. whether it is initiated or reactive in nature), counting the frequency with which people may verbally or physically attack each other has very little meaning (Keating, 2015; Mulroney & Chan, 2005). Similarly, abuse perpetrated by women against men may have very different effects on victims than when the same type of violence is male-to-female perpetrated. While prevalence studies show that men are clearly victims of different forms of IPV and that women can be emotionally, verbally, and physically abusive (Drijber et al., 2013; Mulroney & Chan, 2005), research further reveals that male victims report lower levels of fear and anxiety associated with experiences of DFV (Mulroney & Chan, 2005). Most prevalence studies fail to unpack the context in which people perpetrate or experience DFV. Given the evidence that female perpetrated physical violence especially is often reactive (either in response to or in anticipation of further abuse by the primary aggressor), prevalence studies of female-to-male perpetrated violence remain flawed. Without knowing whether

DFV is experienced by an individual as a primary victim or primary aggressor, interventions cannot be tailored appropriately to the needs of male victims of DFV. Being able to identify and understand context and underlying objectives of abusive behaviours is therefore a crucial element in understanding risk, primary aggressor roles, and related service needs.

In their role as primary victims, men face a number of barriers to help seeking. These include shame and embarrassment associated with having been victimised by a female partner, fears of not being believed or taken seriously when reporting the abuse, and a general lack of suitable services. Specialist victim services, including crisis accommodation and court support services, specifically catering for male victims are rare, especially at the intersection with DFV. Accommodation services primarily cater for men in the context of homelessness rather than post-victimisation. Some jurisdictions (such as the Netherlands) are currently trialling DFV-specific crisis accommodation for men (Drijber et al., 2013). More commonly, DFV-specific services targeting men as victims tend to take the form of online information and telephone helpline services. A lack of available services for victims of DFV has been identified as a significant barrier to help seeking in women (Meyer, 2010) and is likely to have the same effect on men.

In addition to a scarce service landscape catering for men affected by DFV, male victims also report a range of barriers commonly reported by female victims. A recent Dutch study of men's experiences of DFV along with their help-seeking decisions identified that men give similar reasons for staying in an abusive relationship as female victims (Drijber et al., 2013). Some reported being financially dependent on their partner, some feared the loss of access to mutual children, and some simply wanted the abuse but not the relationship to end. In addition, male victims report similar tactics of abuse, control, and isolation employed by the female perpetrator, including threats to leave and take the children away, threats of self-harm, and the strategic isolation from family and friends (Drijber et al., 2013; Mulroney & Chan, 2005). While research shows that the number of male victims who are subject to the same level of abuse and control by a perpetrator of the opposite sex is significantly lower than that of female victims (ANROWS, 2017; Bundeskriminalamt, 2018), it is important to acknowledge and understand the existence of male victimisation along with associated service needs. Specialist services are necessary to address the needs of male victims of DFV. In addition, generalist support services (e.g. police, healthcare professionals) need to have an understanding of different patterns of DFV in a variety of domestic relationships that allows them to respond in a respectful and understanding manner in line with their professional practice standards.

Summary

In this chapter, we unpacked the diverse nature of DFV and the various populations and relationship types it can affect. This chapter has highlighted the current state of knowledge surrounding the experiences and support needs of victims where age, gender, sexual orientation, and/or dependence arising in victim–carer relationships further exacerbate victims' vulnerability. While the different subgroups of victims share some similarities across experiences of violence along with support needs, this chapter also highlights a number of unique factors that need to be understood in the context of victims' individual and situational circumstances to inform service delivery.

This chapter has further highlighted the paucity of research findings relevant to a number of particular subgroups of victims. Despite ongoing advocacy for the rights and protection of particularly vulnerable populations, including people who are elderly or disabled, research evidence remains scarce. In addition, despite the well-established link between childhood exposure to DFV and the role modelling of aggressive and controlling behaviours, little is known about the support needs of parents experiencing DFV at the hands of their adolescent children.

Further, despite a growing awareness and acceptance of gender diversity and diversity in sexual orientation, the experiences of individuals identifying as LGBTIQ remain under-researched. The limited evidence available strongly points to the need for understanding the experiences of DFV by women and men at the intersection of gender and sexual orientation. Both factors substantially contribute to victims' vulnerability over the life course, highlighting the importance of trauma-informed practice when responding to victims in general and victims identifying as lesbian, gay, or bisexual in particular. In the next chapter, we will continue to examine the role of intersectionality in victims' experiences of DFV and their related service needs with a specific focus on indigenous and migrant populations.

References

Australian Law Reform Commission (ALRC). (2010). *Family violence: A national legal response* (ALRC Report 114). Sydney, Australia: ALRC. Retrieved from www.alrc.gov. au/publications/family-violence-national-legal-response-alrc-report-114

Australia's National Research Organisation for Women's Safety (ANROWS). (2017). *Personal Safety Survey 2016 fact sheet*. Retrieved from http://anrowsnationalconference. org.au/fact-sheet-personal-safety-survey-2016/

Bandura, A. (1973). *Aggression: A social learning analysis*. Oxford, England: Prentice-Hall.

Briding, M., & Armour, B. (2015). The association between disability and intimate partner violence in the United States. *Annals of Epidemiology, 25*(6), 455–457.

Bundeskriminalamt. (2018). *Partnerschaftsgewalt: Kriminalstatistische Auswertung – Berichtsjahr 2017*. Wiesbaden: Bundeskriminalamt. Retrieved from www.bka.de/ SharedDocs/Downloads/DE/Publikationen/JahresberichteUndLagebilder/Partnerschaftsgewalt/Partnerschaftsgewalt_2017.pdf

Buzawa, E., & Buzawa, C. (2017a). Introduction: The evolution of efforts to combat domestic violence. In E. Buzawa & C. Buzawa (Eds.), *Global responses to domestic violence* (pp. 1–20). Cham, Switzerland: Springer.

Buzawa, E., & Buzawa, C. (2017b). The evolution of the response to domestic violence in the United States. In E. Buzawa & C. Buzawa (Eds.), *Global responses to domestic violence* (pp. 61–86). Cham, Switzerland: Springer.

Condry, R., & Miles, C. (2014). Adolescent to parent violence: Framing and mapping a hidden problem. *Criminology & Criminal Justice, 14*(3), 257–275.

Cooper, C., Selwood, A., & Livingstone, G. (2008). The prevalence of elder abuse and neglect: A systematic review. *Age & Ageing, 37,* 151–160.

Dank, M., Lachman, P., Zweig, J., & Yahner, J. (2014). Dating violence experiences of lesbian, gay, bisexual, and transgender youth. *Journal of Youth & Adolescence, 43*(5), 846–857.

Dong, X. Q. (2015). Elder abuse: Systematic review and implications for practice. *Journal of the American Geriatrics Society, 63*(6), 1214–1238.

Drijber, B., Reijnders, U., & Manon, C. (2013). Male victims of domestic violence. *Journal of Family Violence, 28*(2), 173–178.

European Union Agency for Fundamental Rights (FRA). (2014). *Violence against women: An EU-wide survey.* Retrieved from http://fra.europa.eu/en/publication/2014/violence-against-women-eu-wide-survey-main-results-report

Fitz-Gibbon, K., Elliott, K. and Maher, J. (2018) *Investigating adolescent family violence in Victoria: Understanding experiences and practitioner perspectives.* Monash Gender and Family Violence Research Program. Melbourne, Australia: Faculty of Arts, Monash University.

Flood, M., Fergus, L., & Heenan, M. (2009). *Respectful relationships education: Violence prevention and respectful relationships education in Victorian secondary schools.* Melbourne, Australia: State Government Victoria.

Foshee, V. A., Bauman, K. E., Arriaga, X. B., Helms, R. W., Koch, G. G., & Linder, G. F. (1998). An evaluation of safe dates, an adolescent dating violence prevention program. *American Journal of Public Health, 88*(1), 45–50.

Frohmader, C. (2014). *Violence against women with disabilities, fact sheet 3.* Women with Disabilities Victoria. Retrieved from www.wdv.org.au/?s=women+with+disabilities

Hague, G., Thiara, R. K., Magowan, P. & Mullender, A. (2008). *Making the links: Disabled women and domestic violence. Full report.* Bristol: Women's Aid.

Hautala, D. S., Hartshorn, K. J., Armenta, B., & Whitbeck, L. (2017). Prevalence and correlates of physical dating violence among North American Indigenous adolescents. *Youth & Society, 49*(3), 295–317. doi: 10.1177/0044118X14559503

Haynie, D. L., & Osgood, D. W. (2005). Reconsidering peers and delinquency: How do peers matter? *Social Forces, 84*(2), 1109–1130.

Ibabe, I., Jaureguizar, J., & Bentler, P. M. (2013). Risk factors for child-to-parent violence. *Journal of Family Violence, 28,* 523–534.

Johnson, S. B., Frattaroli, S., Campbell, J., Wright, J., Pearson-Fields, A. S., & Cheng, T. L. (2005). "I know what love means": Gender-based violence in the lives of urban adolescents. *Journal of Women's Health, 14*(2), 172–179.

Keating, B. (2015). Violence against women: A disciplinary debate and challenge. *The Sociological Quarterly, 56*(1), 108–124.

Kimmel, M. S. (2002). "Gender symmetry" in domestic violence. *Violence against Women, 8*(11), 1332–1363.

Levy, B. (1990). Abusive teen dating relationships: An emerging issue for the 90s. *Response to the Victimization of Women & Children, 13*(1), 5.

Liang, B., Goodman, L., Tummala-Narra, P., & Weintraub, S. (2005). A theoretical framework for understanding help-seeking processes among survivors of intimate partner violence. *American Journal of Community Psychology, 36*(1/2), 71–84.

Malik, S., Sorenson, S. B., & Aneshensel, C. S. (1997). Community and dating violence among adolescents: Perpetration and victimization. *Journal of Adolescent Health, 21*(5), 291–302.

Martin, C., Houston, A., Mmari, K., & Decker, M. (2012). Urban teens and young adults describe drama, disrespect, dating violence and help-seeking preferences. *Journal of Maternal & Child Health, 16,* 957–966.

Mays, J. M. (2006). Feminist disability theory: Domestic violence against women with a disability. *Disability & Society, 21*(2), 147–158.

Meyer, S. (2010). *Responding to intimate partner violence victimization: Effective options for help-seeking* (Trends & Issues in Crime and Criminal Justice Series, No. 389). Canberra: Australian Institute of Criminology.

Mills, T. (2015). Elder abuse. *MedScape.* Retrieved from https://emedicine.medscape.com/article/805727-overview

Mouzos, J., & Makkai, T. (2004). *Women's experiences of male violence: Findings from the Australian component of the International Violence against Women Survey (IVAWS)* (Research and Public Policy Series No. 56). Canberra: Australian Institute of Criminology.

Mulroney, J., & Chan, C. (2005). *Men as victims of domestic violence.* Sydney: Domestic & Family Violence Clearinghouse.

Niolon, P., Vivolo-Kantor, A., Latzman, N., Valle, L., Kuoh, H., Burton, T., . . ., Tharp, A. T. (2015). Prevalence of teen dating violence and co-occurring risk factors among middle school youth in high-risk urban communities. *Journal of Adolescent Health, 56*(2), 5–13.

Oh, J., Kim, H. S., Martins, D., & Kim, H. (2006). A study of elder abuse in Korea. *International Journal of Nursing Studies, 43*(2), 203–14.

O'Keefe, M. (1997). Predictors of dating violence among high school students. *Journal of Interpersonal Violence, 12,* 546–568.

O'Keefe, M., & Aldridge, L. (2005, April). *Teen dating violence: A review of risk factors and prevention efforts.* Harrisburg, PA: VAWnet. Retrieved from www.vawnet.org/applied-research-papers/print-document.php?doc_id=409

Phillips, J., & Vandenbroek, P. (2014). *Domestic, family and sexual violence in Australia: An overview of the issues* (Parliamentary Library Research Paper Series No. 2014–15). Retrieved from http://parlinfo.aph.gov.au/parlInfo/download/library/prspub/3447585/upload_binary/3447585.pdf;fileType=application/pdf

Pillemer, K., Burnes, D., Riffin, C., & Lachs, M. S. (2016). Elder abuse: Global situation, risk factors and prevention strategies. *The Gerontologist, 56*(2), S194–S205.

Salthouse S. & Frohmader C. (2004). *Double the odds: Domestic violence and women with disabilities,* available through Women With Disabilities Australia. Retrieved from: www.wwda. org.au/odds.htm

Shah, S., Tsitsou, L., & Woodin, S. (2016). Hidden voices: Disabled women's experiences of violence and support over the life course. *Violence against Women, 22*(10), 1189–1210.

Silverman, J. G., Raj, A., Mucci, L. A., & Hathaway, J. E. (2001). Dating violence against adolescent girls and associated substance use, unhealthy weight control, sexual risk behavior, pregnancy, and suicidality. *Journal of the American Medical Association, 286*(5), 572–579.

Straus, M. A. (2007). Processes explaining the concealment and distortion of evidence on gender symmetry in partner violence. *European Journal on Criminal Policy and Research, 13*(3–4), 227–232.

Tjaden, P., & Thoennes, N. (2000). *Full report of the prevalence, incidence, and consequences of violence against women: Findings from the national violence against women survey* (NCJ No. 183781). Washington, DC: US Department of Justice.

University of New South Wales (UNSW). (2014). *Calling it what it really is: A report into lesbian, gay, bisexual, transgender, gender diverse, intersex and queer experiences of domestic and family violence.* NSW, Australia: UNSW.

VicHealth. (2016). *Family violence and women with disabilities.* Factsheet prepared in collaboration with the Domestic Violence Resource Centre Victoria. Retrieved from www.betterhealth.vic.gov.au

VicHealth. (2017). *Violence against women in Australia: An overview of research and approaches to primary prevention.* Melbourne, Australia: Victorian Health Promotion Foundation.

Walters, M. L., Chen, J., & Breiding, M. J. (2013). *The National Intimate Partner and Sexual Violence Survey (NISVS): 2010 findings on victimization by sexual orientation.* Atlanta, GA: National Center for Injury Prevention and Control, Center for Disease Control and Prevention.

Wekerle, C., & Wolfe, D. A. (1999). Dating violence in mid-adolescence: Theory, significance, and emerging prevention initiatives. *Clinical Psychology Review, 19*(4), 435–456.

Wolfe, D. A. (2003). Elder abuse interventions: Lessons from child abuse and domestic violence initiatives. In R. Bonnie & R. Wallace (Eds.), *Elder mistreatment: Abuse, neglect, and exploitation in an ageing America* (pp. 501–526). Washington, DC: National Academies Press.

Ziminski Pickering, C. E., & Phillips, L. R. (2014). Development of a causal model for elder mistreatment. *Public Health Nursing, 31*(4), 363–372.

Zweig, J., Dank, M., Yahner, J., & Lachman, P. (2013). The rate of cyber dating abuse among teens and how it relates to other forms of teen dating violence. *Journal of Youth & Adolescence, 42*(7), 1063–1077.

Chapter 8

The vulnerability of the displaced and the dispossessed

Matching services to migrant and indigenous populations

Introduction

Domestic and family violence (DFV) is prevalent in all countries and cultures (Akinsulure-Smith, Chu, Keatley, & Rasmussen, 2013; Barkho, Fakhouri, & Arnetz, 2011), but some populations, such as migrants and indigenous peoples, face additional or increased challenges and are especially vulnerable as a result (Prosman, Jansen, Lo Fo Wong, & Lagro-Janssen, 2011; Reina, Maldonado, & Lohman, 2013). Displacement and dispossession are, we suggest, the overarching factors in the heightened level of risk for these groups. We focus in this chapter on the experiences and typical service needs of populations whose DFV risk is elevated in these ways.

The chapter is in two parts. First, we examine factors that indicate increased vulnerability to DFV among migrant and indigenous groups. Here we use the intersectionality construct to make conceptual sense of the particular challenges faced by these groups. Experiences of DFV in the context of interacting issues – that have to do not just with gender but often with race, class, visa status, and so on – exacerbate social marginalisation and isolation. Having clearly specified and investigated these challenges, in the second part of the chapter we consider appropriate and sensitive responses to victims, perpetrators, and the broader community. Finally, we suggest how these responses might be implemented.

Part 1: displacement and dispossession: the problem

Heightened vulnerability

Some potential clients of DFV services are members of populations that tend to fall outside many of the assumptions about the nature and scope of service provision made by mainstream providers. These persons therefore might not be identified by such services, which are typically poorly resourced to respond anyway (see Ogunsiji & Clisdell, 2017). There are two broad causes of this disjuncture: cultural mismatch and intersectional disadvantage. We begin by investigating the problem of cultural mismatch.

Cultural mismatch here refers to the discrepancy between the broad systems of meaning and understanding that parties may bring to an encounter (i.e. a potential client and those who provide a DFV service). An example of this kind of mismatch is the meanings and understandings around family member roles, and particularly the expectations about marriage-type relationships. A key reason for the failure of services to meaningfully connect with some groups is that the particular needs of the population to which they belong are not focally anticipated by the agency resourced to provide that service (Ghafournia, 2011; Ogunsiji & Clisdell, 2017; Simon-Kumar, Kurian, Young-Silcock, & Narasimhan, 2017). The attention and approaches of mainstream services tend to be guided by normative social values and by thinking informed by predominant theories. These local services tend, perhaps inadvertently, to privilege the needs of those groups that have been readily identified by a mainstream focus. The implications for this divide between need and service with respect to minority populations result ultimately in their heightened and continued vulnerability to DFV (Okeke-Ihejirika et al., 2018). As Ogunsiji and Clisdell (2017) describe, the decreased opportunities for victims to access help, along with exploitation of this predicament by perpetrators, potentially increases both the likelihood that the abuse will occur and that it will endure. Two prominent examples where this failure to connect occurs at a population level are migrant (displaced) and indigenous (dispossessed) groups. The documented DFV experiences of members of these populations provide the focus for this chapter.

Factors affecting access to services

The barriers to client–service engagement outlined above represent markers of vulnerability of particular concern for those affected by DFV within indigenous and migrant groups. Whether these barriers are demonstrable or merely anticipated, the fact remains that they will have real consequences for potential clients. In the case of migrants, these obstacles generally have to do with issues of diminished social networks, limited cultural and linguistic fluency (Ahmad, Rai, Petrovic, Erickson, & Stewart, 2013; Sabina, Cuevas, & Zadnik, 2015), migration-related sources of tension and conflict, socioeconomic insecurity (Hyman et al., 2011), and the risk of deportation (Tartakovsky & Mezhibovsky, 2012).

More generally, researchers have identified a range of variables, which apply to both migrant and indigenous populations, further complicating engagement with services (e.g. Briones-Vozmediano, Agudelo-Suarez, Goicolea, & Vives-Cases, 2014; Childress, 2013; Hyman et al., 2011; Ogunsiji & Clisdell, 2017; Simon-Kumar et al., 2017). Among these are:

- Relationship to the host society/colonising culture
- Level of acculturation
- Helping system receptiveness
- Legal standing and residency status

- Level of ambivalence about the prospect of engaging with DFV services
- Level of trust in government authorities
- Perception and knowledge of service availability

Indeed, migrant and indigenous populations tend to be at a high level of vulnerability to DFV in the first place, and this relates to the second point of disjuncture between these populations and service responses: intersectional disadvantage. Migrant and indigenous populations typically face difficulties related to the broader issues of social disconnection and dislocation emerging from often dramatic, far-reaching, and fundamental changes to their circumstances. We use the term social dislocation in this sense to refer to the experience of being forced to conduct one's life on someone else's terms. In coming into another's culture, there are, for example, a vast number of new social and cultural cues that are very different from those in one's customary environment.

In the case of indigenous peoples, their difficulties might be exacerbated by intergenerational experiences related to colonisation and subsequent dispossession. Dispossession at a population level is of particular relevance here as it refers to the traditional occupation and economic use of land and waterways, but also to customs, spiritual dominion, and lore. Furthermore, the degradation of traditional and enduring systems of welfare and justice compromises a people's ability to contain and respond adequately to social problems that were once autonomously managed (Mackay, Gibson, Huetee, & Beecham, 2015). The replacement of indigenous systems with palpably discriminatory and alien institutions has further damaged these capacities. In examining more closely the experience of both of migrant and indigenous groups, such factors can precede a range of social ills, of which DFV is but one.

Experiencing DFV at the intersection of culture, race, and migration status

Research and practice evidence has repeatedly demonstrated that women born overseas are more vulnerable to DFV victimisation than their locally born counterparts (Burman & Chantler, 2005; Erez, Adelman, & Gregory, 2009; Ghafournia, 2011; Sokoloff & Pearce, 2011). Immigrant women often experience additional barriers to service seeking. Apart from the geographical separation from social supports in their places of origin, as outlined above, these barriers might be associated with limited understanding of local laws and victims' rights, cultural differences that affect understanding of host country definitions of DFV, or perceptions on the appropriateness of external help seeking (Menjivar & Salcido, 2002; Messing, Amanor-Boadu, Cavanaugh, Glass & Campbell, 2013; Phillips & Vandenbroek, 2014). Insufficient access to tangible support such as financial resources, housing, and other welfare services has been identified as a further layer of challenge for some women, especially for those with temporary visa provisions (Crossing & Barassi-Rubio, 2013). Experiences of DFV can be particularly fraught for women with insecure visa arrangements. As a result, immigrant women's help seeking is often limited to informal or community-based arrangements, raising implications for service delivery and identification of risk and related support needs (Messing et al., 2013).

Experiences and service needs of indigenous victims

The complex interaction of colonial history and culturally shaped responses is generally accepted and commonly referenced as the key factor in the current predicament of indigenous people. In an example from Australia, Malcolm Frost (2014) puts it this way: "Aboriginal violence is the achievement of a critical mass of self-generating human psychological dysfunction based on normal human responses to traumatic circumstances" (p. 90). The wide spectrum of challenges facing Australian Indigenous social policy is readily seen in Aboriginal and Torres Strait Islander peoples' highly disproportionate inclusion in negative demographic statistics, such as those surrounding incarceration, mental wellbeing, physical health, housing, education, and social inequalities (Australian Bureau of Statistics, 2014–15). Research and public health data in Australia reveal that family violence has particularly significant ramifications for Indigenous Aboriginal and Torres Strait Islander people, including its elevated prevalence, pervasiveness, and severity (Australian Bureau of Statistics, 2016; Olsen & Lovett, 2016; Phillips & Vandenbroek, 2014; Richards, 2011). This parlous state of affairs stems from a combination of circumstances associated with a detrimental recent history of colonisation, which has resulted in dispersion of kin, fragmentation culture, geographical isolation, and various dimensions of discrimination, disadvantage, and inequality (Cox, Young, & Bairnsfather-Scott, 2009).

In addition, indigenous DFV victims are more likely than non-indigenous DFV victims to have experienced a disrupted parent–child relationship due to their own experiences of regulatory state interventions and being placed in long-term out-of-home care (Haebich, 2001). In Australia, the Stolen Generation refers to a generational cohort of Indigenous children separated from kin by intrusive and punitive state measures (Commonwealth of Australia, 1997; Creative Spirits, 2014). As a result, experiences of violence and abuse, along with other complex family factors, are systemically located within the context of intergenerational trauma (Haebich, 2001; Kwan, 2015). Experiences of separation from their family of origin during childhood, abuse at the hands of a partner or other family member as an adult, and the risk of subsequent child safety interventions all have a compounding effect on victims' help seeking and, in turn, their wellbeing. Such experiences create additional barriers to disclosing abuse and accessing relevant support mechanisms for indigenous victims. Similar to immigrant women, indigenous women therefore often endure prolonged experiences of abuse (Willis, 2011).

Issues of community stigma and shame can create yet more obstacles to victims' help seeking. While many require formal interventions to end the oppression and abuse at the hands of a perpetrator, reaching out to formal support sources often leads to situations that play out in the broader context of oppression of indigenous people by mainstream regulatory interventions (Nancarrow, 2006). Fear of retaliatory violence in close-knit communities (where there is often no place to hide) can hinder help-seeking decision-making, along with doubts about being taken seriously or being adequately supported, even if they were to reach out to formal (typically mainstream) support sources (Cheers et al., 2006; Willis, 2011). In these ways, attempts to seek outside help might be viewed as betrayal – of family, community, or culture – especially where it risks public exposure. Contributing further to already disproportionate representation in child protection and criminal justice systems adds to the community's burden of shame (Cheers et al., 2006; Phillips & Vandenbroek, 2014). As a consequence of colonisation, this unlovely picture is, unfortunately, not at all an uncommon one around the globe as we see in regions such as the Americas and elsewhere in the Pacific. It is a pattern of events that has adversely impacted upon indigenous systems, relationships, and influences.

While there are some clear distinctions between the experiences of indigenous and migrant populations in relation to vulnerability to DFV and service access, there are also similarities. Some researchers argue therefore that despite the level of diversity within, between, and across indigenous and migrant populations, there are some aspects of abuse where both groups experience a higher level of vulnerability than the general population (Erez et al., 2009; Messing et al., 2013). We now consider the implications of three key examples: victim vulnerability to entrapment, the compounding nature of intersectional disadvantage, and intergenerational harm.

Implications for entrapment

The most harmful aspects of DFV, in terms of its invasiveness, persistence, and impact on wellbeing, tend to be related to those forms of abuse characterised by an enduring and pervasive pattern of strategies enacted by one person and intended to establish and maintain interpersonal domination over another. This type of abuse (as introduced in Chapter 2) is variously referred to in the literature by terms such as intimate terrorism (Johnson, 2010; Johnson & Leone, 2005) and coercive control (Stark, 2007). It is experienced by victims as a hostage-like situation and is reinforced through tactics that might be described, in quite literal terms, as torturous. The tools of this kind of confinement and torture are efficient and effective because they rely, to a large extent, on the culturally shaped commitments of the victim and are carried out in the context of ordinary domestic environments. In these ways, entrapment is less easily detected and the goals of the abuser are more readily assured.

While the inequity and oppression inherent in such contexts is seen to reflect normative power relations at wider societal levels, they are, it seems, exacerbated and compounded for the displaced and dispossessed. Victims in these contexts become increasingly enmeshed in a vicious cycle of tension between wishing to honour family and marriage commitments and the urge to escape a life of continual persecution (Murphy, Risley, & Gerdes, 2003). According to Ware, Frost, and Hoy (2010), there are five areas commonly associated with abuse carried out in private spaces: exploitation, secrecy/concealment, collusion, blame-shifting, and victim "grooming" (predatory entrapment). As noted earlier in this chapter, the circumstances of dispossession and displacement that tend to prevail for migrant and indigenous populations result in high levels of isolation and alienation. In such circumstances, personal and family stress, seclusion, restricted options, dependence, and reliance as stressors and facilitators of violence are elevated (Ware et al., 2010). This increased risk is associated with circumstances more easily exploited as strategies of abuse by perpetrators, thus increasing the likelihood and endurance of this coercive controlling type of DFV. For example, where a man feels humiliated and compromised in his masculinity by a lack of access to employment (e.g. because of insecure citizenship, discrimination, lack of educational qualifications, etc.), he might look to a strategy of domination over his wife and family as a means of emotional displacement and ego compensation. His wife – constrained by rigid and narrow gender training, fearful for herself and her children, and perceiving no refuge and few other options – "accepts" the blame that is attributed to her by her husband. In a study of the lived experience of migrant women in the US, Childress (2013) reports how, effectively cut off from sources of help and refuge, these women engaged in desperate attempts to maintain closeness and relationship status while at the same time tried to evade the worst aspects of the abuse. Faced with this predicament, a commonly practiced solution by the women was to respond with an attitude of unquestioning obedience towards their husbands.

The situation these women are in is often particularly precarious because abusive husbands recognise, and look to exploit, their considerable power advantages. Immigrant women often report abusive tactics that relate specifically to their immigrant identity. For instance, in the (not untypical) circumstances where the women's visa arrangements are dependent on those of their partner, perpetrators typically use the victims' vulnerability to their advantage. Threats of reporting the victim to immigration authorities, having her deported and taking away the children are common tactics to maintain power and control over the victim (Messing et al., 2013; Menjivar & Salcido, 2002). To more fully appreciate the impact of such factors on migrant and indigenous populations, the construct of intersectionality (introduced in Chapter 3) is a useful tool in making sense of how they interact with each other to complicate and aggravate DFV.

Intersectional disadvantage and risk

Globally, experiences of indigenous communities in colonised countries (the US, Australia, Canada, and New Zealand, for example) need to be understood in the context of colonisation, dispossession, and cultural oppression in order to address DFV in a culturally informed and culturally appropriate manner. Marginalised community settings, poverty, and racial discrimination (experienced and anticipated), often along with geographic remoteness, all create barriers for potential clients to access services, above and beyond those experienced by those from non-indigenous backgrounds (Cheers et al., 2006; Phillips & Vandenbroek, 2014; Willis, 2011). Nevertheless, they often share common experiences with immigrant communities, primarily around the impact of community marginalisation and racial discrimination (Menjivar & Salcido, 2002; Messing et al., 2013). Like their indigenous counterparts, the experiences of migrant families and communities are mediated by the socio-political context in which the violence occurs and the impact of intersectional factors that result.

In Chapter 3, when discussing relevant theory, we made reference to intersectionality as a useful conceptual tool in understanding the complexity of DFV. By way of reintroducing this term, we draw on Dhamoon and Hankivsky (2011, p. 16):

> Intersectionality is concerned with simultaneous intersections between aspects of social difference and identity (as related to meanings of race/ethnicity, indigeneity, gender, class, sexuality, geography, age, disability/ability, migration status, religion) and forms of systemic oppression (racism, classism, sexism, ableism, homophobia) at macro and micro levels in ways that are complex and interdependent.

As previously described, migrant and indigenous populations are subject to heightened vulnerability to DFV. They also face marginalisation and subjugation in a broader sense because of institutional discrimination. These disadvantaging factors combine, layer, and interlock with DFV to become mutually exacerbating.

Structural factors

As argued in Chapters 2 and 3, we consider DFV to be principally an expression of masculine power and control. Earlier in the current chapter, we used the example of employment to illustrate how these two factors might interact in the emergence and continuation of DFV. In the lives of migrants and indigenous groups, intersectionality theory provides a means to make sense of how masculine hegemony is both mediated and compounded by the impact of displacement and dispossession. For example, because of many of the discriminating features, poor and unsatisfactory levels of employment are common among both indigenous and migrant groups. Due to this reduced access to decent employment along with other markers of power and status, the expression and enactment of traditional forms of masculinity is blocked off or constrained. Furthermore, the impoverishment brought about by these circumstances engenders its own misery and sources of couple and family tension.

Intergenerational patterns of disadvantage and abuse

Not only is disadvantage broadly distributed across groups such as migrant and indigenous populations, theory such as social learning (see Chapter 3) suggest it can also be heritable. In the case of indigenous groups, for instance, members are affected by the oppressive circumstances and damaging impact of colonisation. Typical key impact factors in their history include the atrophy of social resources and withering of institutions, such as kin structure, welfare arrangements, and cultural integrity (Haebich, 2011). These depletions have often resulted in general impoverishment and damage to the wellbeing of such populations across psychological, family, spiritual, and health domains (Haebich, 2001). Blighted by substance misuse, widespread mental and physical health problems, housing inadequacy, and so on, this legacy has endured through generations and continues to disadvantage indigenous populations (Frost, 2014).

Awareness of these matters and the circumstances that give rise to them both suggests ways of responding and provides the ethical impetus to act on them. We now turn to the matter of appropriate service responses, especially where this means different service responses are required for different groups.

Part 2: congruent service provision: the response

Tailoring to diversity

Minority-ethnic populations whose needs do not represent a good "fit" with mainstream thinking and services require different or varied approaches and modalities of practice (see Crichton-Hill, 2001, for example). Ogunsiji and Clisdell (2017) note that this matter has been identified in a number of research studies, producing a stream of recommendations for interventions that are tailored towards addressing this discrepancy. These authors provide a literature review of interventions for intimate partner violence (IPV) among migrants. They conclude that many such interventions have not only succeeded in empowering victims and enhancing their self-esteem but have also resulted in behavioural change for perpetrators. Ogunsiji and Clisdell (2017) note that processes involved in the development of IPV interventions among immigrant populations include an "identification of the theoretical framework that shapes the intervention, utilization of intersectoral approach, and strong emphasis on cultural context" (p. 459).

Cripps and Davis (2012) described some of the promising efforts to reduce indigenous family violence in Australia and overseas, including both government and community initiatives. They found that indigenous-specific programs involving the local people and their senior community members appear to offer distinct advantages. In general, this process suggests shifts in strategy and focus: from centralism to localism and from bureaucrat to elder. Respectful and considerate cultural engagement carried out by culturally competent practitioners working with appropriate partners, it seems, is a gradual but critical process for success in the long-term (Hovane, 2015). In communities that are looking to become more cohesive, the emphasis is often on restorative justice-type initiatives, such as the healing circle based on the well-regarded Hollow Water program in Canada (Native Counselling Services of Alberta, 2001).

Other authors who have studied this problem have added to the discussion on congruent service provision, and we describe significant contributions and encouraging approaches in the remainder of this chapter.

Risk assessment: culturally appropriate service responses

Implications for immigrant populations

As we have described, help seeking for migrant and indigenous peoples can be complicated by an accumulation of variables in their lives and their interaction. Such variables include, but are not limited to: level of cross-cultural fluency (such as language), social location, social ties in the country of residence or to the dominant culture, and culturally specific family and community commitments to preserving the reputation of the community (Erez et al., 2009; Kasturirangan, Krishnan, & Riger, 2004; Mayock, Sheridan, & Parker, 2012). Where circumstances are disadvantageous in relation to these variables, they can contribute to an elevated risk of abuse or re-abuse. For example, a strong commitment to preserving family and community might result in concealing domestic abuse and therefore represent a barrier to help. Based on such known barriers, research evidence has pointed towards the importance of appropriately tailored risk assessment when working with culturally diverse women (Messing, Amanor-Boadu, Cavanaugh, Glass, & Campbell, 2013). Outcomes from this research suggest that when service providers identify potential victimisation, it is important to assess both risk and options for establishing safety (Messing et al., 2013). There are two overarching requirements here. First, a culturally informed response, and second, the availability of a culturally appropriate risk assessment instrument. In this latter requirement, mainstream instruments developed in Western countries may not be able to adequately capture immigrant or indigenous women's risk (Crawford, n.d.).

Respecting values of collectivism and honouring preference

Since culture represents the lens through which we experience the world, it should not be characterised as a separate and discrete obstacle to matching service with need. Felt needs and preferences are inextricably intertwined with one's cultural training. One significant issue here concerns the organisation of one's life with respect to self and others. Western DFV services tend to be designed around the cultural values of liberal individualism. These values encourage, for instance, competitiveness in social and commercial domains and adversarial legal arenas. Moreover, liberal individualism tends to particularise the person as a separate, autonomous, and self-determined being, whose wellbeing is measured by constantly weighing up costs and benefits as they accrue to that individual. The traditional emphasis of Western DFV victim services, therefore, has been on safety achieved through separation and emergency refuge as the woman is encouraged towards an independent life. Yoshioka and Choi (2005) note that non-Western collectivist cultures, by contrast, tend to valorise community-oriented qualities such as commitment, duty, reciprocal obligation, social wellbeing, and harmony. Interestingly, these qualities are emphasised by peoples whose cultural fabric is oriented to a holistic ontology and an instinctively ecological perspective on life and the universe. Such a perspective is typically associated with indigenous cultures. Whereas individualism implies a looseness or separateness of social bonds, collectivism suggests family and social "tightness" (Yoshioka & Choi, 2005) – referring to the centrality of family/tribe/community and one's *membership* of it. So, for example, the principal function of a marriage, according to non-Western cultures, is seen as bringing together two *families*, rather than two individuals, and it is often the case that the wife is considered the responsible partner for maintaining the marriage relationship (Childress, 2013).

Working with resilience and resistance

The circumstances of many within dispossessed and displaced communities can be particularly difficult in regard to DFV, and it might be tempting to conclude in some cases that their situations are hopeless and intractable. Childress (2013), however, reminds us to take into account sources of both potential and proven strength among such persons. She invites practitioners to consider working in collaboration with, for instance, the client's religiosity and spirituality, recruiting these commitments in establishing awareness and appreciation of her worth and contribution to a collectivist culture; the sense of burden and responsibility might be countered with an enlightened appreciation of one's value to family and community in a collectivist worldview. With regard to the perpetrator's role in resisting the use of violence, we might also consider recruiting his culturally inherited strength of family responsibility and commitment as an incentive (Mansley, 2009).

To stay or to leave? Working with (not against) the victim's predicament

While the strategy of assuring safety through separation and independence upheld by mainstream services now has broad social and political support in Western countries, this solution may be associated with harsh community sanction among collectivist cultures. Yoshioka and Choi (2005) note the ambivalence expressed by non-Western clients towards this victim service strategy and wonder whether a more flexible and client-centred approach might achieve better outcomes in some circumstances through family preservation. Indeed, safety might be better served by identifying expressed need (thereby honouring cultural preference), rather than assumed need. Yoshioka and Choi (2005) examine the experience of working with the HIV/AIDS community where practitioners frequently encountered "high-risk" behaviour but eventually accepted the complex realities of the field, reconciling to working with preference – successfully. These authors reinforce their argument by citing the benefits of responding empathically and sympathetically, thus better promoting client engagement and readiness through service inclusiveness and flexibility.

Ghafournia (2011) weighs the merits of both sides of this argument. In what she calls *universalist* thinking, she first considers the view that there ought to be a singular approach to all instances of DFV. This reflects the hard-line protective position advocating for the independence of the woman as the best strategy for protecting her and promoting the man's accountability. Ghafournia (2011) compares this universalist position with a *relativist* stance, which promotes the view that each case must be decided in its distinctive cultural context. This latter perspective argues that the universalists stand for interventionism, thereby reflecting a strategy of assimilationist colonialism. This author goes on to deconstruct this harsh binary by promoting a third position and proposing a midway policy of being resolute in implacable opposition to abuse, while at the same time taking a collaborative approach to bring about safety. Ghafournia (2011, p. 212) concludes:

> We need to take a moderate approach. This approach will accept the cultural differences while avoiding relativist views and constructively attempt to reach not only women but also male counterparts and their underlying belief of their violence. Their so-called cultural belief, whether considered cultural or not, needs to be challenged and no excuse should justify abusive behavior.

This position is also taken up by Simon-Kumar and colleagues (2017). Their research reflects the views of a small group of practitioners in anti-violence interventions with minority-ethnic groups in Aotearoa, New Zealand. In summarising this, they suggest that, rather than seeking to erase culture, efforts should go towards *mobilising* culture and that the language of service should be directed towards *family* safety, rather than towards women's safety per se.

Mobilising culture

As described earlier, mainstream DFV services in Western countries tend to emphasise a strategy based around separation and sanctuary for victims, and this has become established into service logic. As we contend, however, there can be multiple and considerable difficulties around "imposing" this strategy upon persons from migrant and indigenous cultures, and ethical challenges arise where this directly contradicts the wishes expressed by clients. We have considered alternative ways of approaching these disjunctures, such as a change in emphasis from the explicit promotion of individual safety to the goal of family safety (Simon-Kumar et al., 2017).

Among the adaptations appropriate for working with these vulnerable communities is the need to take into account the fraught history of their relationship with the state. Moreover, service providers commonly cite the need to be inclusive, consultative, and respectful. The principle of "doing with" (that is, "alongside") rather than "doing to" is especially important given the reluctance and wariness of mainstream, and especially state, service representatives. Australian history – even recent history – is replete with accounts of local Indigenous community leaders working hard to implement local initiatives only to have their work overturned by the state government implementing larger-body oversight (see Moran, 2016).

Grounding interventions within an apposite cultural context requires high levels of cultural competency and familiarity with good practices. Supporting a "trajectory of agency" (Kennedy, 2005) goes beyond culturally competent practice, however. Working with culturally diverse populations to promote safety involves what Simon-Kumar and colleagues (2017) refer to as "mobilising" culture. In their study of culturally informed interventions in Aotearoa, New Zealand, these authors identify this as a core strand of practice in anti-violence work across cultures. Among strategies used to mobilise culture, the study found that practitioners called upon practices that took a family approach, engaged men in their interventions (even functionally reinforcing gendered roles and accountability where appropriate), and deployed cultural tropes (e.g. around spirituality).

Such work is consistent with the sentiment that it is both discriminatory and erroneous to assume cultures that have been oppressed and subjugated are somehow intrinsically morally faulty. As Simon-Kumar and colleagues (2017, p. 1388) suggest, "interventions into domestic violence can be framed around resisting, challenging and changing 'oppressive' cultures". Citing authors such as Haldane (2009), they make reference to "an emergent scholarship that sees culture not merely as the dominant cause of violence, but rather as an asset in its intervention" (Simon-Kumar et al., 2017, p. 1388). Indeed, these authors see culture as having transformatory potential. In order for that potential to be realised, however, cultures must be detached from their characterisation as inveterately counter to the interests of women. Rather, culture is recognised as

> complex, with the potential to have multiple implications for women, not all of which are negative. . . . Within each culture there exist locally relevant concepts that can be consciously and purposely mobilised to reaffirm identity and demarcate community boundaries, as well as to focus attention and generate institutional commitment towards rethinking gender violence.
>
> (Simon-Kumar et al., 2017, p. 1388)

Employing a strengths-based orientation and a community development approach, these authors bring attention to strategies that took important cultural tropes such as family and community fidelity and worked with them as assets, endowing them with energy to recognise the importance of the role and strength of women in achieving collective family and community goals.

In translating this to practice among indigenous communities, for instance, we would see approaches based on respectful consultation with elders and informed by the notion that a sole individual will not necessarily be comfortable in making decisions unilaterally. It is important here that there is a strong investment in the ownership and self-determination of the local community. Such investment means taking *time* – often much longer than the circumscribed periods assigned for evaluation studies – to develop relationships founded on *trust*, which must be won back (see Moran, 2016). Tackling DFV in these circumstances might mean taking into account generations of dislocation and trauma (sometimes intergenerational), and its implications for flexibility in relation to healing. In many respects, this is the mirror image of working with persons who have been victimised, the difference being that here we are talking about a community and a population that has been victimised and has collectively taken on the characteristics of a survivor. It stands to reason that this approach needs to apply to working with those in affected communities who have perpetrated DFV, as they are simultaneously victims in this light. Service providers working in these contexts argue that a position of accountability needs to be founded on a platform of healing (Thomas & Thomson, 2012).

Summary

Many of the vulnerabilities faced by those affected by DFV from majority-culture victims, such as those resulting from gender inequality and other forms of disadvantage, tend to be magnified for immigrant and indigenous populations by virtue of cultural mismatch, structural intersectional disadvantage, and the legacies of colonial exploitation. These issues typically combine and intersect with other issues surrounding culture, race, and class to exacerbate the experiences of people affected by DFV. Once afflicted, alienation, isolation, lack of familiarity, and discrimination become further barriers between communities and services.

However, the implications of such abuses and barriers are not restricted to migrant and indigenous peoples. It can be said that every encounter is a cross-cultural encounter to some extent. Moreover, in the field of DFV practice there is a significant power differential at work; service providers typically have authority over service seekers by means of official reporting or direct imposition. Learnings from the experiences of practice with dispossessed or displaced communities – such as the principle of doing with rather than doing to – have real implications for all clients of DFV services. In Chapters 9 and 10, where we consider the application of good practice, we reincorporate some of these learnings.

References

Ahmad, F., Rai, N., Petrovic, B., Erickson, P. E., & Stewart, D. E. (2013). Resilience and resources among South Asian immigrant women as survivors of partner violence. *Journal of Immigrant and Minority Health*, 15(6), 1057–1064.

Akinsulure-Smith, A. M., Chu, T., Keatley, E., & Rasmussen, A. (2013). Intimate partner violence among West African immigrants. *Journal of Aggression, Maltreatment and Trauma*, 22(2), 109–126.

Australian Bureau of Statistics. (2016). *Migration, Australia, 2016–17* (Cat. No. 3412.0). Retrieved from www.abs.gov.au/ausstats/abs@.nsf/mf/3412.0/

Australian Bureau of Statistics (ABS). (2014–15). *National Aboriginal and Torres Strait Islander Social Survey, 2014–15*. Retrieved from www.abs.gov.au/ausstats/abs@.nsf/mf/4714.0

Barkho, E., Fakhouri, M., & Arnetz, J. E. (2011). Intimate partner violence among Iraqi immigrant women in Metro Detroit: A pilot study. *Journal of Immigrant and Minority Health*, 13(4), 725–731.

Briones-Vozmediano, E., Agudelo-Suarez, A., Goicolea, I., & Vives-Cases, C. (2014). Economic crisis, immigrant women and intimate partner violence services: A qualitative study of professionals' perceptions in Spain. *International Journal for Equity in Health*, 13(1), 44–63.

Burman, E., & Chantler, K. (2005). Domestic violence and minoritisation: Legal and policy barriers facing minoritized women leaving violent relationships. *International Journal of Law and Psychiatry*, 28(1), 59–74.

Cheers, B., Binell, M., Coleman, H., Gentle, I., Miller, G., Taylor, J., & Weetra, C. (2006). Family violence: An Australian Indigenous community tells its story. *International Social Work*, 49(1), 51–63.

Childress, S. (2013). A meta-summary of qualitative findings on the lived experience among culturally diverse domestic violence survivors. *Issues in Mental Health Nursing*, 34(9), 693–705.

Commonwealth of Australia. (1997). *Bringing them home* (Report of the National Inquiry into the Separation of Aboriginal and Torres Strait Islander Children from Their Families). Retrieved from www.humanrights.gov.au/sites/default/files/content/pdf/social_justice/bringing_them_home_report.pdf

Cox, D., Young, M., & Bairnsfather-Scott, A. (2009). No justice without healings: Australian Aboriginal people and family violence. *Australian Feminist Law Journal*, 30(1), 151–162.

Crawford, L. (n.d.). *Cross agency risk assessment tool: Domestic and family violence: An Aboriginal perspective*. Submitted to the Reference Group Committee, April 2008.

Creative Spirits. (2014). *A guide to Australia's Stolen Generations*. Retrieved from www.creativespirits.info/aboriginalculture/politics/stolen-generations/a-guide-to-australias-stolen-generations

Crichton-Hill, Y. (2001). Challenging ethnocentric explanations of domestic violence. *Trauma, Violence & Abuse*, 2(3), 203–214.

Cripps, K., & Davis, M. (2012). Communities working to reduce Indigenous family violence. *Indigenous Justice Clearinghouse*. Brief 12. Retrieved from www.indigenousjustice.gov.au/wp-content/uploads/mp/files/publications/files/brief012-v1.pdf

Crossing, B., & Barassi-Rubio, C. (2013). *Women on temporary visas and domestic violence*. Sydney, NSW: Australian Domestic & Family Violence Clearinghouse.

Dhamoon, R. K., & Hankivsky, O. (2011). Why the theory and practice of intersectionality matter to health research and policy. In O. Hankivsky (Ed.), *Health inequities in*

Canada: Intersectional frameworks and practices (pp. 16–50). Vancouver: University of British Columbia Press.

Erez, E., Adelman, M., & Gregory, C. (2009). Intersections of immigration and domestic violence: Voices of battered immigrant women. *Feminist Criminology, 4*(1), 32–56.

Frost, M. (2014). The three rules of being Aboriginal: Anxiety and violence in Central Australia. *Australian Aboriginal Studies, 1,* 90–97.

Ghafournia, N. (2011). Battered at home, played down in policy: Migrant women and domestic violence in Australia. *Aggression and Violent Behavior, 16*(3), 207–213.

Haebich, A. (2001). Between knowing and not knowing: Public knowledge of the Stolen Generations. *Aboriginal History, 25,* 70–90.

Haebich, A. (2011). Forgetting indigenous histories: Cases from the history of Australia's Stolen Generations. *Journal of Social History, 44*(4), 1033–1046.

Haldane, H. (2009). The provision of culturally specific care for victims of family violence in Aotearoa/New Zealand. *Global Public Health, 4*(5), 477–489.

Hovane, V. (2015). Improving outcomes through a shared understanding of family violence in Aboriginal communities: Towards an Aboriginal theory of family violence. *InPsych: The Bulletin of the Australian Psychological Society Ltd, 37*(5), 18–19.

Hyman, I., Mason, R., Guruge, S., Berman, H., Kanagaratnam, P., & Manuel, L. (2011). Perceptions of factors contributing to intimate partner violence among Sri Lankan Tamil immigrant women in Canada. *Health Care for Women International, 32*(9), 779–794.

Johnson, M. P. (2010). *A typology of domestic violence: Intimate terrorism, violent resistance, and situational couple violence.* Boston: Northeastern University Press.

Johnson, M. P., & Leone, J. M. (2005). The differential effects of intimate terrorism and situational couple violence: Findings from the National Violence against Women Survey. *Journal of Family Issues, 26*(3), 322–349.

Kasturirangan, A., Krishnan, S., & Riger, S. (2004). The impact of culture and minority status on women's experiences of domestic violence. *Trauma, Violence & Abuse, 5*(4), 318–331.

Kennedy, A. C. (2005). Resilience among urban adolescent mothers living with violence: Listening to their stories. *Violence against Women, 11*(12), 1490–1514.

Kwan, J. (2015). From taboo to epidemic: Family violence within aboriginal communities. *Global Social Welfare, 2*(1), 1–8.

Mackay, E., Gibson, A., Huetee, L., & Beecham, D. (2015). *Perpetrator interventions in Australia: Key findings and future directions* (Compass Research to Policy and Practice Issue No. PP01). Sydney, NSW: Australian Domestic & Family Violence Clearinghouse.

Mansley, E. A. (2009). *Intimate partner violence: Race, social class, and masculinity.* El Paso, TX: LFB Scholarly Pub.

Mayock, P., Sheridan, S., & Parker, S. (2012). Migrant women and homelessness: The role of gender-based violence. *European Journal of Homelessness, 6*(1), 59–82.

Menjivar, C., & Salcido, O. (2002). Immigrant women and domestic violence: Common experiences in different countries. *Gender & Society, 16*(6), 898–920.

Messing, J. T., Amanor-Boadu, Y., Cavanaugh, C. E., Glass, N. E., & Campbell, J. C. (2013). Culturally competent intimate partner violence risk assessment: Adapting the Danger Assessment for immigrant women. *Social Work Research, 37*(3), 263–275.

Moran, M. (2016). *Serious whitefella stuff: When solutions became the problem in indigenous affairs.* Melbourne, VIC: Melbourne University Press.

Murphy, S. B., Risley, C. C., & Gerdes, K. (2003). American Indian women and domestic violence: The lived experience. *Journal of Human Behavior in the Social Environment*, 7(3), 159–181.

Nancarrow, H. (2006). In search of justice for domestic and family violence: Indigenous and non-Indigenous Australian women's perspectives. *Theoretical Criminology*, 10(1), 87–106.

Native Counselling Services of Alberta. (2001). *A cost: Benefit analysis of Hollow Water's community holistic circle healing process*. Alberta, Canada: Solicitor General Canada.

Ogunsiji, O., & Clisdell, E. (2017). Intimate partner violence prevention and reduction: A review of literature. *Health Care for Women International*, 38(5), 439–462.

Okeke-Ihejirika, P., Yohani, S., Muster, J., Ndem, A., Chambers, T., & Pow, V. (2018). A scoping review on intimate partner violence in Canada's immigrant communities. *Trauma, Violence, & Abuse*. Advance online publication. doi: 10.1177/1524838018789156

Olsen, A., & Lovett, R. (2016). Australia's National Research Organisation for Women: Existing knowledge, practice and responses to violence against women in Australian Indigenous communities: *Landscapes: State of knowledge paper*. Issue 2 January. ANROWS: Sydney.

Phillips, J., & Vandenbroek, P. (2014). *Domestic, family and sexual violence in Australia: An overview of the issues* (Parliamentary Library Research Paper Series No. 2014–15). Retrieved from http://parlinfo.aph.gov.au/parlInfo/download/library/prspub/3447585/upload_binary/3447585.pdf;fileType=application/pdf

Prosman, G. J., Jansen, S. J., Lo Fo Wong, S. H., & Lagro-Janssen, A. L. (2011). Prevalence of intimate partner violence among migrant and native women attending general practice and the association between intimate partner violence and depression. *Family Practice*, 28(3), 267–271.

Reina, A. S., Maldonado, M. M., & Lohman, B. J. (2013). Undocumented Latina networks and responses to domestic violence in a new immigrant gateway: Toward a place-specific analysis. *Violence against Women*, 19(12), 1472–1497.

Richards, K. (2011). *Children's exposure to domestic violence in Australia* (Trends and Issues in Crime and Criminal Justice Series, No 419). Canberra: Australian Institute of Criminology. Retrieved from www.aic.gov.au/media_library/publications/tandi_pdf/tandi419.pdf

Sabina, C., Cuevas, C. A., & Zadnik, E. (2015). Intimate partner violence among Latino women: Rates and cultural correlates. *Journal of Family Violence*, 30(1), 35–47.

Simon-Kumar, R., Kurian, P., Young-Silcock, F., & Narasimhan, N. (2017). Mobilising culture against domestic violence in migrant and ethnic communities: Practitioner perspectives from Aotearoa/New Zealand. *Health & Social Care in the Community*, 25(4), 1387–1395.

Sokoloff, N. J., & Pearce, S. C. (2011). Intersections, immigration, and partner violence: A view from a new gateway: Baltimore, Maryland. *Women & Criminal Justice*, 21(3), 250–266.

Stark, E. (2007). *Coercive control: How men entrap women in personal life*. Oxford, UK: Oxford University Press.

Tartakovsky, E., & Mezhibovsky, S. (2012). Female immigrant victims of domestic violence: A comparison between immigrants from the former Soviet Union in Israel and Israeli-born Women. *Journal of Family Violence*, 27(6), 561–572.

Thomas, J., & Thomson, K. (2012, November). *Men's healing circles*. Paper presented at the No to Violence Conference, Melbourne.

Ware, J., Frost, A., & Hoy, A. (2010). A review of the use of therapeutic communities with sexual offenders. *International Journal of Offender Therapy and Comparative Criminology, 54*(5), 721–742.

Willis, M. (2011). *Non-disclosure of violence in Australia Indigenous communities* (Trends & Issues in Crime and Criminal Justice No. 405). Canberra: Australian Institute of Criminology. Retrieved from www.aic.gov.au/media_library/publications/tandi_pdf/tandi405.pdf

Yoshioka, M., & Choi, D. (2005). Culture and interpersonal violence research: Paradigm shift to create a full continuum of domestic violence services. *Journal of Interpersonal Violence, 20*(4), 513–519.

Chapter 9

Tackling domestic and family violence

Primary, secondary, and tertiary prevention

Introduction

The overarching aim of prevention strategies is to reduce (or prevent) the occurrence or reoccurrence of a specific problem. This is not limited to DFV – preventative and reactive interventions exist for a broad range of social and behavioural issues (Krug, Mercy, Dahlberg, & Zwi, 2002), for example bullying, substance misuse, or parental neglect. Throughout this chapter, we will unpack three overarching tiers of interventions designed to stop DFV and discuss their aims and objectives, along with some of their overlapping elements. Prevention strategies are often categorised into primary, secondary, and tertiary prevention tiers. You will notice that these concepts or categories are not static. Instead, they are dynamic and often intertwined (Michau, Horn, Bank, Dutt, & Zimmerman, 2015).

In line with the gendered framework applied throughout this book, the focus on prevention programs in this chapter takes a primarily gendered approach. The need for such an approach arises from the underlying factors contributing to risk and manifestation of DFV discussed in Chapters 2 and 3 Key drivers include social norms and attitudes that foster environments in which violence against women is permissible. As a result, a wide range of prevention strategies to address the issue of DFV focus on addressing the wider social context in which DFV occurs (Storer, Casey, Carlson, Edleson, & Tolman, 2016). It is important to note (as highlighted in Chapter 7) that research and practice evidence, albeit limited in some areas, identifies a diverse range of relationships that can be affected by DFV, including same-sex couple, adult child–parent, and other extended family relationships. The general concepts of prevention can be applied beyond a gendered paradigm. However, you will notice that many prevention strategies adopt a gendered focus on intimate partner and dating violence, informed by the gendered pattern of DFV and its underlying social attitudes and beliefs, addressed in Chapters 2 and 3.

What is prevention?

Globally, the prevention of violence against women, including DFV, is strongly informed by public health approaches that aim to address an issue of social and community concern (in this case DFV; Krug et al., 2002; Storer et al., 2016). In Australia, the National Public Health Partnership (NPHP) (2006, p. 5) defines public health as the "organised response by society to protect and promote health and to prevent injury, illness and disability". The public health approach mainly has primary prevention as its goal; in other words, it "aims to prevent through an organised effort, the occurrence of health problems in whole populations before they occur" (NPHP, 2006, p. 5). The ultimate goal here, therefore, is to pre-empt the occurrence of DFV through community education and awareness. However, given the pervasive nature and prevalence of the issue, other strategies are required to tackle DFV where it has already manifested in the form of victimisation, perpetration, or children's exposure to DFV. When addressing existing and persistent social problems, such as DFV, prevention strategies often take a more holistic approach, incorporating primary, secondary, and tertiary strategies. In the following section, we will explore the different tiers of prevention along with the benefits and challenges associated with each.

Primary, secondary, and tertiary prevention

So, what do we mean by primary, secondary, and tertiary prevention, and how can we apply these approaches to prevention when targeting DFV? We offer an adapted version of national and international definitions used primarily in public health approaches to prevention (Storer et al., 2016; Wolfe & Jaffe, 1999). When reviewing the literature around prevention, you will notice that secondary prevention is also often referred to as "early intervention" due to its proactive approach towards cases where there is an increased risk of DFV. The following section provides a snapshot of the aims of different prevention approaches in the context of DFV:

- Through addressing underlying causes, **primary prevention** approaches aim to prevent DFV across whole populations before it occurs
- **Secondary prevention** (or early intervention) approaches aim to change practices or to build skills of individuals or groups who are at an elevated risk of perpetrating or experiencing DFV
- **Tertiary prevention** refers to approaches in response to identified occurrences of DFV and those affected by it, such as provision of crisis accommodation to victims and children, or punitive and rehabilitative responses to perpetrators

As indicated earlier on in this chapter, these different tiers of prevention frequently complement each other, as highlighted by Flood (2014, p. 9):

> rapid and coordinated responses to individuals perpetrating . . . violence can reduce their opportunities for and likelihood of further perpetration, while effective responses to victims and survivors can reduce the impact of victimisa-

tion and prevent re-victimisation. In short, the effective and systematic application of tertiary strategies complements and supports primary prevention.

Other writers agree that the different tiers of prevention not only complement each other but also overlap to some extent. Instead of being clear-cut, static categories, they can be fluid in their objectives and outcomes. Storer and colleagues (2016), for example, unpack the nature of certain crisis responses (i.e. tertiary prevention) to DFV as having the capacity to protect children from subsequent exposure to DFV by interrupting the cycle of violence and thus reducing the risk of intergenerational transmission of DFV (i.e. primary and secondary prevention).

Primary prevention

As per the aforementioned definition, primary prevention has a very clear target population and aim. That is, to prevent the occurrence of a particular problem (in this case DFV) through educating a whole population that has not yet experienced the problem (i.e. the target population). Due to its broad approach to educating whole populations (such as through school-based intervention programs or awareness campaigns run via media outlets), at-risk populations may logically be captured, albeit not forming the primary target population. However, their already elevated level of risk may minimise their responsiveness to such campaigns. However, the objective of primary prevention is to generate awareness of and intolerance to attitudes and practices that support DFV among the wider population to prevent them from occurring in our communities.

In 2015, for example, Australia took a national approach to developing a framework for changing individual and community attitudes around gender inequality and related forms of abuse, such as DFV, by releasing *Change the Story: A Shared Framework for the Primary Prevention of Violence Against Women and Their Children in Australia*.

According to this framework (Our Watch, 2015, p. 17):

> Primary prevention requires changing the social conditions, such as gender inequality, that excuse, justify or even promote violence against women and their children. Individual behavioural change may be the intended result of prevention activity, but such change cannot be achieved prior to, or in isolation from, a broader change in the underlying drivers of such violence across communities, organisations and society as a whole. A primary prevention approach works across the whole population to address the attitudes, practices and power differentials that drive violence against women and their children.

This approach highlights the need for a combination of primary prevention approaches, including early education around respectful relationships targeting young people as well as wider awareness-raising campaigns targeting men, women, and the community as a whole.

Primary prevention strategies targeting young people

Primary prevention approaches frequently refer to "respectful relationships" (see for example Flood, Fergus, & Heenan, 2009; Le Brocque, Kapelle, Meyer, & Haynes, 2014). Not only are these meant to be modelled by a diverse range of people, but particular focus is placed on respectful relationships education and its implementation in educational settings for young people. Respectful relationships education is a popular example of what primary prevention can look like, particular in the form of an integrated educational strategy as part of national curricula to provide early education around DFV, including dating violence, to all students (Foshee et al., 2004; Le Brocque et al., 2014; Our Watch, 2015).

Curriculum-based educational programs are designed to teach young people how to identify healthy – or respectful – interpersonal relationships. They take a skill-based approach to equip young people with the necessary skills to identify prosocial and respectful attitudes, beliefs, and habits, utilise them appropriately, and challenge those who do not. Evaluations show that in order to be effective, these types of primary prevention programs need to be implemented as part of a whole-of-school approach to generate and model an environment of respectful relationships that goes beyond the classroom content (Flood et al., 2009; Le Brocque et al., 2014).

While respectful relationships programs are highly regarded by many practitioners, researchers, and policymakers, they present some challenges. As with most types of intervention, there is usually no one-size-fits-all approach. Social issues, such as DFV, are highly complex, and target populations for educational programs can be highly diverse. One of the challenges associated with primary prevention approaches such as school-based interventions is that they often fail to capture high-risk populations, such as those displaying frequent truant behaviour. Frequent truancy is often associated with complex family issues. Some research suggests a correlation between truancy and the occurrence of DFV in families with complex needs (Martin, 2002; Richards, 2011). As a result, school-based prevention programs may not reach students in greatest need of primary prevention and/or early intervention.

Another challenge associated with standardised school-based prevention programs is their mainstream approach to respectful relationships education. In order to address the educational needs of all young people, prevention programs need to be tailored towards a diverse range of audiences of varying religious and cultural backgrounds, differences in sexual identity and orientation, and varying degrees of cognitive abilities and language skills. Failing to acknowledge the diversity of young people and their (dating) relationships increases the risk of alienating a broad range of young people, including those most vulnerable, due to diversity and associated marginalisation. As an example, when delivering prevention programs to students from migrant or refugee backgrounds in national or international settings, programs need to be culturally informed and conducted by suitable personnel. In some cases, culturally sensitive prevention programs may be most effective when conducted at a community level by suitable community stakeholders rather than in mainstream educational settings.

Primary prevention strategies targeting whole populations

International research evidence highlights the need for a whole-of-community approach to ensure that what young people learn at school is further supported and modelled within the family and the broader community (Krug et al., 2002; Storer et al., 2016; Our Watch, 2015). This strongly links to the initial definition provided earlier in this chapter, whereby these approaches prevent DFV across whole populations.

Some prominent examples of primary prevention, targeting the wider community through education and awareness raising, include media campaigns, such as the global NO MORE Project (The NO MORE Project, 2018) and similar campaigns addressing DFV and sexual assault, in countries like Australia, the UK, and the US. In line with the overarching objectives of primary prevention, these campaigns aim to:

- Raise awareness of the various habits and practices that constitute DFV
- Educate people that there is no excuse or tolerance of such behaviour in the wider community
- Raise awareness around relevant resources available to support those directly affected by DFV, those wanting to change their behaviour, or those (e.g. family and friends) concerned for someone's safety or someone's behaviour towards their partner or family
- Raise awareness around how to respond or intervene if witnessing DFV as a third party (bystander intervention education)

Most of these types of campaigns raise awareness and understanding around what constitutes DFV, the impact it can have at the individual, family, and broader social levels, and the support available to those affected or in need of further information. In addition, bystander approaches specifically aim to equip the target population with the confidence and skills required to intervene when observing signs of DFV. Bystander interventions have gained increasing interest among communities, organisations, and government departments in recent years by promoting the message that DFV is a matter of public concern and is thus everybody's responsibility to address (Jewkes, Flood, & Lang, 2015). This message is promoted via televised and online media campaigns, such as the Australian #dosomething or #besomeonewhodoessomething campaigns (Department of Premier and Cabinet, 2018), as well as specifically tailored bystander interventions. An internationally renowned example of a primary prevention program to equip potential bystanders with the necessary awareness, understanding, and skills to intervene is the American Mentors in Violence Prevention (MVP) program. Founded in the early 1990s by Jackson Katz, this program aims to change social norms and attitudes that foster the use and tolerance of abusive behaviour. Over the last two decades, a range of international locations and community settings have adopted the MVP program (including organisational, educational, and sports settings) to tackle different types of violence, such as DFV, sexual violence, and bullying (Jewkes et al., 2015; Katz, 1995; Katz, Heisterkamp, & Fleming, 2011; Williams & Neville, 2017).

Unlike primary prevention programs designed to educate young people about healthy relationships, the bystander approach incorporates a range of strategies to prevent DFV and other forms of violence (Katz, 1995; McMahon & Dick, 2011), with a focus on:

- Educating individuals and the wider community to identify early warning signs
- Equipping individuals with the relevant skills and confidence to take action
- Fostering a responsibility to act when identifying such signs through increased awareness

Secondary prevention

As indicated under the brief definitions of the different tiers of prevention earlier in this chapter, secondary prevention is also frequently referred to as early intervention. Unlike primary prevention, which targets whole populations in an attempt to stop DFV before it occurs, secondary prevention targets groups and individuals that have been identified as being at-risk. So-called at-risk populations include anyone who – based on the analysis of a research or practice evidence base – is known to be at an elevated risk of becoming a victim or perpetrator of DFV. One prominent example is children with past or current exposure to DFV in their family home. As discussed in Chapter 6, research on children's exposure to DFV has repeatedly identified the elevated risk of later life victimisation and/or perpetration of DFV among children exposed to parental DFV (Herrenkohl & Rousson, 2018; Richards, 2011; Whitfield, Anda, Dube, & Felitti, 2003).

The aim of early interventions here is to address underlying risk factors that foster the use and/or tolerance of abusive behaviours within intimate and family relationships. Risk factors include learnt or adopted attitudes, values, and beliefs, as well as the role of trauma in making children (especially girls) more vulnerable to violent victimisation by a future intimate partner. Common secondary prevention strategies to address such risk factors include educational programs targeting young people to assist them in developing age-appropriate, respectful social and interpersonal relationship skills, and trauma counselling to minimise the impact of childhood exposure to DFV (Krug et al., 2002; Wolfe & Jaffe, 1999). As discussed in Chapter 6, childhood exposure to DFV can have a range of short- and long-term effects, including mental health problems, self-harming behaviours, low self-esteem, and early onset substance misuse (Devaney, 2015; Dube, Anda, Felitti, Edwards, & Williamson, 2002). By addressing children's vulnerabilities associated with childhood exposure to DFV, these intervention strategies aim to prevent children's subsequent use of, or exposure to, DFV in their own teenage and adult relationships.

Tertiary prevention

Tertiary prevention covers a wide range of responses to known victims and perpetrators of DFV. While some tertiary interventions aim to prevent subsequent victimisation or perpetration of violence by limiting immediate opportunities for such experiences, others focus on generating long-term behaviour change. As alluded to earlier in this chapter, tertiary prevention strategies at times cut across multiple prevention tiers. Especially where children are involved, preventing the repeat victimisation of a parent also prevents children's ongoing exposure to DFV and thus has the potential to break the intergenerational cycle of DFV through different elements of prevention.

Immediate and short-term forms of tertiary prevention

Unlike primary prevention, which targets whole populations, tertiary prevention takes an individual-level approach by responding to the individual circumstances of known victims and perpetrators of DFV (Storer et al., 2016; Wolfe & Jaffe, 1999). In some instances, tertiary prevention aims to prevent future occurrences of DFV by removing the victim and/or perpetrator from the current situation and thus "disabling" or "incapacitating" them from being exposed to or engaging in the same behaviours in the immediate or short-term future. This type of prevention does not focus on behaviour change. Instead, it primarily focuses on creating an environment where reoffending/revictimisation is prevented by either removing the victim (and children) from the abusive situation (e.g. by offering crisis accommodation) or by removing the perpetrator (e.g. through arrest) and/or placing a protection order (also referred to as a restraining order in some jurisdictions) on him/her.

In some instances, these immediate responses of "incapacitation" can have a long-term prevention effect. For example, the immediate arrest or punishment of a perpetrator can have a long-term deterrent effect on his/her abusive behaviour. It is important to note that this is not the result of change in the underlying drivers of DFV (such as social norms, attitudes, and beliefs). Instead, this form of tertiary prevention achieves its goal through either incapacitation (i.e. by removing either the victim or perpetrator and thus the opportunity for further violence to occur) or deterrence (i.e. by creating fear of undesirable repercussions for the perpetrator). This differs from more long-term focused, rehabilitative approaches discussed in the next section.

Long-term tertiary prevention

Long-term tertiary prevention efforts often aim to prevent future occurrences of DFV by addressing the underlying and ongoing risk factors associated with victimisation and/or perpetration of DFV. Victim empowerment and offender rehabilitation are two key strategies of long-term tertiary prevention. The empowerment of victims can be supported through specialised victim support services. The overall objective here is to strengthen victims in their journey towards a life free from violence. This may require a range of holistic services, including counselling to help victims recover from the trauma associated with the exposure to DFV; access to affordable, safe, and sustainable housing and employment opportunities; and, in many cases, legal support (Meyer, 2014, 2015). Victim empowerment plays a crucial role in preventing victims' subsequent experiences of abuse and supporting their journeys towards safety (Meyer, 2012, 2015).

While victim-focused tertiary prevention strategies aim to build resilience and confidence in future help seeking to prevent subsequent exposure to DFV, perpetrator-focused strategies aim to change harmful attitudes, beliefs, and behaviours and thus reduce the risk of reoffending. The primary objective here is to generate behaviour change through psychoeducational, cognitive behavioural, and, at times, trauma-informed interventions. The most prominent type of intervention under this category are men's behaviour change programs (MBCPs), also referred to as batterer intervention programs (BIPs) or domestic violence perpetrator programs (DVPPs). In most cases, these programs complement other types of tertiary prevention (such as where the perpetrator has previously been arrested and prosecuted).

Similar to the short-term tertiary prevention strategies, the long-term variants, focusing on victim empowerment and perpetrator behaviour change, also cut across the different tiers of prevention. Men who successfully engage in MBCPs not only have a positive impact on their (ex-)partner's safety and wellbeing but also further reduce their children's exposure to DFV (where applicable, i.e. for men who are fathers or have a male carer role; Michau et al., 2015; Storer et al., 2016). In addition, men with changed and respectful attitudes towards women, gender equality, and relationship expectations can show a greater willingness to intervene as bystanders when observing signs of DFV within their social networks or the wider community (Storer et al., 2016).

The nature and suitability of tertiary prevention approaches, especially immediate ones, frequently relies on an identification of the level of risk posed by the perpetrator. Here, the level of risk identified when police and/or DFV specialist services respond to calls for help tends to inform subsequent measures such as perpetrator arrest or removal from the scene, as well as victims' relocation into crisis accommodation. Exceptions include jurisdictions where, for example, mandatory arrest policies are in place. In such instances, arrest is a common and legislated response rather than one informed by an individual risk assessment process, conducted by attending officers. Risk identification and assessment can further inform longer-term approaches to tertiary prevention. For example, intake processes into MBCPs as well as trauma counselling for victims and children can involve risk assessment processes to identify any current and ongoing risk to victims, children, and potentially perpetrators themselves (Stanley & Humphreys, 2014). While risk assessment is seen as good practice across a range of service systems that respond to victims, perpetrators, and/or whole families affected by DFV, research continues to observe persistent gaps in the use of risk assessment tools and processes (Hazel, Hamilton, Jaffe, & Campbell, 2013; Office of the State Coroner, 2014). We discuss the nature and role of risk assessment tools along with risk assessment processes hereafter.

Risk assessment tools

Risk assessment tools have predominantly been informed by risk factors associated with DFV escalating into fatal outcomes (Olszowy, Jaffe, Campbell, & Hamilton, 2013). It has been suggested that deaths occurring in the context of DFV and/or related relationship separation are the most preventable form of homicides due to their association with a wide range of identifiable risk factors. These include a history of DFV and specific types of abuse, prior agency contact by victims and/or perpetrators, and individual victim and perpetrator characteristics (Hazel et al., 2013; Office of the State Coroner, 2014). Risk factors informing commonly used risk assessment tools therefore include a focus on both victim and perpetrator characteristics and backgrounds.

While risk assessment tools have been informed by evidence derived from fatality reviews and are often used to predict (and avoid) fatal incidents of DFV, their use is not restricted to fatality-related outcomes. Different types of tools have been designed to predict different DFV outcomes. Moreover, their usefulness goes beyond addressing only DFV-related homicides (which, while a clearly significant issue, represent only a statistically small proportion of DFV outcomes; Bundeskriminalamt, 2018; Campbell et al., 2009). As part of the focus on risk assessment as a form of tertiary prevention, we provide an overview of three different risk assessment tools here, before discussing the implications of these tools and processes for violence prevention.

In the following subsections, we examine the Danger Assessment (DA), the Ontario Domestic Assault Risk Assessment (ODARA), and the Brief Spousal Assault Form for the Evaluation of Risk (B-SAFER). There are other forms of risk assessment available, including the original Spousal Assault Risk Assessment (SARA), which informed both the ODARA as well as the B-SAFER. In addition, other assessment tools are often adapted from the ones mentioned here by different agencies or service areas to meet specific service or client needs (Campbell et al., 2003; Olszowy et al., 2013). We chose the ones discussed here due to their evidence-based nature and their suitability across a range of service settings without requiring clinical administration and assessment skills (Campbell, Webster, & Glass, 2009; Olszowy et al., 2013).

Danger Assessment

The Danger Assessment (DA) was originally developed in 1985 to assess women's lethality risk in the context of DFV. It has since been revised into the Danger Assessment–Revised (DA-R) and is also used to identify victims' risk of revictimisation in general, rather than just lethality risk (Campbell et al., 2009). The DA (in its original as well as its revised form) is probably the most widely used and validated risk assessment tool (Campbell et al., 2009; Olszowy et al., 2013). It comprises two overarching sections. The first consists of a "diary", which asks victims to complete questions around experiences of DFV in the past 12 months. By having to recall specific incidents along with their severity and consequences on a calendar timeline, victims' memory is prompted, which then assists in identifying patterns of escalating severity. This is an improvement on the less reliable approach of simply asking whether the abuse has escalated in the past year. Research conducted to validate the DA found that in over one-third of cases where victims initially said that abuse severity and/or frequency had not changed in the past 12 months, their diary entries identified a clear pattern of increasing severity and/or frequency (Campbell et al., 1995). The second part of the DA focuses on identifying the presence or absence of risk indicators for intimate partner homicide. This section consists of 15 items in the original instrument and 20 items in the revised DA (Campbell et al., 2009).

Risk indicators screened for in the DA have been included based on research evidence derived from earlier research into intimate partner homicide. In addition to the assessment of increasing severity, the revised version includes the following 20 items (Campbell et al., 2009):

1   Increase in severity or frequency of physical violence in past 12 months
2   Perpetrator's access to a firearm
3   Separation
4   Perpetrator's employment status (unemployment is a risk factor)
5   Prior use of or threats with a weapon by perpetrator
6   Prior threats to kill the victim
7   Perpetrator has avoided arrest in the past
8   Victim has a child from a previous relationship residing with her/him
9   Perpetrator has forced the victim to have sex in the past
10   Attempted choking/strangulation
11   Perpetrator uses illicit substances
12   Perpetrator drinks excessively
13   Perpetrator shows controlling behaviour
14   Sexual jealousy
15   DFV during pregnancy
16   Perpetrator has threatened suicide
17   Perpetrator has threatened to harm the children
18   Victims believes perpetrator is capable of killing her/him

19 Perpetrator stalks victim
20 Victim has threatened or contemplated suicide

For a full overview of the checklist used for the DA, please see Campbell and colleagues' (2009) paper, or you can visit www.dangerassessment.org. For the purpose of "rating risk" of clients, the DA has a weighted score system, assigning different values to different items, depending on their level of risk (as identified by empirical evidence). DA scores allow the categorisation of victims into four levels of risk: variable danger, increased danger, severe danger, and extreme danger (Campbell et al., 2009). Some of the indicators identified as particularly risky include the perpetrator's access to a firearm, the use of a firearm in past threats or violent incidents, impending or recent separation after living together, and a pattern of controlling behaviour. When predicting the risk of women being killed by a male intimate (ex-)partner in a review of 220 individual cases, Campbell and colleagues (2003) found that a victim's risk of being killed by her abusive partner increases nine-fold if the couple had recently separated and the abusive partner was highly controlling. Even more concerning was the abuser's use of a gun to threaten or harm the victim in a past abusive incident, which increased victims' risk of being killed by a factor of 41. Overall, this study found that controlling behaviour, recent separation, and perpetrators' access to a firearm is a particularly dangerous combination for victims of DFV (Campbell et al., 2003). Other factors considered critical risk indicators are, for example, past threats to kill the victim, past incidents of attempted strangulation, constant jealousy, and forced sex (Women's Justice Center, 2004). Victims of intimate homicide are significantly more likely to experience a number of these risk indicators (i.e. have significantly higher-risk scores when their cases are reviewed against these items) compared to victims of DFV where fatal violence does not occur (Campbell et al., 2003; Campbell et al., 2009). Indeed, Campbell and colleagues (2009) found that seven or more of the common risk indicators are present in the majority of intimate partner homicides.

While this assessment tool has been tested and validated across different studies and populations and is said to be 90% accurate in predicting the different risk levels (Olszowy et al., 2013; Campbell et al., 2009), authors of the DA emphasise that "even at the lowest level (variable danger), the risk of lethal violence is never negligible and can change quickly" (Campbell et al., 2009, p. 662). This highlights that the risk associated with repeat victimisation of DFV is dynamic and needs to be reassessed over time by services or individuals who have ongoing contact with victims and/or perpetrators of DFV in order to maximise prevention of subsequent victimisation. Unlike some risk assessment tools, the DA does not require clinical skills or access to particular information systems (e.g. criminal justice records) and can therefore be used by any service provider coming into contact with victims of DFV (e.g. child protection, healthcare, specialist victim support services, legal services; Campbell et al., 2009).

In addition to its validation around predicting adult risk of revictimisation, the DA has been tested regarding its suitability to predict and prevent the risk of fatal acts of DFV targeting children (Olszowy et al., 2013). Overall, the tool was not able to predict differences between domestic homicides involving adult victims only and child victims (with or without the involvement of adult victims). However, one item, threats to harm the children, was significantly more common among cases where children had been targeted (Olszowy et al., 2013). This suggest two things. First, where victims are identified at risk of lethal violence, their children should be considered at risk as well and should therefore be included in any safety planning strategies. Second, where perpetrators make threats to harm the children, these need to be taken seriously, and unsupervised access to children needs to be carefully assessed and restricted until deemed safe.

Ontario Domestic Assault Risk Assessment (ODARA)

Unlike the DA, the ODARA is not an assessment tool to identify lethality risk. While it uses some similar perpetrator-based risk indicators to the ones used in the DA (e.g. history of DFV, abuse during pregnancy, threats to kill victim, children, or other people relevant to the victim, substance abuse problems, and perpetrator's stepchildren in the home), it has a number of items specifically focused on law enforcement responses. These include criminal history (other than DFV-related), history of violence (other than DFV-related), and any violation of protection, probation, or parole orders. In addition, this assessment tool includes an item on victims' barriers to accessing support (e.g. geographic isolation, language barriers, lack of access to transport). The ODARA is a 13-item assessment tool, specifically designed for use by law enforcement. It is based on the original SARA but is shorter and more simplified to suit the needs of law enforcement professionals, who tend to face time restrictions and lack the clinical training required to administer the original SARA (Hilton et al., 2004; Olszowy et al., 2013). The ODARA has been tested and validated across a number of studies. Identified risk scores have been found to correlate with those of the DA and SARA, suggesting that the ODARA is able to accurately predict risk of re-assault and re-assault severity by an intimate (ex-)partner (Hilton et al., 2004; Olszowy et al., 2013).

For more detail on the ODARA, please refer to the following website:

> https://novascotia.ca/pps/publications/ca_manual/ProsecutionPolicies/
> ODARA%20RISK%20ASSESSMENTS%20IN%20SPOUSAL
> PARTNER%20CASES%20ALL.pdf

Brief Spousal Assault Form for the Evaluation of Risk (B-SAFER)

Like the ODARA, the B-SAFER is based on the original SARA. Designed for use by law enforcement (especially police officers), the B-SAFER has been reduced from 20 items down to a 10-item perpetrator-focused tool (Olszowy et al., 2013). Its underlying objective is to go beyond identifying risk of re-assault and inform risk management by police and other law enforcement professionals (Storey et al., 2014). Unlike the SARA, it does not require clinical psychology skills associated with assessing the presence of mental health issues captured by other instruments. Further, like the ODARA, the B-SAFER has been designed to predict risk of re-assault rather than risk of fatal violence. This assessment tool comprises two overarching sections. The first comprises five items identifying perpetrator risk-associated behaviour, including violent acts, violent threats, escalation of abuse, violation of court orders, and holding violent attitudes (Petersson, Strand, & Selenius, 2019). The second section comprises items identifying perpetrators' psychosocial adjustment, including history of general (non-DFV) criminality, intimate relationship problems (e.g. struggling to form or maintain intimate relationships), employment problems, substance misuse problems, and mental health problems (Petersson et al., 2019). This tool allows assessors to distinguish antisocial from family-only offenders and identify their level of risk (Petersson et al., 2019). Research shows that antisocial offenders are more likely to re-assault their victim and that their pattern of violence is more likely to escalate (Loinaz, 2014; Petersson et al., 2019; Storey, Kropp, Hart, Belfrage, & Strand, 2014).

The B-SAFER was originally developed in English and has been translated into various languages, including Italian, Norwegian, Portuguese, and Swedish (Storey et al., 2014). Validation of the B-SAFER has been by indirect means, as it was derived from the validated SARA tool. However, a number of studies have evaluated the effectiveness of the B-SAFER in identifying and managing risk and have revealed positive results, especially for identifying and managing high-risk cases (Loinaz, 2014; Olszowy et al., 2013; Storey et al., 2014). A recent study by Petersson and colleagues (2019) found that the B-SAFER is able to accurately predict risk of severe and potentially deadly violence in around 75% of antisocial offenders and 89% of family-only perpetrators. The B-SAFER is particularly appealing and suitable to frontline law enforcement professionals due to its succinct nature and the fact no specific clinical skills are required to accurately identify risk.

Implications for tertiary prevention

The various aspects of DFV-related homicide (with a particular focus on intimate partner homicide) raise a number of implications for practice. First and foremost, they highlight that risk assessment tools and processes play a substantial role in predicting risk of revictimisation and thus informing relevant tertiary prevention strategies (Campbell et al., 2009; Hilton et al., 2004; Loinaz, 2014; Petersson et al., 2019; Olszowy et al., 2013; Storey et al., 2014). The evidence base discussed here raises some key implications of the potential benefit of tertiary prevention approaches to DFV:

- The use of risk assessment across service systems to prevent revictimisation

- Practitioner awareness of the key risk indicators predicting an increased risk of repeat and potentially fatal victimisation
- Practitioner understanding of overlap between risk for the non-abusive parent and risk for any children in the household
- Organisational and practitioner awareness of assessment tools suitable to their area of practice (e.g. justice professionals may benefit from using a tool that has been specifically designed for this area of practice)
- Practitioner awareness of implications of different risk factors (e.g. safeguards required for working with separating victims)
- Availability of clear referral pathways to ensure immediate responses to high-risk clients (e.g. through an established integrated response to DFV or other collaborative approaches)

The latter is particularly significant because risk assessment is only one element informing tertiary prevention approaches. Risk management strategies surrounding decisions to arrest the perpetrator, refer a perpetrator into an MBCP, and/or relocate a victim and children into crisis accommodation are equally important. As emphasised by Storey and colleagues (2014), risk assessment tools should not only be used to identify risk but also to further manage the risk to prevent revictimisation through informed responses. Some victims may require immediate crisis accommodation, whereas others may wish to remain in their current place of residence with a safety plan in place. Essentially, risk assessment tools are designed to identify elevated levels of risk to inform subsequent service responses. Not all victims are ready (or want) to leave the abusive partner when encountering different service systems. It is therefore important to ensure that initial risk assessment is followed by informed risk management strategies, which may include safety planning, referrals to other relevant services, assisting with obtaining a protection order (also referred to as restraining orders in some jurisdictions), and ensuring that children are considered in the overall risk assessment and safety planning. This is where holistic responses to victims, perpetrators, and families affected by DFV become relevant. The role and nature of such responses is further examined in the following chapter on good practice in responding to DFV.

Summary

In this chapter, we described in detail the three overarching tiers of prevention and their role in responding to victims, perpetrators, families, and wider communities affected by DFV. Ranging from whole-population approaches to working with individual victims and perpetrators, the first part of this chapter highlighted the diverse range of prevention strategies available and the target populations that exist. In the second part of this chapter, we examined the role of risk assessment in informing tertiary prevention strategies. We discussed three examples of internationally used risk assessment tools suitable for different service settings, including the Danger Assessment, the ODARA, and the B-SAFER. All evidence-based, these tools are used to identify risk of revictimisation more broadly as well as risk of fatal outcomes. Implications discussed throughout this chapter for different areas of practice highlighted that the different tiers of prevention are most effective if applied in a holistic approach to violence prevention. In other words, while the use of and exposure to DFV is an individual-level experience, its prevention requires individual-level responses that are embedded into wider whole-population approaches, drawing on education and awareness raising (Krug et al., 2002; Michau et al., 2015; Storer et al., 2016). We further discuss the role of good practice in DFV prevention and service delivery in the next chapter.

References

Bundeskriminalamt. (2018). *Partnerschaftsgewalt: Kriminalstatistische Auswertung – Berichtsjahr 2017*. Wiesbaden: Bundeskriminalamt. Retrieved from www.bka.de/SharedDocs/Downloads/DE/Publikationen/JahresberichteUndLagebilder/Partnerschaftsgewalt/Partnerschaftsgewalt_2017.pdf

Campbell, J. C. (1995). *Assessing dangerousness*. Newbury Park, CA: Sage Publications.

Campbell, J. C., Webster, D. W., & Glass, N. (2009). The Danger Assessment: Validation of a lethality risk assessment instrument for intimate partner femicide. *Journal of Interpersonal Violence, 24*(4), 653–674.

Campbell, J. C., Webster, D. W., Koziol-McLain, J., Block, C., Campbell, D., Curry, M. A., . . ., Sharps, P. (2003). Risk factors for femicide in abusive relationships: Results from a multisite case control study. *American Journal of Public Health, 93*(7), 1089–1097.

Department of Premier and Cabinet (Queensland). (2018). *Bystander campaigns*. Retrieved from https://campaigns.premiers.qld.gov.au/dosomething/when-to-do-something.aspx

Devaney, J. (2015). Research review: The impact of domestic violence on children. *Irish Probation Journal, 12*, 79–94.

Dube, S. R., Anda, R. F., Felitti, V. J., Edwards, V. J., & Williamson, D. F. (2002). Exposure to abuse, neglect, and household dysfunction among adults who witnessed intimate partner violence as children: Implications for health and social services. *Violence & Victims, 17*(1), 3–17.

Flood, M. (2014). Preventing violence against women and girls. In R. J. Burke & D. J. Major (Eds.), *Gender in organizations: Are men allies or adversaries to women's career advancement?* (pp. 405–427). United States: Edward Elgar Publishing Ltd.

Flood, M., Fergus, L., & Heenan, M. (2009). *Respectful relationships education: Violence prevention and respectful relationships education in Victorian secondary schools*. Victoria: Department of Education and Early Childhood Development. Retrieved from https://eprints.qut.edu.au/103414/

Foshee, V. A., Bauman, K. E., Ennett, S. T., Linder, G. F., Benefield, T., & Suchindran, C. (2004). Assessing the long-term effects of the Safe Dates program and a booster in preventing and reducing adolescent dating violence victimization and perpetration. *American Journal of Public Health, 94*(4), 619–624.

Hazel, L., Hamilton, A., Jaffe, P., & Campbell, M. (2013). Assessing children's risk for homicide in the context of domestic violence. *Journal of Family Violence, 28*(2), 179–189.

Herrenkohl, T., & Rousson, A. (2018). IPV and the intergenerational transmission of violence. *Family & Intimate Partner Violence Quarterly, 10*(4), 39–46.

Hilton, N. Z., Harris, G. T., Rice, M. E., Lang, C., Cormier, C. A., & Lines, K. J. (2004). A brief actuarial assessment for the prediction of wife assault recidivism: The Ontario Domestic Assault Risk Assessment. *Psychological Assessment, 16*(3), 267–275.

Jewkes, R., Flood, M., & Lang, J. (2015). From work with men and boys to changes of social norms and reduction of inequities in gender relations: A conceptual shift in prevention of violence against women and girls. *The Lancet, 385*(9977), 1580–1589.

Katz, J. (1995). Reconstructing masculinity in the locker room: The Mentors in Violence Prevention Project. *Harvard Educational Review, 65*(2), 163–175.

Katz, J., Heisterkamp, H. A., & Fleming, W. M. (2011). The social justice roots of the mentors in violence prevention model and its application in a high school setting. *Violence against Women, 17*(6), 684–702.

Krug, E. G., Mercy, J. A., Dahlberg, L. L., & Zwi, A. B. (2002). The world report on violence and health. *The Lancet, 360*(9339), 1083–1088.

Le Brocque, R., Kapelle, R., Meyer, S., & Haynes, M. (2014). *Respectful relationships evaluation, final report, prepared for Department of Social Services.* Brisbane: The University of Queensland. Retrieved from www.dss.gov.au/sites/default/files/documents/01_2016/3-1-respectful-relationships-evaluation-summary-of-findings.pdf

Loinaz, I. (2014). Typologies, risk and recidivism in partner-violent men with the B-SAFER: A pilot study. *Psychology, Crime & Law, 20*(2), 183–198.

Martin, S. G. (2002). Children exposed to domestic violence: Psychological considerations for health care practitioners. *Holistic Nursing Practice, 16*(3), 7–15.

McMahon, S., & Dick, A. (2011). "Being in a room with like-minded men": An exploratory study of men's participation in a bystander intervention program to prevent intimate partner violence. *Journal of Men's Studies, 19*(1), 3–18.

Meyer, S. (2012). Why women stay: A theoretical examination of rational choice and moral reasoning in the context of intimate partner violence. *Australian & New Zealand Journal of Criminology, 45*(2), 179–193.

Meyer, S. (2014). *Victims' experiences of short- and long-term safety and wellbeing: Findings from an examination of an integrated response to domestic violence* (Trends and Issues in Crime and Criminal Justice No. 478). Canberra: Australian Institute of Criminology.

Meyer, S. (2015). Examining women's agency in managing intimate partner violence and the related risk of homelessness: The role of harm minimisation. *Global Public Health, 11*(1–2), 198–210.

Michau, L., Horn, J., Bank, A., Dutt, M., & Zimmerman, C. (2015). Prevention of violence against women and girls: Lessons from practice. *The Lancet, 385*(9978), 1672–1684.

National Public Health Partnership. (2006). *The language of prevention.* Melbourne: NPHP. Retrieved from www.nphp.gov.au

The NO MORE Project. (2018). *NO MORE: Together we can end domestic violence & sexual assault, Global Project.* Retrieved from https://nomore.org/

Office of the State Coroner. (2014). *Annual report 2013–2014.* Queensland Courts.

Olszowy, L., Jaffe, P. G., Campbell, M., & Hamilton, L. H. A. (2013). Effectiveness of risk assessment tools in differentiating child homicides from other domestic homicide cases. *Journal of Child Custody, 10*(2), 185–206.

Our Watch, Australia's National Research Organisation for Women's Safety (ANROWS), & VicHealth. (2015). *Change the story: A shared framework for the primary prevention of violence against women and their children in Australia.* Melbourne: Our

Watch. Retrieved from www.ourwatch.org.au/getmedia/0aa0109b-6b03-43f2-85fe-a9f5ec92ae4e/Change-the-story-framework-prevent-violence-women-children-AA-new.pdf.aspx

Petersson, J., Strand, S., & Selenius, H. (2019). Risk factors for intimate partner violence: A comparison of antisocial and family-only perpetrators. *Journal of Interpersonal Violence, 4*(2), 219–239.

Richards, K. (2011). *Children's exposure to domestic violence in Australia* (Trends and Issues in Crime and Criminal Justice Series, No 419). Canberra: Australian Institute of Criminology. Retrieved from www.aic.gov.au/media_library/publications/tandi_pdf/tandi419.pdf

Stanley, N., & Humphreys, C. (2014). Multi-agency risk assessment and management for children and families experiencing domestic violence. *Children & Youth Services Review, 47*(1), 78–85.

Storer, H., Casey, E., Carlson, J., Edleson, J., & Tolman, R. (2016). Primary prevention is? A global perspective on how organizations engaging men in preventing gender-based violence conceptualize and operationalize their work. *Violence against Women, 22*(2), 249–268.

Storey, J. E., Kropp, P. R., Hart, S. D., Belfrage, H., & Strand, S. (2014). Assessment and management of risk for intimate partner violence by police officers using the Brief Spousal Assault Form for the evaluation of risk. *Criminal Justice and Behavior, 41*(2), 256–271.

Whitfield, C., Anda, R., Dube, S., & Felitti, V. (2003). Violent childhood experiences and the risk of intimate partner violence in adults: Assessment in a large health maintenance organization. *Journal of Interpersonal Violence, 18*(2), 166–185.

Williams, D. J., & Neville, F. G. (2017). Qualitative evaluation of the Mentors in Violence Prevention pilot in Scottish high schools. *Psychology of Violence, 7*(2), 213–223.

Wolfe, D. A., & Jaffe, P. G. (1999). Emerging strategies in the prevention of domestic violence. *The Future of Children, 9*(3), 133–144.

Women's Justice Center. (2004). *Domestic violence homicide risk assessment.* Women's Justice Center. Retrieved from http://justicewomen.com/tips_dv_assessment.html

Chapter 10

Responding to domestic and family violence

Good practices

Practice and pragmatics

Let us first be clear about what we mean by "good" practice. As highlighted throughout this book, the DFV field is subject to controversy. We can assume that one person's good practice could be another's misguided time-wasting – or worse.

In Chapter 3, we reviewed various strands of theory relevant to DFV. We concluded that several of these strands, both separately and together, can be helpful in informing practice. However, when the prevalence and severity of violence against women, their children, and other family members is taken into account, we reasoned that a feminist gender analysis, informed by post-structuralist thinking, provides the most compelling and comprehensive account of DFV as a social problem. Here in Chapter 10, we operationalise this analysis with a view to substantiate the "good" in good practice. While this view sidelines alternative (and sometimes deeply antagonistic) perspectives, we maintain that a gendered violence focus provides a consistent model that best supports the integrated practice framework, which itself represents the core of most contemporary efforts in the field of DFV responses. It is also broadly consistent with the majority of current practice approaches (Gondolf, 2007, 2012; Kelly & Westmarland, 2015; Trabold, McMahon, Alsobrooks, Whitney, & Mittal, 2018) and program standards (Colorado Domestic Violence Offender Management Board, 2016; Hansen, 2016). This provides, we argue, a more cohesive and pragmatic formula to help make sense of the complex circumstances that are typically found in DFV practice.

We consider that this view distinguishes our approach in a progressive sense from reductionist approaches, which seek to tease out discrete individual factors – incidents, isolated "behaviours" disconnected from context, deficits, antecedents, or personality characteristics (Aaron & Beaulaurier, 2017). Such approaches refer to disembodied causative mechanisms – such as drives, pressures, stresses, strains, and blocks – that tend to imbue events with impelling qualities while inhibiting the recognition of intention and agency in persons. We favour a framework for practice that privileges holism and targets intention and pattern over mechanistic reductionism, which revolves around incident and algorithm. This latter perspective is related to the so-called evidence-based practice movement. While advocating for a rigorously scientific approach to identifying best practice, it prescribes characterisations of practice that might be both problematic in translating to real-world settings (Breckenridge & Hamer, 2014; Wagers, Pate, & Brinkley, 2017) and potentially alienating of practitioners (Gondolf, 2012; Velonis, Cheff, Finn, Davloor, & O'Campo, 2016). Although certainly not demoting the function and significance of research, we promote the importance of an inclusive, collaborative, and therefore integrated conceptualisation of the research endeavour in such a contested field. This is in fact more consistent with the original conception of evidence-based practice, and we tend to agree with Breckenridge and Hamer's (2014) conclusion that a critical and reflexive engagement with formal evidence is the defining feature of "best practice" and thus an effective response to DFV.

An example might be useful at this point. In terms of the implications for practice of the approach we advocate, we use the illustration of work in the area of men's behaviour change (MBC). Specifically, let us imagine the practitioner is concerned with developing an understanding of a man's abusive conduct. Practice approaches influenced by structuralist or functionalist theory strands (see Chapter 3) might pose the question "what *caused* this man to act violently towards his partner and children?" This enquiry may be inspired by the urge to make sense of factors relating to the man's abusive actions (e.g. his past experiences and his interpretation of those experiences based on his cognitive skills, which in turn might be shaped by his experiences, etc.) so that transformative change might be planned. However, this question around causation shines only a dim light on the man's intentions and personal agency – his *will*: in short, what he is uniquely responsible for and might be expected to exercise volition over. Richer and more inclusive material, we argue, is more likely to emerge from this broader enquiry as embodied in the question "what was the *context* in which this man *chose to use* violence?" This is not to deny that people experience constraints in their lives and restraints in relation to how they act (such as when they are faced with humiliation or threat), but such experiences, we argue, do not "cause" their actions. Furthermore, these actions might well have more to do with their relative position of power. Moreover, this latter question, by opening up possibilities for action by the man, provides room for him to exercise responsibility and, ultimately, accountability. Let us now move on to consider the application of this position to the purpose and principles of DFV practice. This is a matter about which, interestingly, there is broad agreement.

Two principles for practice: seeking common ground

From what we have established in this book, the clearest area for agreement among researchers and practitioners in DFV work is in terms of broad purpose and principles. The commonly accepted twin purpose of the work is to promote a) victim safety and b) perpetrator accountability. To be more specific, we could have some confidence in assuming agreement in the sector that the work should result in the wellbeing (safety, security, self-determination) of those who have been victimised, as well as the successful transfer of accountability to those who have perpetrated this kind of violence. Accountability could be taken to mean taking action to restore justice and to act with safety and respect in future on the basis of a felt sense of responsibility and commitment (Kelly & Westmarland, 2015). Extending this common-ground approach further allows us to identify a shared target for change: DFV itself. While this might at first appear a simplistic and obvious conclusion, we suggest that this shared focus on combating abuse per se concentrates effort on the problem and not on personal blameworthiness or on some broadly defined group. One useful corollary of this reasoning is that the notion of gender becomes a free-floating tool of analysis – a construct attached to aspects of the person's values, preferences, and commitments – rather than being inextricably tied to one's identity as man, woman, or any other sexual identity. In order to more clearly bring these abstract ideas closer to their implications for practice, let us next consider their application to principles of safety and accountability.

Safety

Understandably, feminist-based social activism, which has to a large extent impelled social responses to DFV, initially focused its efforts on the immediate safety of women and children, especially by means of providing physical refuge and then helping to restore independence and autonomy. In the broader picture, however, promoting safety in terms of *confronting* abuse is a consideration for everyone involved in that endeavour – including bystanders, practitioners, and particularly those with a history of using abuse. For this latter group, their contribution to safety is not merely in terms of ceasing violent practices or even desisting from those practices. A more active role and characterisation is in actively *resisting* violence in their lives and purposefully *refusing to engage* with it. This brings us back to the second common principle: accountability.

Accountability

The meaning of perpetrator accountability is another area of contention in this work. Set against the recognition of the often considerable harm experienced by DFV victims, the notion of accountability is sometimes understandably framed in a retributive sense. "Holding men accountable" is a phrase that regularly appears in service standards, mission statements, and agency goals. It is an injunction that is used readily in the face of blame-shifting tactics of perpetrators and its historical context of public semi-tolerance. This phrase might imply that the perpetrator should be spotlighted and shamed into admitting his culpability, thereby unburdening those who have carried guilt along with the many other legacies of abuse. Indeed, in some ways, it makes a great deal of pragmatic sense to continually monitor and report upon the subsequent actions of the man in a bid to manage ongoing risk. However, this kind of management should not be confused with the intention to objectify him. This would be tantamount to resorting to the tactics he is likely to have used in the course of abuse himself – and, surely, practitioners should not take up the tactics they seek to oppose. Rather, we suggest that accountability should take on an active sense in which the ongoing cessation of violence and attending to its consequences becomes, as soon and as far as possible, the responsibility of the perpetrator. Furthermore efforts should be made to recruit him into this undertaking by inviting him to take up an active role in the common purpose of resistance toward abuse.

In recent literature, there has been a good deal of attention on addressing men's *lack* of accountability (e.g. Cape & Garvin, 2009; Hamel, 2012). Arguably, this has directed perpetrators towards considering what they *should not* be (controlling, aggressive, possessive) and perhaps less towards what they *could* be. From a psychological perspective, "avoidance goals" (focusing on what one is trying to avoid) appear to be more difficult to achieve than "approach goals" (focusing on what one is trying to achieve; Ward & Stewart, 2003). Following this logic, then, MBC interventions should be conducted in a manner that encourages perpetrators to achieve human goods (such as competence, mastery, inner peace, intimacy, and belonging; Ward & Gannon, 2006) through templates for masculinity that promote non-abusive means and through relationships that foster mutual respect. A focused analysis that deconstructs masculinities should inform this intention. Alan Jenkins' book, *Becoming Ethical: A Parallel, Political Journey with Men Who Have Abused* (2009), as the title suggests, is oriented to the hopeful notion of the man becoming the partner/father he would prefer to become, rather than a sustained but static analysis of the partner/father he "is". Using the ideas of the philosopher Deleuze, Jenkins (2009) argues that the latter strategy is more likely to inadvertently invite the man to take up an entrenched position, but the former is more likely to be generative of change. According to this transformational way of thinking, in establishing "approach goals" for men who seek to commit to change, or who might consider such change, we should consider presenting models of masculinity that are both rewarding to the man *and* respectful of others.

Making sense of this important clinical goal of inviting accountability is well served in MBC practice with regard to the man's intentionality over time. We have discussed how making intentionality, as well as responsibility, central in this work can restore a sense of dignity and agency and also offer a pathway to restoration. The same applies to those who have experienced abuse. A sense of mastery is enabled when a woman's active attempts to escape and resist abuse are emphasised over characterising her response in terms of the absence of action and intention (DeKeseredy & Schwartz, 2009; Enander & Holmberg, 2008). In order to track intentionality, however, we need to address the pattern of resistance *over time* rather than as a series of separate, isolated acts of defence. Taking the defence out of context, a woman's use of physical force, for instance, might result in an inaccurate attribution of purpose and therefore an incorrect assignment of intention. Indeed, in studying how perpetrators evade responsibility, Kelly and Westmarland (2016) discovered that perpetrators relied on a description of separate and decontextualised events to account for their lack of culpability. We made brief reference to this phenomenon in Chapter 3, and next we turn to consider in greater detail the significance of it as a focus for practice.

Pattern or incident?

The practice of measuring DFV by enumerating incidents of violent events and then attributing these events to combinations of single-factor "triggers" (such as anger or alcohol) is attractive in its simplicity but problematic in at least two ways. In the first place, mere records of the incidents themselves tend to ignore more sinister and enduring patterns of conduct. Secondly, references to triggers and causes of DFV lend themselves to excusing violence by characterising it as a manifestation of seemingly irresistible drives and forces, such as addiction or rage.

We know from the experiences of those who are victimised through DFV that the nature of such harm is principally to do with the impact of experiences of oppression and confinement, reinforced by an enduring sense of fear fostered within the family or domestic context. The terms "coercive control" (Stark, 2007) and "intimate terrorism" (Johnson, 2010) have been coined to represent the strategies of perpetrators and the experiences of victims and are based on research related to the accounts of the lived experience of those who have survived this systematic and enduring abuse. Such outcomes have little to do with spikes of heightened emotion from someone "driven to breaking point" (by which we tend to excuse men – but, interestingly, rarely women) or accounts of bottled-up flows of testosterone. This kind of systematic abuse is better explained with reference to a purposeful and sustained pattern of conduct. Here, the *intention* of the man has to do with securing control and compliance of family members; the strategy is to induce fear though the invasive and intrusive tactics of intimidation, confinement, restriction, surveillance, isolation, and threat. Unlike other manifestations of violence that occur outside the home, this is enabled by culturally shaped expectations of marital roles, the legacy of protecting the "privacy" of the family environment, and much wider gender-based imbalances of power. This motivation for abuse, however, is rarely addressed in public media, and such tactics are, by design, difficult for its victims to report or for others to detect. It is easier to see the bruises and breakages that might well be the result of a tactic (physical violence) that is typically only used as a final resort – if at all (Crossman, Hardesty, & Raffaelli, 2016). More efficient tactics for the perpetrator are the telling gesture, the "accidental" barge, or "that look" – which has the rest of the household trained to be on alert and "walking on eggshells" (Jenkins, 1990) in fear of a possible escalation to overt violence. As a result, actions that are often considered types of abuse in themselves (psychological, emotional, sexual, or financial) might be more helpfully characterised as tactical tools in an overarching strategy of coercion and control.

In these ways, it is the pattern of abusive conduct and choices based on intention and enabled by power differentials (cf. "behaviours" motivated by "drives") that constitutes the kind of violence that we are principally concerned with in DFV practice. It makes sense, therefore, to investigate context and choice as much as "causation". A significant context for practice is the setting where practice takes place and the processes that might ensue. Thus, we turn to the form and process of practice and its dynamics of power.

DFV practice is political

Domestic and family violence is, we suggest, more helpfully addressed in practice as a *process* in a particular setting rather than as a series of discrete events. In contrast to tailoring interventions to people based directly and narrowly on an individually measured set of risk-causing and risk-preventing factors, an approach based on context and accountability also considers the intentions and commitments of persons to self, family, and community. This implies promoting a more inclusive perspective on risk assessment, and one that takes into account the constantly changing risk context, as well as "protective" resources. Approaches characterised by the desistance paradigm (McNeill, 2006; Morran, 2010), Jenkins' restorative model (1990; 2009) or the Good Lives framework (Ward, 2002; Ward, Yates, & Willis, 2012) represent intervention methods that engage persons' broader intentions for their lives. They tend to take into account the wider social and political environment from which DFV emerges, and in which interventions take place. They acknowledge that people are inextricably and actively connected through, and immersed in, that environment.

In presenting a mode of practice for working with men with a history of using DFV, Jenkins' restorative model (2009) emphasises the "parallel journey" of the practitioner and client. This notion recognises that both occupy a similar cultural space in the sense of gender role and stratification biases. In invoking this metaphor, the practitioner avoids moralistic distinctions by, for instance, applying moral labels to the man with a history of DFV, or by attributing narrow motivations to him. In this way, Jenkins (2009) seeks to neutralise power differentials and to avoid objectifying or subjugating practices. Furthermore, by avoiding a defensive response through these measures, the man is more open to electing his own ethical journey with respect to his abuse. This approach also makes way for "reaching out to the world of the other", a process that Jenkins (2009) identifies as seminal in the man appreciating the hurt his actions have caused and in avoiding superficial attempts at restoration.

Based on tenets of narrative therapy, and invoking what he refers to as an invitational approach, Jenkins (1990, 2009) describes a nuanced but rigorous paradigm in which he carefully communicates respect while persistently inviting accountability. This process is perhaps seen at its most distinctive in the handling of *shame*. Jenkins shuns not only the conventional psychological/psychiatric edict of avoiding shame by resolving it as *guilt* but also the hard-line "shaming" approach of, for example, "concept-based" correctional programs conducted in the US (Main, 1977). Instead, he endorses an attitude that invites the man to face up authentically and wholeheartedly to the consequences of his abusive conduct. This is intended not to punish, to provoke distress, or even to achieve emotionally empathic resonance, but rather to bring the offender face-to-face with his abusive conduct in order to honour himself and those he has harmed. The enactment and experience of this painful emotion, according to Jenkins, exposes underlying values. While these values might have been undermined in terms of the abuse he has perpetrated, it does point to their importance to him. Once identified in this way, these values might be explored and amplified. By way of contradistinction to some other approaches, Jenkins eschews expressions of remorse or apology for their own sake.

In this work, Jenkins' appeal to common humanity is not just an ethical and political stance but also reflects the broader recognition of the social and community roots of DFV and the preference for a response based largely on community development rather than psychotherapeutic disciplines or mainstream criminal justice interventions. This approach is supported by outcome evaluations, which tend to suggest that the extent to which MBC programs (MBCPs) are effective is a function of the extent to which they collaborate with other DFV practice systems and community resources (Gondolf, 1999, 2004).

A coordinated community response

Agencies and services have often faced criticism for working in separate policy and legislative silos and faced accusations that this has sometimes dangerously hampered the efficiency of response efforts (see for example, Diemer, Humphreys, Laming, & Smith, 2015). From his extensive and longstanding experience as a researcher and author on the subject of the effectiveness of interventions among men who perpetrate, Gondolf (2012) concludes that the effectiveness of MBCPs is closely linked to the "system" in which these operate and are embedded. He is referring here to the critical importance of an integrated response across agencies, departments, and community in responding to DFV offenders and offending. While this is in part to do with the *content* of the information, data, and insights that are communicated and shared, its value is also in terms of the *act* of sharing and the relational quality of the collaborations among the service community. It follows, then, that the nature of violence and abuse enacted in private spaces is best understood as that which reflects this systemic approach. Those who live their life according to "traditional" masculine principles and understand their identity as reflected in those ideals are responding to deeply embedded traditional, and consequently highly opaque, templates for the performance of gender. Identifying risk factors, attributing their genesis and history within circumstances, and inviting perpetrators to accept responsibility for managing them requires a practice model that will synthesise and integrate these factors in a manner that can direct practitioners in ways that address their relationship to social justice concerns, such as gender and power.

Countering cultural opacity

It is precisely this embeddedness of DFV within sociocultural structures, however, that lends it a cloak of invisibility. Such violence might be "hidden in plain sight" as relatives, neighbours, and passers-by turn a blind eye or excuse it as an artefact of family and relationship. Even those with a history of DFV themselves who have committed to change offer explanations of their abuse that are entrenched in culturally dominant beliefs and assumptions about masculinity, and thus fail to confront the abusiveness of their actions because of the conflation of gender with essentialist characteristics of manhood (Dobash & Dobash, 2011, 2015; Flood, 2016). Cultural aphorisms, such as "boys will be boys", reflect tropes that give voice to these assumptions.

For these reasons, we must constantly recognise that the possibilities for tackling DFV cannot be understood without reference to the wider economic and political context. In highly stratified societies, this work is produced, practiced, and developed within a constructed system of power and privilege; that is, within a specific set of hierarchical social relations, including relations based on gender. Arguably, this system of oppressive/abusive structures demands a systemic response. Kelly and Westmarland (2015), based on their research into the experiences of women, children, and their advocates in the UK, argue that DFV perpetrator programs should not be narrow, self-contained entities, but instead should contribute widely to the field through women's and children's services, as a point of reference in the field and in their reporting. This holistic and integrated conceptualisation of the work is also the point of connection with requirements to meet the wider needs of child and adult victims along with perpetrators.

Collaborative practices in men's behaviour change practice: systems work

The research literature suggests that MBCPs are most effective and function most appropriately when their contribution is considered in relation to the other components of the DFV response system – child protection, victim advocacy, criminal justice agencies, and so on (Gondolf, 2002, 2012). It follows that the more tightly these are aligned with and supported by other parts of this system in a collaborative community response, the more effective the overall system (Diemer et al., 2015). It also follows that the higher the internal consistency of MBCPs, in terms of program integrity and program logic, the more efficiently they will interlock with these other agencies and services (Day, Chung, O'Leary, & Carson, 2009). It is neither useful nor appropriate, then, to think of an MBCP as a standalone conveyer belt that "processes" clients as input, throughput, and output (Vlais, 2014).

Here, we are considering the practices of MBCPs in relation to the goodness of fit with the broader DFV response and accountability system. This is done on the basis of broad practice principles and goals for the sector and in relation to a range of current policy guidelines and standards. The focus, then, is on *systems* work rather than self-contained program work. In terms of program logic, the principles of MBCP practice need to be set alongside the critical considerations of coordination and timing with regard to other components of DFV intervention. A man's readiness for potential involvement with forums that might involve (ex-)partners and children must consider not only basic safety and wellbeing but also outcomes that are *just*. This is MBC integration in practice.

One attempt to operationalise this collaborative integrative philosophy has been in the form of "affiliational" or "one-stop-shop" organisations, which provide social services from multiple agencies within a single location. An example is the Family Justice Centres established by the US Department of Justice (Gwinn, Strack, Adams, Lovelace, & Norman, 2007; Townsend, Hunt, & Rhodes, 2005). Here, a principal "navigator" manages each case and liaises with other organisations within a hub of physically adjacent services. The emphasis is on efficiency of service provision and on convenience for clients who may otherwise have to engage with representatives from multiple agencies and tell their often harrowing story several times. Having to navigate a system unfamiliar to many, having to find suitable services they may not be aware of, and having to rely on more mainstream services are all examples of hindrances and delays that the one-stop organisation might mitigate. These agencies might also make help seeking more manageable by catering for practical needs such as on-site childcare, managing time off work, and travel.

Specifically, these organisations can potentially offer a gateway to all services. Plus, as most clients have multiple needs, agencies work in multidisciplinary teams to manage clients together. This enables agencies to:

- Reduce the number of meeting that clients need to attend
- Develop and manage highly integrated treatment plans
- Co-author court reports and other administrative duties

Working with diversity: practices of inclusion

The politics of DFV also play a key role in encompassing diversity. The guiding ideology of evolving feminisms have put a spotlight, for instance, on masculinity and the persistence of the traditional blueprint for its performance. This blueprint is seen to have a powerful and damaging influence in shaping expectations, for men especially, and these expectations often appear to outstrip men's capacity to conform to it, especially under the pressure of other factors such as poverty and underemployment (e.g. Irvine, Livingstone, & Flood, 2018). This power is seen throughout our cultural and colonial histories and constitutes aspects of a broader oppressive system. As argued in Chapters 3 and 8, the theory of intersectionality accounts for how disadvantage is layered and intersects with other drivers of DFV.

Cultures and their institutions, blighted by political forces such as colonisation, can be compromised in the capacity of their communities to counter and resist DFV. The hegemonic influence of colonisation can also blind practitioners to their power in defining realities for indigenous peoples. Almeida and Dolan-Delvecchio (1999, p. 654), in commenting on immigrant communities, make this point:

> Too frequently the impact of culture is either minimised or dangerously misunderstood by domestic violence practitioners embedded within treatment approaches that are guided by dominant – that is White-centric – theories. Minimization of the full meaning and impact of culture occurs, for example, when culture is theorised as an "add-on" characteristic. . . . The presumption is that "those people are just like us (Whites)" except for certain idiosyncratic patterns that one needs to keep in mind.

These authors go on to present the example of White practitioners in the US working with South Asian American women assuming that "cultural sensitivity" is expressed by characterising these women as uniquely duty-bound to husband and family. Rather than engage this group in exploring their broader preferences, intentions, and family and cultural commitments, practitioners see it as their singular duty to help the women to find ways to leave their marriages. This represents a form of discrimination that is consistent with cultural blindness and is rendered potentially oppressive in a cross-cultural context where one culture has power over another. A further and more pernicious extension of this thinking is where culture is seen to provide the *explanation* for DFV. A common experience reported by MBC practitioners from majority cultures is that clients from minority cultures claim that their violence towards women and children is normative. This, of course, is not an explanation that is likely to be countenanced by a practitioner from the man's own ethnic culture (Almeida & Dolan-Delvecchio, 1999).

This example of working in a context of ethno-cultural diversity is emblematic of the issues that arise in seeking to be inclusive in MBC practice while at the same time accommodating diversity. Attempts to conduct integrated practice must be wary of not promoting *exclusive* practice. The implications for working effectively with forms of diversity need to be reconciled with what are considered core elements of "mainstream" services in a process of tailoring intervention to the person and in and with their social environment. An ethical and socially responsible response in DFV practice takes into account both the cultural milieu in which DFV is generated as well as the direct implications for clients. This acknowledges those who have experienced abuse as survivors, as perpetrators, or both. Appropriate and effective practice nevertheless must respond to both need and responsibility.

Relating to clients as ethical agents

So far in this chapter we have focused on the far-reaching, constraining influences of history, social structure, and cultural expectation surroundings DFV. However, promoting realistic change through intervention is incomplete without recognising the agency of the person in efforts to resist such influences and to engage their preferences and commitments in living abuse-free lives. Failure by practitioners to actively appreciate such personal agency risks undermining client volition and instilling a sense of hopelessness in both those who use these services and those who provide them. In other words, practice needs to honour the felt sense of self-determination of the person. This, however, creates multiple challenges. For instance, in working with a man who has a history of DFV, the practitioner must take into account the socialised gender training that the man has experienced (but is probably only dimly aware of). At the same time, the practitioner is expected to engage the man in a way that is consistent with his recognition of his responsibility for the abuse he has enacted and his accountably for putting things to right. For those working with victims, how does the worker respect the intentions of a woman who is acting in accordance with her identity preferences and commitments to family and marital continuity, while also acting to preserve her safety? It is surely dangerously patronising to proceed as if he (the perpetrator) is merely enacting social learning and she (the victim) is merely the passive product of abuse. Respecting her efforts to resist violence must not only be acknowledged but also be placed front and centre around which efforts to assist are deployed.

In the remainder of this chapter, we address such challenges on the basis of our stance on practice principles and their implications, followed by considering implications in more detail, referring to examples from the literature about current practices. We do this by first reviewing implications for working with those who have a history of using violence, and then for those who have been subject to such abuse. We conclude with a summary of the key features of current practice strategies.

Perpetrator intervention

As described in Chapter 4, the most common approach to perpetrator intervention, alongside criminal justice efforts, are group-based programs based on feminist psychoeducational (i.e. Duluth model; Pence & Paymar, 2003) and cognitive behavioural principles (e.g. Hamberger, 1997, 2002; Jennings, 1987; Sonkin & Durphy, 1997; Wexler, 2000). This refers to program objectives that involve consciousness-raising around the unequal nature and oppressive features of patriarchal society alongside teaching strategies for challenging the kind of thinking and the actions that support violence against women. While the Duluth model remains the approach of choice for a majority of jurisdictions (Corvo, Dutton, & Chen, 2009) and provides an overarching framework that is appropriate for most perpetrator groups (Gondolf, 2012), programs that use it also need to tailor their interventions to the circumstances of particular cases (e.g. Voith, Logan-Greene, Strodthoff, & Bender, 2018).

The big issues

There is wide international agreement across research, policy, and community sectors that essential components of violence prevention include promoting gender equity and addressing multiple and intersecting forms of discrimination and disadvantage that place women at risk of violence (Garcia-Moreno & Watts, 2011). This includes engaging all sectors of society in confronting unhelpful entrenched beliefs, cultural norms, and patterns of behaviour that lead to discrimination against women, as well as stereotyped roles that underpin gender inequalities. While, as described in Chapter 9, there is clearly a significant need for primary (preventive) intervention, and while such preventive strategies continue to gain momentum and funding, there remains an imperative to address DFV at an acute, here-and-now level (i.e. tertiary prevention) where those with a history of such violence who remain at risk have been identified.

Kristin Anderson's (2005) theoretical examination of the relevance of gender to intimate partner violence (IPV) deconstructs the individualised "anatomy-is-destiny" conceptualisation to consider an interactionist and structuralist analysis. By shedding light on the contextual, multidimensional components of gender and applying them to IPV, Anderson argues that a more finely tuned response to the influences of gender is warranted. Gender, according to this argument, is not something "resident" in the individual man or woman, but is constituted – played out or "performed" – according to setting and context. So, for instance, in response to the constraints of structural inequalities and enduring blueprints of femininity and their complementarity to similar masculinity blueprints, women's pursuit of security and wellbeing *tends* to be shaped towards a strategy of seeking partners who are older, physically larger, and who earn higher incomes than themselves. Such socialised preferences exacerbate vulnerability to abuse.

In terms of MBC work, then, it is important that the client comes to identify and appreciate not only ways in which he has exploited such gender-based inequalities in his relationships but also how he has relegated more respectful and non-abusive values. In a complementary fashion, we might assume perhaps that narrow blueprints for masculinity act as restraints on men seeking nurturance and emotional support outside of their relationships with women. They might use their position of relative power in these relationships to seek such human goods by means of coercion. This thinking goes beyond the narrow individualist construction of gender that leads to the conclusion that sex in some way "causes" violence. Gender expectations can be readily exploited by those with relative power. To do so, however, is the result of choice. At the practice level, then, the assumptions around explicit references to characteristics and properties of men (e.g. "boys will be boys") and women (e.g. "bringing a feminine touch") need to be examined closely for their usefulness to clients in living abuse-free lives, rather than being "natural", taken-for-granted aspects of men's and women's lives.

Intervention targets: program content

Program coherence and effectiveness

As referred to earlier, Gondolf (2012) has concluded that, while the effectiveness of MBCPs was dubious as a standalone response, there are good grounds for optimism in regard to their collaborative and coordinated efforts alongside other agencies and services engaged in countering DFV. Another program feature that is likely to contribute to their effectiveness is their groundedness in practices that are consistent with principles established in the field (Vlais, 2014). Along with the commonly held principles of prioritising the safety of women and their children and the accountability of offenders, these principles also include the successful targeting of "central dynamic risk factors" (Vlais, Ridley, Green, & Chung, 2017). These factors represent certain features associated with the man and within his control that are considered the most predictive of further abuse.

Debate arises, however, as to how such accountability is operationalised in MBC work, and what distinguishes a dynamic risk factor as "central". Recent Australian policy documents, such as the Centre for Innovative Justice Report (2016), have become more explicit and assertive in respect to these questions. They promote, for example, notions of the *visibility* of perpetrators (in relation to accountability) and the identification of core "criminogenic needs" (derived from dynamic risk factors; Andrews & Bonta, 2010; Stewart, Gabora, Kropp, & Lee, 2014) regarding DFV-related attitudes and beliefs (e.g. hostility towards women, enduring beliefs about male entitlement; Stewart, Flight, & Slavin-Stewart, 2013). Vlais and colleagues (2017, p. 67), reflecting on what they consider less central risk factors, such as substance abuse or compromised mental health, make the following comment:

> Unlike the more central risk factors, they do not drive risk, and hence interventions directed specifically towards these risk factors are generally insufficient to produce sustained risk reduction or long-term behaviour change.

In contrast, these central factors refer to the highly gendered nature of this kind of violence.

The tone and character of MBCPs

Scholarly analysis of DFV leads to the conclusion that there is an association with primary issues of human rights violation and inequality. We infer from this that the nature of restitution for these wrongs need to align with the provision of justice. Certainly, during the early endeavours of the feminist movement, there was a strong focus on having DFV recognised as malicious conduct and tantamount to other forms of criminal violence. Perhaps partly because of this reasoning, it was seen as necessary to have perpetrators treated in the same way as other criminals in order to express society's abhorrence. Consequences for offenders, in this way of thinking, should therefore include arrest and the strongest criminal justice responses. Two developments in thinking have countered this reasoning. One is that punishment is demonstrably not an efficient way of bringing about behaviour change in relation to violence (Boonin, 2008; Crockett, Keneski, Yeager, & Loving, 2015). The other is that the singular and authoritarian nature of criminal justice can act to mute the voices of women and children who have been subjected to DFV, sidelining their individual and particular preferences and concerns. This effect can be at least patronising, potentially disempowering, and contrary to the preferences of those persons, exacerbating their experience of deprivation in terms of autonomy and agency.

Integrating MBCP practices as a response to DFV

The complexity surrounding DFV practice stems from a number of factors. In the first place, practitioners are surrounded by fiercely competing theories and the contending ideologies that inform them. Yet there is also the sheer scope – the depth and breadth – of the issues involved. In seeking to help bring about change, the practitioner must take into consideration both the fine-grain detail of the case in front of her, as well as its broader interpersonal and social context. These requirements are related, but at very different levels of generality. MBCP practitioners work primarily with the specific, here-and-now aspects of individual cases, such as how the man is conducting himself in the setting of the group program alongside the pattern and dynamics of abuse in his relationship. However, these matters are, in turn, related to earlier experiences, family histories, cultural backgrounds, and so on.

To be effective in practice with men who have used violence in family relationships, practitioners need to find ways of addressing these disparate elements in a coherent fashion. This entails going beyond standard individually targeted criminal offender rehabilitation approaches. In part, this requires a closer examination of the aforementioned integrative approach: purposefully weaving MBC initiatives within the overall DFV prevention project. Based on the issues we have raised concerning about gender, it should also take into account persons, families, and systems involved from the perspective of transition and fluidity in interaction, role, and identity. Fortunately, some recently developed practice models and rehabilitation frameworks show promise here. We briefly discuss these under the labels of invitational practice, the Good Lives Model, and the desistance paradigm.

Invitational practice

Jenkins, in proposing a way of working with men, labels his approach as invitational theory and has described this process in the title of his book: *Becoming*

Ethical: A Parallel, Political Journey with Men Who Have Abused (Jenkins, 2009). This approach explicitly acknowledges practitioners' engagement with clients in the context of power relations and the need to undertake the work of resisting inequality and abuse as a collaborative project to develop ethical practices. Moreover, Jenkins' approach seeks to make explicit the ethical strivings of clients and holds these in ironic contrast to the habits and practices by which persons have tried to attain them. For instance, Zed, a man engaged in a men's behaviour change program, acknowledges that he had always hoped for his son to develop the independence that he, Zed, had always wished for himself. In acknowledging that he resorted to coercive tactics in trying to achieve this with his son, he is now confronted with the contradiction between his intentions and what he has done, and faces the shame of treating his son in this way. Non-aggressively but "irresistibly" confronting men with such contradictions constitutes a critical and significant element in this practice.

The Good Lives Model

Jenkins' highlighting of ironic intention is also a feature of Tony Ward's Good Lives Model (Ward, 2002; Ward et al., 2012). At the heart of this model of offender rehabilitation is the idea that in the process of "offending" (such as the use of abusive practices), attempts to attain "primary human goods" are ultimately frustrated by the "criminal" means one goes about achieving them.

Good Lives Model proponents claim their alternative framework fits under the rubric of "strengths-based" approaches. Essentially, the Good Lives Model considers that criminal conduct reflects offenders' misguided or distorted attempts to achieve these universal human goods, such as competence, mastery, and a sense of connectedness. The corollary is that offenders' attempts to attain them without taking into account the needs, feelings, and rights of others is highly problematic. Rehabilitative efforts, then, are steered towards assisting them to meet these needs in more prosocial, satisfying, and, ultimately, successful ways (Langlands, Ward, & Gilchrist, 2009).

The desistance paradigm

Authors such as McNeill (2006) and Morran (2010), representing a desistance approach to rehabilitation, argue that the transformational efforts put into MBC work ultimately support family safety and the interests of the community. At the same time, they would be reluctant to employ terms such as "treatment" because of their association with a paradigm that emphasises efficiencies in numbers rather than quality of service. They argue that the "best practice" paradigm, where programs are "delivered" rather than conducted and offenders "managed" rather than engaged, is disembodying of practice. The argument here is that the language around services, and the approach it reflects, detracts from the personal agency and active engagement that are at the heart of MBC work. A key message of the desistance paradigm is that clients are not commodities but citizens, and that change is not an event but a process.

Finally, having considered matters surrounding the *process* of practice – the tone and character of intervention; *how* it is conducted alongside *what* is transacted, we consider the contribution of the *context* of these programs, and especially the role of the group setting.

Group work: the context and process of MBCPs

The majority of MBCPs rely predominantly on a group format for their direct work with clients. Increasingly, however, participation in these programs is becoming more than simply attending a series of group sessions. The group, as a platform for MBCPs, has long been seen as advantageous. One obvious advantage is its efficiency – inputting the same number of hours but delivering a more economically favourable staff–client ratio and generating more "outputs". Another advantage conferred by the group format is the opportunity for mutual challenge among group participants and less dependency on the efforts of practitioners. In corrections work, for instance, which is generally heavily cognitive behavioural therapy-focused (Morgan & Flora, 2002), criminal offenders – as fellow group members – are considered to provide a more plausible source of critique for confronting the individual's "cognitive distortions", such as denial, blame-shifting, minimisation, and rationalising (or excuse-making).

Some writers (e.g. Frost, Ware, & Boer, 2009; Jennings & Sawyer, 2003; Ward, 1998) have argued for complementing this *confronting* intention of groups in the corrections field with a *process-focused* intention. Relationship-focused group work has long recognised the capacity of the well-run group to contribute to interpersonal support and personal growth among its individual members. Such an approach, based on carefully established norms of trust and openness, provides the platform for authentic "here-and-now" interpersonal encounters. For correctional settings, this immediacy affords the opportunity to progress beyond merely confronting abuse-supportive thinking to promoting personal capability for clarifying and meeting more appropriate interpersonal goals. These goals are linked to personally valued attributes such as interpersonal competence, which might help replace abuse-related perceptions of the need to impose control over others.

Adapting group work for MBCPs

Yalom and Leszcz (2005) note that when a group is both supportive and challenging, it is *engaging*. One of the challenges for these clients is to modulate the limits of their behaviour, as well as the impact that behaviour has on others. The group sessions therefore might emphasise skill rehearsal and applying learning in a very practised manner. This allows the best opportunity when men return to a relationship to be able to take up the social and emotional responsibilities that are inherently part of domestic life.

By nature and definition, group work requires a range of interactions between participants that differ significantly from both working with individual clients and a practitioner working with a client "audience". Empirically, group work is an excellent modality for enacting change, provided it is structured and that the group *as a whole* and its properties are exploited (e.g. Donigian & Malnati, 1977). To this end, a good grasp of group process is critical to the delivery of effective group interventions. We now turn to outline a number of core ideas that underpin therapeutic group work and relate these to how they might typically work within an MBCP context.

An important point to emphasise in this discussion is that the offer of support by MBCPs is firmly contingent upon the man's commitment to change. This is not to say that reluctance is not tolerated, but rather that any advocacy on the man's behalf is in relation to his movement towards MBC-related goals. In this sense, the tone and tenor of MBC groups needs to be consistent with anti-abusive and respectful practice, and collusion with sexist discourse needs to be consistently challenged. The group format in which most MBC work takes place is critical, here. Given that the group constitutes a "social microcosm" (Yalom & Leszcz, 2005), norms that develop in the group will be magnified – for better or for worse.

This reference highlights the centrality of group work to MBCPs. The dynamics and processes that occur naturalistically among a group of people who meet regularly and with purpose provide a wide range of opportunities for intervention. This is not just in relation to the "content" of the program but also because of the opportunities offered by the interactional nature of the group. Practitioner skill in group work is an important tool in the belt of MBC practitioners for these reasons.

A critical subskill is co-facilitation. Due to the gendered underpinnings of DFV, mixed-gender co-facilitation is, where circumstances allow, an industry standard (Apps & Gregory, 2011). Group workers are alert to any form of oppression that might surface in the group. Rather than summary dismissal, however, these incidents can be taken up (if not welcomed) as opportunities to sensitise members to the power relations that fuel DFV.

Victim intervention

In this section, we briefly examine the types of interventions available to victims of DFV and efforts to address trauma and the risk of revictimisation before concluding with a message about the essence of good practice.

Crisis accommodation

A number of interventions for victims affected by DFV are located in and driven by the women's sector, including its specialised victim services. Women's shelters remain a substantial component of service provision. While often thought of as an accommodation provider (and regularly funded as such), many such services go far beyond crisis accommodation, although that is their primary focus. For example, according to Putt, Holder, and O'Leary (2017, p. 3):

> At the frontline, workers interact with women in circumstances where the women and children's safety is of paramount importance, but the women's situation is not necessarily self-evident during crisis contact. The women may have taken the step of contacting the service, but many are hurt, vulnerable, confused and uncertain.

As highlighted in a report provided to the Queensland Government in Australia (Quixley, 2015), shelters are much more than "just a bed". Interventions provided by many shelters include counselling for women and children, education, advocacy, and empowerment programs for women, and transitional housing support, which assists in enabling the move into safe and sustainable housing following the initial period of crisis accommodation.

Consistent with the integrated approach to DFV mentioned earlier in this chapter, many shelters also work closely with other agencies and organisations to ensure adequate referral pathways so as to link women affected by DFV and their children with other services, including medical, financial support, legal, childcare, employment, and specialised trauma counselling services. As a result, crisis accommodation providers have long argued for funding agreements that reflect the diversity of their treatment modalities, which go well beyond the provision of housing (Bowstead, 2015; Quixley, 2015).

The effectiveness of shelters depends significantly on the definition of intended outcome. If it is assumed that their effectiveness is primarily associated with providing safe housing for women and their children escaping DFV, then outcomes are likely to be effective in most cases where women are able to access available shelter space. However, national and international research consistently suggests that shelter space is limited. In Australia, for example, most shelters are said to be at full capacity on any given night and those that do have vacancies usually already have a referral on the way (Malone, 2017). Similar observations have been reported for women's access to crisis accommodation in the UK (Bowstead, 2015).

International research has shown that crisis accommodation is capable of addressing the immediate need for accommodation and psychosocial support. Often, however, this type of service cannot adequately provide longer-term safe and sustainable housing solutions unless funded to do so, or where they form part of a broader, integrated response capable of responding to this need (Meyer, 2014; Spinney, 2012). Overall, the effectiveness of programs and interventions in empowering women to rebuild a life free from victimisation and to support their transition into safe and sustainable housing following shelter services is often highly dependent on the level of integration of services (Meyer, 2014). Holistic and integrated responses have been labelled as "best practice" in relation to "treatment effectiveness" of victim-focused interventions (Putt et al., 2017; Quixley, 2015; Wilcox, 2010).

Specialised DFV support services

Specialised non-residential walk-in services have been described by independent agencies for women with DFV as their core business (Putt et al., 2017). These agencies provide a range of information, including that around legal and clinical issues, although they might not necessarily profess to have expertise in such matters. Collectively, however, they also offer a range of treatment services for victims (and in many cases, children; Campbell, Vargas-Whale, & Olson, 2018).). While interventions and responses vary depending on service size, location, mandate, and funding agreement, they often include a number of the following:

- Crisis responses
- Community education
- Counselling
- Early intervention
- Legal support
- Parenting programs
- Primary prevention programs
- Professional training for external agencies
- Referral pathways to other relevant agencies
- Safety upgrades for the victim's home
- Translation services
- Women's support groups

Similar to the evidence around to the effectiveness of shelter-based interventions, the effectiveness of responses offered by specialised DFV support services varies with their level of integration and the service's capacity under its relevant funding agreement (Wilcox, 2010). Key features associated with the effectiveness of treatment types for victims – especially those focusing on "education", empowerment, and recovery from trauma – include format and duration (Eckhardt, et al., 2013). While a one-off contact or information session can have some benefit in some instances, optimal safety, recovery, and overall quality-of-life outcomes are more likely where intervention has involved multiple sessions or points of contact. As noted by Eckhardt and colleagues (2013), it seems the active ingredients are:

- A developed working relationship with the service provider
- A step-by-step process addressing issues relevant to emotional wellbeing, safety strategies
- Qualities of the parent–child relationship

As with MBC services, the key to success in victim services, whether as crisis responses or more specialised and ongoing interventions, appears to lie in their affiliation with and combination into a coordinated community response (Shorey,

Tirone, & Stuart, 2014). A broader "ecological" approach, incorporating community-wide agencies – such as victim advocate organisations, criminal justice system, healthcare systems, and educational/vocational programs – serves to helpfully extend such a response network (Sullivan, 2006).

Summary

While *good* practice can encompass a considerable range and many types of practice across both perpetrator and victim services, we reiterate that it is in their coordinated combination that they are likely to be most successful. Like pieces of a jigsaw puzzle, all these components (MBCP, crisis accommodation, DFV support services, criminal justice system interventions, child safety interventions) together are in a powerful position to monitor perpetrator risk, support and empower victims and children, and generate change (whether behavioural or recovery). It is critical that DFV services, regardless of their designation, play their part in purposeful efforts to construct the bigger picture of the abusive scenario. That is to say, they are engaged in promoting mutual understanding, shared language and definitions, and clear protocols to allow those in possession of information to share it safely where necessary and appropriate. This involves respectfully inviting clients, as violators or violated, into an active and allied role in resisting abuse. In these ways, the gaps and silences in which DFV thrives are more readily identified, and closed or filled.

References

Aaron, S., & Beaulaurier, R. (2017). The need for new emphasis on batterers' intervention programs. *Trauma, Violence & Abuse*, 18(4), 425–432.

Almeida, R. V., & Dolan-Delvecchio, K. (1999). Addressing culture in batterers intervention: The Asian Indian community as an illustrative example. *Violence Against Women*, 5(6), 654–683.

Anderson, K. L. (2005). Theorizing gender. *Sex Roles*, 52(11/12), 853–865.

Andrews, D. A., & Bonta, J. (2010). *The psychology of criminal conduct* (5th ed.). Newark, NJ: Matthew Bender.

Apps, J., & Gregory, R. (2011). "You're only there cos you're a woman": A study of women who co-facilitate men's behaviour change group programs. *Women against Violence*, 23, 29–39.

Boonin, D. (2008). *The problem of punishment*. New York: Cambridge University Press.

Bowstead, J. C. (2015). Why women's domestic violence refuges are not local services. *Critical Social Policy*, 35(3), 327–349.

Breckenridge, J., & Hamer, J. (2014). *Traversing the maze of "evidence" and "best practice" in domestic and family violence service provision in Australia* (Issues Paper No. 26). Sydney, NSW: Australian Domestic & Family Violence Clearinghouse. Retrieved from www.anrows.org.au/resources/news/new-adfv-clearinghouseanrows-paper-domestic-and-family-violence-best-practice

Campbell, K., Vargas-Whale, R., & Olson, L. (2018). Health needs of children of women seeking services for and safety from intimate partner violence. Advance online publication *Journal of Interpersonal Violence*. doi: 10.1177/0886260518754871

Cape, J. K., & Garvin, D. J. H. (2009). *Operationalizing accountability: The domains and bases of accountability*. Washtenaw, MI: Catholic Social services of Washtenaw County, Alternatives to Domestic Aggression.

Centre for Innovative Justice. (2016). *Pathways towards accountability: Mapping the journeys of perpetrators of family violence: Report to Department of Premier and Cabinet*. Melbourne, VIC: RMIT University.

Colorado Domestic Violence Offender Management Board. (2016). *Standards for treatment for court ordered domestic violence offenders*. Lakewood, CO: State of Colorado. Retrieved from https://cdpsdocs.state.co.us/dvomb/Standards/standards01.pdf

Corvo, K., Dutton, D., & Chen, W. (2009). Do Duluth model interventions with perpetrators of domestic violence violate mental health professional ethics? *Ethics & Behavior, 19*(4), 323–340.

Crockett, E. E., Keneski, E., Yeager, K., & Loving, T. J. (2015). Breaking the mold: Evaluating a non-punitive domestic violence intervention program. *Journal of Family Violence, 30*(4), 489–499.

Crossman, K., Hardesty, J., & Raffaelli, M. (2016). "He could scare me without laying a hand on me": Mothers' experiences of nonviolent coercive control during marriage and after separation. *Violence against Women, 22*(4), 454–473.

Day, A., Chung, D., O'Leary, P., & Carson, E. (2009). Programs for men who perpetrate domestic violence: An examination of the issues underlying the effectiveness of intervention programs. *Journal of Family Violence, 24*(3), 203–212.

DeKeseredy, W. S., & Schwartz, M. D. (2009). *Dangerous exits: Escaping abusive relationships in rural America*. New Brunswick, NJ: Rutgers University Press.

Diemer, K., Humphreys, C., Laming, C., & Smith, J. (2015). Researching collaborative processes in domestic violence perpetrator programs: Benchmarking for situation improvement. *Journal of Social Work, 15*(1), 65–86.

Dobash, R. E., & Dobash, R. L. (2011). What were they thinking? Men who murder an intimate partner. *Violence against Women, 17*(1), 111–134.

Dobash, R. E., & Dobash, R. L. (2015). When men murder women. *Policing, 10*(4), 456–457.

Donigian, J., & Malnati, R. (1977). *Systemic group therapy: A triadic model*. Pacific Grove: Wadsworth.

Eckhardt, C. I., Murphy, C. M., Whitaker, D. J., Sprunger, J., Dykstra, R., & Woodward, K. (2013). The effectiveness of intervention programs for perpetrators and victims of intimate partner violence. *Partner Abuse, 4*(2), 196–231.

Enander, V., & Holmberg, C. (2008). Why does she leave? The leaving process(es) of battered women. *Health Care for Women International, 29*(3), 200–226.

Flood, M. (2016). Involving men in ending violence against women: Facing challenges and making change. *Graduate Journal of Social Science, 12*(3), 12–29.

Frost, A., Ware, J., & Boer, D. (2009). An integrated groupwork methodology for working with sex offenders. *Journal of Sexual Aggression, 15*(1), 2–38.

Garcia-Moreno, C., & Watts, C. (2011). Violence against women: An urgent public health priority. *Bulletin of the World Health Organization, 89*, 2.

Gondolf, E. (1999). A comparison of re-assault rates in four batterer programs: Do court referral, program length and services matter? *Journal of Interpersonal Violence, 14*, 41–61.

Gondolf, E. (2002). *Batterer intervention systems issues, outcomes, and recommendations*. Thousand Oaks, CA: Sage Publications.

Gondolf, E. (2004). Evaluating batterer counseling programs: A difficult task showing some effects and implications. *Aggression and Violent Behavior, 9*(6), 605–631.

Gondolf, E. (2007). Theoretical and research support for the Duluth Model: A reply to Dutton and Corvo. *Aggression and Violent Behavior, 12*(6), 644–657.

Gondolf, E. (2012). *The future of batterer programs: Reassessing evidence-based practice.* Boston, MA: Northeastern University Press.

Gwinn, C., Strack, G., Adams, S., Lovelace, R., & Norman, D. (2007). The family justice center collaborative model. *Saint Louis Public Law Review, 27,* 79–120.

Hamberger, L. K. (1997). Cognitive behavioral treatment of men who batter their partners. *Cognitive and Behavioral Practice, 4*(1), 147–169.

Hamberger, L. K. (2002). The men's group program: A community-based cognitive behavioral, profeminist intervention program. In E. Aldarondo & F. Mederos (Eds.), *Men who batter: A handbook for clinicians, practitioners, and prevention strategies in a diverse society.* Kingston, NJ: Civic Research Institute, Inc.

Hamel, J. (2012). "But she's violent, too!" Holding domestic violence offenders accountable within a systemic approach to batterer intervention. *Journal of Aggression, Conflict and Peace Research, 4*(3), 124–135.

Hansen, J. (2016). *Standards for treatment with court ordered domestic violence offenders: A process evaluation.* Colorado Domestic Violence Offender Management Board. Retrieved from https://cdpsdocs.state.co.us/dvomb/Research/Evaluation.pdf

Irvine, H., Livingstone, M., & Flood, M. (2018). *The man box: A study on being a young man in Australia.* Melbourne: Jesuit Social Services. Retrieved from https://jss.org.au/what-we-do/the-mens-project/the-man-box/

Jenkins, A. (1990). *Invitations to responsibility: The therapeutic engagement of men who are violent and abusive.* Adelaide, SA: Dulwich Centre Publications.

Jenkins, A. (2009). *Becoming ethical: A parallel, political journey with men who have abused.* Lyme Regis, UK: Russel House.

Jennings, J. L. (1987). History and issues in the treatment of battering men: A case for unstructured group therapy. *Journal of Family Violence, 2*(3), 193–214.

Jennings, J. L., & Sawyer, S. (2003). Principles and techniques for maximising the effectiveness of group therapy with sex offenders. *Sexual Abuse: A Journal of Research and Treatment, 15*(4), 251–267.

Johnson, M. (2010). *A typology of domestic violence intimate terrorism, violent resistance, and situational couple violence* (Northeastern Series on Gender, Crime, and Law). Lebanon: Northeastern University Press.

Kelly, L., & Westmarland, N. (2015). *Domestic violence perpetrator programs: Steps towards change.* London and Durham: London Metropolitan University and Durham University. Retrieved from www.dur.ac.uk/resources/criva/ProjectMirabalfinalreport.pdf

Kelly, L., & Westmarland, N. (2016). Naming and defining "domestic violence": Lessons from research with violent men. *Feminist Review, 112*(1), 113–127.

Langlands, R. L., Ward, T., & Gilchrist, E. (2009). Applying the Good Lives Model to male perpetrators of domestic violence. *Behaviour Change, 36*(2), 113–129.

Main, T. F. (1977). Concept of the therapeutic community: Variations and vicissitudes. *Group Analysis, 10*(2), S2–S16.

Malone, U. (2017, 19 October). Women leaving domestic violence living in car as homeless fill shelters. *ABC News.* Retrieved from www.abc.net.au/news/2017-10-19/domestic-violence-shelters-filled-with-homeless-women/9063860

McNeill, F. (2006). A desistance paradigm for offender management. *Criminology and Criminal Justice*, 6(1), 39–62.

Meyer, S. (2014). *Victims' experiences of short- and long-term safety and wellbeing: Findings from an examination of an integrated response to domestic violence* (Trends and Issues in Crime and Criminal Justice, No. 478). Canberra, ACT: Australian Institute of Criminology. Retrieved from http://search.informit.com.au/fullText;dn=420984536242378;r es=IELHSS

Morgan, R. D., & Flora, D. B. (2002). Group psychotherapy with incarcerated offenders: A research synthesis. *Group Dynamics: Theory, Research and Practice*, 6(3), 203–218.

Morran, D. (2010). Re-education or recovery? Re-thinking some aspects of domestic violence perpetrator programs. *Probation Journal*, 58(1), 23–36.

Pence, E., & Paymar, M. (2003). *Creating a process of change for men who batter: An education curriculum*. Duluth, MN: Domestic Abuse Intervention Project.

Putt, J., Holder, R., & O'Leary, C. (2017). *Women's specialist domestic and family violence services: Their responses and practices with and for Aboriginal women: Key findings and future directions*. Sydney, NSW: Australian Domestic & Family Violence Clearinghouse. Retrieved from http://media.aomx.com/anrows.org.au/s3fs-public/Women's%20specialist%20domestic%20and%20family%20violence%20services_Putt_CompassFINAL.pdf

Quixley, S. (2015). *More than just a bed: The contribution of women's refuges in Queensland*. Brisbane, QLD: Combined Women's Refuge Group. Retrieved from www.cwrg. org/#!position-paper-more-than-just-a-bed-/bp705

Shorey, R. C., Tirone, V., & Stuart, G. L. (2014). Coordinated community response components for victims of intimate partner violence: A review of the literature. *Aggression and Violent Behavior*, 19(4), 363–371.

Sonkin, D. J., & Durphy, M. (1997). *Learning to live without violence: A handbook for men* (4th ed.). Volcano, CA: Volcano Press.

Spinney, A. (2012). *Home and safe? Policy and practice innovations to prevent women and children who have experienced domestic and family violence from becoming homeless* (AHURI Final Report No. 196). Melbourne, VIC: Australian Housing and Urban Research Institute.

Stark, E. (2007). *Coercive control: How men entrap women in personal life*. Oxford, UK: Oxford University Press.

Stewart, L., Flight, J., & Slavin-Stewart, C. (2013). Applying effective corrections principles (RNR) to partner abuse interventions. *Partner Abuse*, 4(4), 494–534.

Stewart, L., Gabora, N., Kropp, P. R., & Lee, Z. (2014). Effectiveness of risk-needs-responsivity-based family violence programs with male offenders. *Journal of Family Violence*, 29(2), 151–164.

Sullivan, C. M. (2006). Interventions to address intimate partner violence: The current state of the field. In J. R. Lutzker (Ed.), *Preventing violence: Research and evidence based intervention strategies* (pp. 195–212). Washington, DC: American Psychological Association.

Townsend, M., Hunt, D., & Rhodes, W. (2005). *Evaluability assessment of the President's Family Justice Center initiative*. Cambridge, MA: Abt Associates. Retrieved from www. familyjusticecenter.org/resources/evaluability-assessment-presidents-family-justice-center-initaitive/

Trabold, N., McMahon, J., Alsobrooks, S., Whitney, S., & Mittal, M. (2018). A systematic review of intimate partner violence interventions: State of the field and implications for practitioners. *Trauma, Violence & Abuse.* Advance online publication. doi: 10.1177/1524838018767934

Velonis, A., Cheff, R., Finn, D., Davloor, W., & O'Campo, P. (2016). Searching for the mechanisms of change: A protocol for a realist review of batterer treatment programmes. *BMJ Open*, 6(4), 1–9.

Vlais, R. (2014). *Domestic violence perpetrator programs: Education, therapy, support, accountability "or" struggle?* Melbourne: No to Violence, Male Family Violence Prevention Association.

Vlais, R., Ridley, S., Green, D., & Chung, D. (2017). *Family and domestic violence programs: Issues paper of current and emerging trends, developments and expectations.* Perth, Australia: Stopping Family Violence Inc.

Voith, L., Logan-Greene, P., Strodthoff, T., & Bender, A. (2018). A paradigm shift in batterer intervention programming: A need to address unresolved trauma. *Trauma, Violence & Abuse.* Advance online publication. doi: 10.1177/1524838018791268

Wagers, S. M., Pate, M., & Brinkley, A. (2017). Evidence-based best practices for batterer intervention programs: A report from the field on the realities and challenges batterer intervention programs are facing. *Partner Abuse*, 8(4), 409–428.

Ward, D. (1998). Groupwork. In R. Adams, L. Dominelli, & M. Payne (Eds.), *Social work: Themes, issues and critical debates*. London: Macmillan.

Ward, T. (2002). Good lives and the rehabilitation of offenders: Promises and problems. *Aggression and Violent Behavior*, 7(5), 513–528.

Ward, T., & Gannon, T. (2006). Rehabilitation, etiology, and self-regulation: The Good Lives Model of rehabilitation for sexual offenders. *Aggression and Violent Behavior*, 11(1), 77–94.

Ward, T., & Stewart, C. A. (2003). The treatment of sex offenders: Risk assessment and the Good Lives Model. *Professional Psychology, Research and Practice*, 34(4), 353–360.

Ward, T., Yates, P. M., & Willis, G. M. (2012). The Good Lives Model and the risk need responsivity model: A critical response to Andrews, Bonta, and Wormith. *Criminal Justice and Behavior*, 39(1), 94–110.

Wexler, D. B. (2000). *Domestic violence 2000: An integrated skills program for men.* New York: W.W. Norton.

Wilcox, K. (2010). Connecting systems, protecting victims: Towards vertical coordination of Australia's response to domestic and family violence. *UNSW Law Journal*, 33, 1013–1037.

Yalom, I., & Leszcz, M. (2005). *The theory and practice of group psychotherapy* (5th ed.). New York: Basic Books.

Chapter 11

Conclusion

We briefly review DFV as a site of complexity and diversity, and the theoretical antagonism surrounding it. We argue that practitioners must confront and reconcile the reality of these difficulties in order to provide appropriate services. This challenge is at the core of the book's purpose. Our response to this challenge has been to propose a decisive characterisation of the problem as a social and public health issue, and to suggest coherent theory as the basis for an integrated response.

Confronting difficulty and complexity

Part of the "difficulty" of the topic of DFV lies in its inherent unpleasantness. Its nature, persistence, and prevalence are dismal features that threaten to instil a sense of hopelessness in those who seek to tackle it. Nevertheless, practitioners in and students of this field are typically motivated to action by these very features and are often inspired to join in a common cause to resist the influence and hold of DFV.

In describing the topic as difficult, we are also referring to its complexity. Family relationship and other intimate and kinship settings become the tangled and enduring contexts in which a systematic abuse of power is often played out. These settings themselves are diverse, and there is considerable heterogeneity among both victims and perpetrators. Yet even then, there is uncertainty about *what* is being perpetrated towards *whom*. The term "domestic violence" has tended to conjure up images of the bruised and battered faces of women and children peering from doors ajar or parted blinds. The term clearly implies violence among intimates, family, or kinfolk. However, these initial stereotypical and simplistic representations have been gradually and incrementally revised over decades of research to reveal a far more intricate picture. It has become clear that the impact of DFV on victims is multifaceted and potentially pervasive across all aspects of their lives, impinging on the fundamental freedoms and liberties that are widely considered to be basic human rights. This has led some to propose that the depth and pervasiveness of these experiences are not adequately covered by the term "violence" and might be better represented as a form of abuse.

The increasing recognition of the diversity of DFV has in part been made possible by researchers who have proposed, investigated, and refined categories and types of DFV. This has challenged the original assumptions of modernist feminist scholars and activists who characterised the problem as uniformly about men's violence against women. Another contribution to broadening the scope of understanding the issue has been that of post-structuralist feminism, which has forced the field to consider the experiences of victims across culture, sex, class, and circumstance. While we agree that the tradition of research in this field has been distracted from, for instance, the experiences of men as victims, and would benefit from a better understanding of these cases, we have been clear that the core focus of this book is on the most pernicious form of abuse in terms of severity, persistence, and pervasiveness. This form of DFV is perhaps best characterised as coercive control and predominantly involves men's use of violence against women and their children.

There needs to be a way of accounting for this gender bias. Because of the obvious exceptions to the violent man/victimised woman scenario, any explanation as to why violence occurs cannot be restricted to some intrinsic quality of men or women per se. Indeed, some academics in the field continue to maintain that the traditional view of the male perpetrator and female victim does not reflect their alternative conclusion that there is a more or less equal distribution of violence between men and women. These academics, however, base their conclusion on research that focuses on individual instances of violence in these settings rather than the purposes and intentions of the perpetrator, and the contexts in which they occur. While we do not concur with this conclusion, the fact that women, quite commonly, do resort to acts of violence needs to be accommodated in the integrated conception that we propose. In this sense, post-structuralist feminism has been useful in characterising gender not as an essential feature of men or women but as a social construct and culturally shaped expectation, requiring that social actors engage in gender "performance" in order to form and maintain their social identity. The argument here is that dominant blueprints for these gender performances, and for masculinity particularly, play a vital role in the maintenance of the problem. Indeed, the blueprint for masculinity presents a role that is narrow and rigid in form and competitive, power-oriented, and aggressive in nature. The violence of men therefore tends to be motivated by attempts to secure possession and power through means of fear and threat. The violence of women in most situations is, we conclude, motivated by other reasons – typically as resistance to this oppressive abuse perpetrated by men. We consider this variation on the understanding of violence against women as a progressive development of earlier feminist articulations using the concept of gender. It accounts for the variations observed on the theme of asymmetry while retaining the argument that men's violence over women is at the core of the problem.

It is clear then that the phenomenon of DFV cannot be simply explained away as some aberrant form of conduct (as some strands of theory have attempted to do) – it is far too common ("normal") for that. Nevertheless, DFV remains aberrant in the sense that its existence is antithetical to any well-functioning social system. It is plain from the above that we must accept that complexity is part and parcel of DFV, and that if we are serious about making sense of this problem in order to tackle it, then we must not only accept but also embrace it as a central challenge for practitioners.

Nevertheless, deep ideological divisions in this field remain. Indeed, positions are still so far at odds that they are holding up progress in the field and therefore remain a stumbling block to well-informed practice. It is useful, then, to identify some principles of the field that are common to all perspectives. In this way, practitioners might be better able to reconcile the diverse and antagonistic approaches to DFV with which they are faced.

Identifying a common adversary: two accepted principles

We maintain that the first step in achieving common ground for a cohesive response to DFV is in recognising that the most significant and common thread across approaches is that it is a problem of injustice. That is to say, at the heart of anti-DFV efforts, there is a need to put wrongs to right. Such realisation presents a unifying presupposition in that, regardless of the strategy for understanding the problem, there exists a common foe: DFV itself. Thus, instead of singling out a "problem" group to target, refute, or vilify (such as men, feminists, researchers, and so on), it is recognised that DFV exists as a social and therefore a systemic problem. In this sense, men, women, feminists, scientists, social workers, psychologists, researchers, and practitioners are, philosophically at least, united: ultimately, no one will prosper from the continuation of DFV. Moreover, the enmity between opposing camps has the ironic and unproductive effect of trying to solve adversity with adversity. Happily, there are at least two apparently universally accepted goals in the endeavour to tackle DFV: victim safety and perpetrator accountability. Useful responses, then, should accommodate this dual objective, galvanise a common purpose, and consolidate efforts around it. We argue this goal should be approached by characterising neither those violated as helpless and passive victims, nor those violating as malice-driven monsters incapable of change. In this, we recognise also that all protagonists in the field, whether as clients or colleagues, violated or violators, or practitioners or researchers are not simply cogs in machines but embodied actors engaged in navigating human relationships. At the same time, we believe that refuting binary extremes in our understanding of the problem and treating those with whom we work with respect and dignity is more likely to lead to respectful, non-abusive outcomes.

Knowledge foundations of a practice response

As we have argued, an effective and ethical practice response to DFV must be based upon knowledge that makes sense of practice situations. In other words, such a response must be able to be rendered understandable, relevant, and appropriate to the actual circumstances confronted by practitioners. In this book, we have argued that a feminist analysis of gender within an intersectional framework satisfies these prerequisites. This approach reconciles circumstances associated with vulnerability to DFV (such as historical structural oppression, social marginalisation, and current social conditions) balanced with an appreciation of personal intention and agency (such as the motivation and capacity to resist abuse). That is to say, this strand of theorising blends the general (i.e. context) with the particular (i.e. people immediately affected by DFV). This holistic manner of conceptualising the problem refutes the "incidentalising" of DFV and instead considers it in a context of human intention and behavioural patterning over time, which thus more authentically represents the nature of the phenomenon. This is consistent with Kelly's (1988) notion of "continuum thinking", which places the concept of gender at the heart of the problem as an embedded and interactional phenomenon, rather than attaching its influence to the lives of persons in the form of internal or external forces driving particularised and discrete "behaviours".

According to a feminist analysis, the central and independent feature of influence here is gender power relations rather than, for example, anger, personal pathology, or the presence of intoxicants (although these features might have a mediating role). Men, who are traditionally invited to take up an identity based on competitive masculinity, are inclined to exercise coercive control over family members in order to experience a compensatory sense of power when confronted by circumstances where they perceive that other options to do so are limited. They may resort to various forms of violence in order to reinforce such control, thereby supplementing other resource advantages typically available to men, such as access to money, authority, and legal advantage.

At the same time, from a post-structuralist feminist perspective, persons and communities are considered in relation to properties of choice and agency. Opportunities to exercise such choice and agency, however, are either restricted or promoted according to circumstance, such as wealth, employment, immigration status, or other relative benefit or privilege. Gender ascription is considered a core influence in accessing these resources. Yet gender does not represent an essential characteristic of persons. Rather, it is a social construction with which persons are compellingly invited to identify according to sex and to perform according to role – traditionally as either men or women. According to a post-structuralist feminist view, DFV emerges from people trying desperately to both conform to and enforce the typically narrow and rigid versions of these gender expectations in the context of power relations. It is therefore social tolerance of, and personal ascription to, these restraining gender expectations that is at question rather than some essential characteristic of the persons involved. This also applies to the organisations and agencies that are involved in working with those persons in their experiences of DFV. As Boyle asserts, "[the] Feminist Anti-Violence Movement . . . is a movement *against* violence against women" (Boyle,

2019, p. 2; italics in original), making it clear that this is an active endeavour confronting gendered violence as a target for change rather than characterising the persons implicated as helpless or intractable. In DFV practice, this confrontation is rightly to do with the influence of gendered violence in the lives of persons rather than ascribed attributes or personal faults. Intervention, then, is to do with intention and pattern over the course of a relationship rather than the examination of a series of discrete acts. The latter is a strategy that tends to reinforce denial of responsibility and therefore deter accountability (Kelly & Westmarland, 2016). This interpretation is helpful to practice in that it is hopeful and optimistic in terms of transformation.

Assessing the violent situation

DFV at its core represents an attack on the rights of women and children. Yet it can be seen as the culmination of practices of oppression and abuse, both locally and broadly, proximally, and distally – affecting individuals, families, and communities through their lives and often across generations. The abuse is experienced in such a way as to threaten security, constrain liberty, and restrict choice (Stark, 2007). At the local, proximal level, it tends to be experienced by victims specifically in terms of control – isolation, immobilisation, impoverishment, and confinement (Stark, 2007). This control is typically maintained by fear of explicit violence and reinforced by symbols or reminders of that explicit violence (Johnson & Ferraro, 2000). The wider context of this is convincingly explained by its embeddedness in enduring patriarchal power structures, experiences of displacement, and the influence of community dispossession. Women and children tend to be at the sharp end of these abuses because of their relative social disadvantage and because of the roles they are expected to take up within society. As we referred to above, although some articulations of feminism have been criticised for painting a uniform picture of men's abuse of women and their children, and for not taking into account the use of violence of others, broad spectrum evidence suggests a lopsided reality of the impact of DFV by men against other family members – primarily women. Based on this reality, a gendered portrayal of violence against women suggests the potential for the exploitation of men over women is ever present, and that the line between a controlling interpersonal style and abuse might be quite fine. This analysis underlines once more Kelly's (1988) notion of DFV as a continuum rather than a specific act, a process rather than an event.

Practitioners nevertheless will be faced with here-and-now cases in which they will be required to assess the likelihood of (further) DFV. Particular cases will be assigned to a high-risk category and here, especially, a finely grained risk assessment will be called for. Risk assessment tools, based on research into many such cases and calibrated by actuarial calculation, have been designed to estimate the likelihood and level of DFV. While the clamour for such information is understandable and justified, the here-and-now circumstances must be considered in their unique context. The choice of risk assessment instrument would thus ideally be tailored to the circumstances of the situation with respect to ethnic, cultural, relational, and historical circumstances – as risk factors are not evenly weighted. Therefore, realistically, other factors must be taken into account by means of the assessor's judgement or incorporation of matters such as disability or age. Also, in order to gain a realistic appraisal of the likelihood and severity of risk, the protective factors (such as the resistance of both perpetrator and victim towards such abuse) should be taken to account by assessing not only the risks but also the resources available to persons. To open up possibilities for change, the *performance* of gender should be illuminated and *acts* of resistance to abuse promoted. This might mean balancing prescriptions for immediate safety with longer-term wellbeing, security, and acts of respect. Clearly this is not a straightforward task and is one that should, as far as possible, incorporate the intentions and experiences of those being assessed.

All this reinforces our conclusion that tackling DFV is a complex matter. However, it does not detract from our secondary conclusion that this complexity must be confronted, even embraced. In the final section, we will synthesise our overview of an intervention that returns to the important notion of integration in the field where we apply it to a practice response.

An integrated response

Throughout this book, we have emphasised the importance of expanding and amplifying the picture of DFV in order to encompass the issues that reflect its global reach and pervasiveness in the lives of diverse people and communities. We have argued against competing hypotheses that rest on notions that abuse within relationships, families, and kinship communities resides in their internal properties, or results from psychological or social "forces". We have also resisted ideas that intervention should be reduced to attending to distinct events, isolated factors, or categories of pathology. Instead, we have promoted the view that the problem should be seen in terms of enduring patterns, continuum, human agency, and intention.

In this final section of the book, we return to the notion of holism to propose principles for how practice might be conceptualised and carried out on the basis of these ideas. Our intention here is to bring together the arguments for a rounded view of the problem combined with an integrated model for responding to it. Although we support the idea of reframing DFV as a public health problem (as opposed to a private individual problem) the key word here is *public* – we are not in favour of pathologising it, which is a way of pretending it is epidemiologically aberrant. In our view, this reinforces the unhelpful idea that it concerns a limited number of abnormal or helpless individuals rather than being reflective of its pervasive broader reality.

The intention in applying this holistic lens is to advocate for an integrated approach to practice. In the same way as an individualistic diagnostic and prescriptive approach to private individual problems is unlikely to be a successful strategy for tackling a widespread public health problem, we conclude that an effective response to DFV needs to be a coherent, coordinated, collaborative, and broad-based effort. This means strongly promoting preventative measures to address what is a socially heritable problem with intergenerational consequences. This toxic legacy is not confined to individuals and families but applies to whole cultures where systematic abuse has taken place by means of colonising (dispossession) or exclusionary (displacement) strategies. Here we are convinced of the need for common language and practices between different agencies and service occupations that allow for information sharing, coordination, and purposeful timing of intervention. For example, child protection services, as well as attributing protective responsibilities to mothers, must be able to respond to social restraints and compromised capacities, as well as inviting the duties and accountabilities of fathers. This also implies sensitivity to and appreciation of culturally shaped preferences of partners and parents in diverse communities, and the mobilisation of the resources to empower them. For victims of DFV, this might mean an initial focus on safety and security, whereas for violators this might mean initial efforts should centre on expectations of accountability in relation to partnerhood and parenthood. In either case, assurance of safety is balanced with respect for ethical agency. Because of the restrictive and narrow influences of gender role expectations, service efforts should take the direction of opening up approach-focused possibilities for clients rather than avoidance-focused prescription and injunction. Restoring the agency of victims and the responsibility to perpetrators is, we believe, a more productive long-term strategy than regulation and management or the imposition of guilt and shame.

The responses of practitioners to the impact of DFV are often heavily constrained by public clamour for decisive action in relation to those affected by DFV. This is often translated, through political reactivity, into departmental and agency policy that might place simplistic but considerable and urgent expectations on mothers to protect themselves and their children. The sometimes explicit expectation to separate and leave might be compromised or obscured by an individual's own experiences as a victim and countered by cultural expectation or preference that they stay in the family relationship. With regard to perpetrators, the ubiquitous requirement that they are "held to account" might be interpreted not as inviting them to take up commensurate responsibility in a parenting or restorative role, but as a form of retribution for their behaviour. Imposition and injunction (especially by means of shame – perhaps the most painful of emotions) and the advocacy of goals based on avoidance, however, are rarely successful in promoting wellbeing or behaviour change.

We advocate for integrative practice approaches that identify preference, elicit motivation, and support personal agency in countering DFV. It is in this way that personal narratives of resistance to DFV are likely to emerge. This is helpful, we believe, in that the telling of these stories of resistance to DFV helps to counter the centuries of silence and blindness to this endemic social problem.

In the same way as the global #metoo movement has provided "permission" and impetus to the telling of stories involving sexual abuse that hitherto could not be told – either because of a sense of victim blameworthiness or the absence of an audience willing to listen (Plummer, 1995) – supporting a social habit of such storytelling counters one of the most powerful allies of abuse: silence. Positioning clients as object rather than subject, on the other hand, serves to mimic the strategies of DFV itself.

Having followed the logic of this encompassing and holistic argument as a practitioner or student of this topic, you may well be thinking: "This is all very well, but how do I put this philosophy into practice? I imagine myself being faced with a traumatised family and a perpetrator who is not only unrepentant but actively defensive". Here we emphasise practice integration. The safety of women and children was established as the original goal of all DFV services. Even at this foundational level, however, the ethic of integrated services is relevant. It is evident to practitioners that providing a secure roof and safe bed is only the most urgent of needs. While these services might play a key role in attending to immediate wellbeing, this is just the beginning of the relationship between victims and services. Such services are ideally extended to include counselling and trauma-informed intervention; they are the potential site of information provision, referral options, and, where applicable, court support and programmed services.

Similarly, in a recent summing up of the considerable research and intervention efforts put into "batterer" programs, Gondolf (2012) concluded that "the system matters". In other words, he concludes that confining attention to the circumscribed setting of the program space and trying to isolate and measure change factors related directly to that experience is fraught and that outcomes are ambiguous. However, when the intelligence derived from such programs is aggregated with the experience of victims, shared with criminal justice entities, and combined with the input of women's advocates, the picture is somewhat clearer – and more optimistic. Moreover, it seems that it is not just the measurable quantum of knowledge sharing and data production that is of value; it is the factors of synergy, community of practice, social capital – in fact the totality of the interactions – that is of value to safety, accountability, and behaviour change. The message for policymakers and practitioners is clear: adopting a systemic lens and developing consistent language and a shared, coherent framework while engaging purposefully with other components of the DFV practice systems (through information sharing, coordination, and cooperation) is associated with success in this endeavour. The breadth and complexity of the problem behoves us to move beyond the silos of insular responsibility, professional jealousy, and fragmentation of services – arrangements that, through their blinkeredness, inadvertently mimic the nature of abuse itself.

The same argument applies to services for victims: it is the system that determines effectiveness. We need to address the bigger picture for women and children to foster not only immediate protection, but lasting safety, security, and wellbeing. Services are also far more accessible if they form part of a larger, integrated response. Together, these pieces (i.e. men's behaviour change programs (MBCPs), crisis accommodation, DV support services, criminal justice agencies, child safety interventions) are in a powerful position to monitor perpetrator risk, support and empower women and children, and potentially to promote change.

The integration of services is indeed an emerging trend in this field (as we reported in Chapter 10), but it is the professional spirit of cooperation and collaboration behind such enterprises that is also of vital importance. This spirit of integration might be incorporated better into other areas of practice. We mentioned two examples of significance within this book: service evaluation research and the group work component of MBCP.

A fully integrated response to DFV, of course, goes beyond the immediate responsibility and purview of practitioners. A coherent and cohesive service ethic supporting a consistent and unified response will go a long way, but when witnesses to such abuse do not hesitate to act, when bystanders to sexism intervene, and when men turn their back on such exploitation, we will know the job is complete.

References

Boyle, K. (2019). What's in a name? Theorising the inter-relationships of gender and violence. *Feminist Theory*, 20(1), 19–36. doi: 10.1177/1464700118754957

Gondolf, E. (2012). *The future of batterer programs: Reassessing evidence-based practice*. Boston, MA: Northeastern University Press.

Johnson, M., & Ferraro, K. (2000). Research on domestic violence in the 1990s: Making distinctions. *Journal of Marriage and Family*, 62(4), 948–963.

Kelly, L. (1988). *Surviving sexual violence*. Cambridge: Polity Press.

Kelly, L., & Westmarland, N. (2016). Naming and defining "domestic violence": Lessons from research with violent men. *Feminist Review, 112*, 113–127.

Plummer, K. (1995). *Telling sexual stories: Power, change, and social worlds*. London: Routledge.

Stark, E. (2007). *Coercive control how men entrap women in personal life*. New York: Oxford University Press.

Index

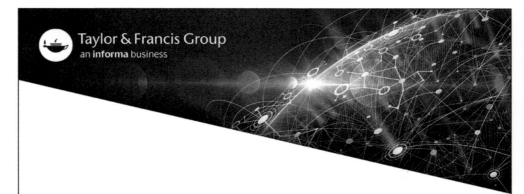

9781138552739